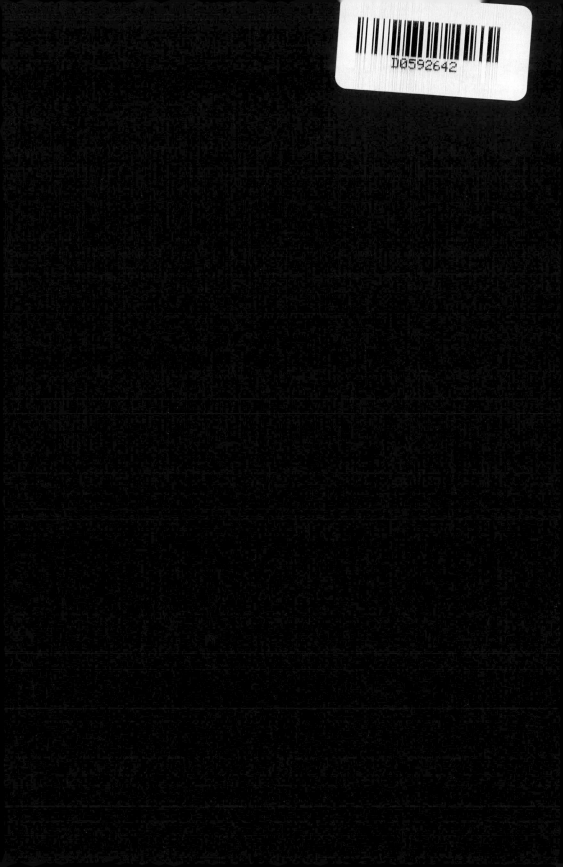
D0592642

NARRATING SOCIAL ORDER: AGORAPHOBIA AND
THE POLITICS OF CLASSIFICATION

SHELLEY Z. REUTER

Narrating Social Order

Agoraphobia and the Politics of Classification

UNIVERSITY OF TORONTO PRESS
Toronto Buffalo London

ISBN-13: 978-0-8020-9088-1
ISBN-10: 0-8020-9088-5

∞

Printed on acid-free paper

Library and Archives Canada Cataloguing in Publication

Reuter, Shelley Z. (Shelley Zipora), 1968–
   Narrating social order : agoraphobia and the politics of classification /
Shelley Z. Reuter.

   Includes bibliographical references and index.
   ISBN-13: 978-0-8020-9088-1
   ISBN-10: 0-8020-9088-5

   1. Agoraphobia.   2. Mental illness – Classification.   3. Social psychiatry.
I. Title.

   RC552.A44R49 2007   306.4'61   C2006-904771-5

This book has been published with the help of a grant from the Canadian
Federation for the Humanities and Social Sciences, through the Aid to
Scholarly Publications Programme, using funds provided by the
Social Sciences and Humanities Research Council of Canada.

University of Toronto Press acknowledges the financial assistance to its
publishing program of the Canada Council for the Arts and the
Ontario Arts Council.

University of Toronto Press acknowledges the financial support for its
publishing activities of the Government of Canada through the Book
Publishing Industry Development Program (BPIDP).

'Is everyone mad, do you think?' Sybil asked, recovering her poise. 'One way or another, do you think it could be so?'

Jung gave one of his shrugs and said: 'There are degrees of madness, of course. I have found some traces of it in myself, I do confess.' He waved his hand. 'But madness is a crafty beast and cannot be caught with theories. Over time, I have learned not only to be distrusting of theories, but to actively oppose them. Facts are what matter. And the facts regarding each individual's madness are all we have. General theories regarding madness merely get in the way of discovering its true nature in each patient, one by one by one. My own madness is quantified by parentheses – just as all madness is. And because of that, I have learned not only to deal with it, but to live with it. And most importantly, as any person must, to function in its presence. It is mine – my own and only mine.'

(Timothy Findley, *Pilgrim*, 1999)

Contents

Acknowledgments

Having begun as a dissertation, this book would not have been possible without the support and direction of my doctoral committee. Roberta Hamilton, then and since, has shouldered most of the burden of teaching me how to be a historical sociologist, guiding this project from its first tentative words to its present, post-Ph.D. form. She has read and commented on the manuscript many more times than can reasonably be expected of one person. Numerous conversations with Jacalyn Duffin as well – about medical history, epistemology, and, in particular, the concept of disease – directly inform the arguments I make here. Anthony Synnott, Bart Simon, and David Lyon were also generous with their insights and feedback, helping me shape a curious observation into a situated and defensible argument. For all this attention, I am in their debt.

My gratitude also extends to several others who worked with me on the manuscript at various stages: Jennifer Shea and Sandra Smele for their research assistance; three anonymous reviewers for their useful comments; and Len Husband, Frances Mundy, and Theresa Griffin of the University of Toronto Press for their editorial guidance and suggestions.

I am also grateful to the following family, friends, and colleagues for their support of this project and of me, but above all for helping me to keep things in perspective: Nehama Reuter, Moshe Reuter, Orit Reuter, Tali Hassan, Fiona Green, Barry Edginton, Susanne Ottenheimer, Richard Day, Jeffrey Cormier, Geoffrey Smith, and Katherine Lagrandeur. Thank you all.

Funding for this project was provided by the Social Sciences and Humanities Research Council, the National Chapter of Canada IODE, and Queen's, Memorial, and Concordia Universities.

NARRATING SOCIAL ORDER: AGORAPHOBIA AND
THE POLITICS OF CLASSIFICATION

1 Introduction:
A Sociology of Psychiatry

agoraphobia (ăg"ō-ră-fō'bē-ă) [Gr. *agora*, marketplace, + *phobos*, fear]. Overwhelming symptoms of anxiety, often leading to a panic attack. This may occur in a variety of everyday situations (e.g., standing in line; eating in public; in crowds of people; on bridges or in tunnels; while driving) in which a person might have an attack and be unable to escape or get help, or suffer embarrassment. Panic attack symptoms often include rapid heartbeat, chest pain, difficulty breathing, gastrointestinal distress, faintness, dizziness, weakness, sweating, fear of loss of control or of going crazy, dying or impending doom. People with these symptoms often avoid phobic situations, even to the point of staying at home for their entire lives.

(*Taber's Cyclopedic Medical Dictionary*, 17th ed., 1993)

Zoom in, floor level. Opera plays in the background, and we see a heavy steel apartment door opening slowly. An arm emerges and feels around. A woman peers out to see her newspaper lying just out of reach.

'Not again!' she snaps, and slams the door.

Zoom out.

The door opens again. On her knees, now she's armed with a broom. Her eyes averted, her diaphragm heaving, suddenly the broom flails out. She tries dragging the newspaper in with it ... damn!

Can't get it.

Out of breath she pulls back, aggravated, muttering, tossing aside both broom and eyeglasses. Quietly, she begins reciting the names of U.S. presidents.

She's not giving up.

Gripping the doorframe, one eye peering anxiously out, she leans forward again. Still whispering presidents' names, she slowly gets up on her feet, ever so careful not to look out into the corridor. Desperate, she finally hurls her whole body towards the newspaper and lands face first, on the floor.

But she's got it.

Quickly she slides back into the apartment. She's inside. She's safe. She closes the door, leans against the wall, relieved, trying to catch her breath ...[1]

Imagine. So many people – mostly women – endure this type of ordeal every single day.

The Scope of the Problem

Since its symptoms include 'frightening palpitations and tachycardia,' agoraphobic panic is commonly mistaken for a cardiovascular problem, and can lead patients to the nearest emergency room convinced that they are dying of a heart attack. As it turns out, a high percentage of cardiology patients with chest pain actually have undiagnosed panic disorder (Ballenger, 1987). The nausea and abdominal distress experienced by many agoraphobics is likewise often mistakenly attributed to gastrointestinal problems – from which we can conclude that there are far more people suffering from the disease than reports would indicate. One study has estimated that agoraphobia is present in as much as 2 per cent to 5 per cent of the population (Rosenbaum et al., 1995), with roughly 80 per cent of the sufferers being married women. In fact, women are between 2.5 and 4 times more likely than men to develop agoraphobia/panic disorder (Sheikh et al., 2002; also Joyce et al., 1989), and being female increases the likelihood of a person's developing one of a range of anxiety disorders by as much as 85 per cent (Cloitre et al., 2004).

In the U.S. context, a prevalence rate as high as 5 per cent translates into millions of people, mostly urban-dwelling (George et al., 1986), some too fearful of public spaces to leave their homes even to step a few feet to their mailboxes. So it is not surprising that many people know someone with agoraphobia, a disease that touches the lives of the 'ordinary' and the 'famous' alike. Marilyn Monroe, Kim Basinger, and Howard Hughes have been associated with it (Insane Asylum, 1998).[2] Sigmund Freud told a colleague he had experienced agoraphobia (Reik, 1949); Emily Dickinson and Charles Darwin may have suffered from it too (Adler, 1997; Barloon and Noyes, 1997a, 1997b; Colp, 1997; FitzGibbon, 1997; Fuss, 1998; Garbowsky, 1989; Gordon, 1997).

An Internet search (www.google.com) for the term 'agoraphobia' generates hundreds of thousands of hits, with links to sufferers, reams of personal statements, and websites for support groups and information resources. ABC's newsmagazine, *20/20* (ABC News, 1999) and 'Canada's national newspaper' the *Globe and Mail* (Huang, 2000; also Young, 2004) have dealt with the topic, and in 2001, *Time* magazine did a special report on phobias, which included a self-test based on criteria from the American Psychiatric Association's official *Diagnostic and Statistical Manual of Mental Disorders*: 'Do you have a persistent and excessive fear of ... being in a public place from which there is no escape?' 'Do you have an excessive and ongoing fear of social situations, such as going to the mall, the movies, or a restaurant?' 'Do you fear traveling without a companion?' (Kluger, 2001:59).[3] Agoraphobia also has inspired novels (Daigle, 1999; Hollingshead, 1992) films (*Copycat, The Fear Inside*), and television shows, having once been featured in a plot line on *ER*. Even Loblaws, the Canadian grocery chain, not long ago tucked a short piece on agoraphobia in and among the recipes in its self-published *President's Choice Magazine* (Underwood, 1999). One can also find numerous items for sale, including self-help videos and audiocassettes with titles like 'Agoraphobia: A Prison without Bars,' 'Fight or Flight? Overcoming Panic and Agoraphobia,' and 'Pass through Panic.' Searches at barnesandnoble.com and amazon.com turn up more than ninety books on agoraphobia – for sufferers, by sufferers, for friends and family of sufferers, and for therapists. Agoraphobia is also a major source of revenue for pharmaceutical companies, whose annual sales of the indicated antidepressants and minor tranquillizers reached a combined total exceeding $1 billion in 2002 alone.

As profitable as the disorder has been, it comes at great personal cost to those who suffer from it, especially, as epidemiological and clinical studies have shown, in terms of quality of life (see Mendlowicz and Stein, 2000). For instance, people with anxiety disorders sleep less, and lack of sleep along with the drugs many of them take to manage their disorders place them at greater risk of having automobile accidents. Their spouses, children, and extended families pay a social and psychological price, so the sufferers' ability to sustain healthy family relationships and to enjoy life is also affected. From an economic perspective, there are both direct and indirect costs, both of which can be considerable. The direct costs include hospital visits or outpatient appointments, or even unnecessary tests (e.g., cardiac); the indirect costs consist of the sufferers' lost economic productivity and the lost earning time of friends and family charged with the responsibility of bringing them to clinics for treatment. In general, patients with chronic psychiatric disorders have difficulty maintaining continuous employment, and agoraphobia in particular may contribute to significant work incapacity (Edlund, 1990). We must also consider the fact that agoraphobics simply do not go out and shop as much as 'normals' do (Goffman, 1963), and their absence from the marketplace puts additional strain on the economy.

For these and other reasons, agoraphobia has gained increasing notoriety in recent decades. But evidence of phobias can be found in the ancient writings of Hippocratic physicians, who described 'men who feared that which need not be feared' (Errera, 1962). The ancient writers classified the symptoms of phobia under the category of melancholia (black bile), one of the three major types of insanity delineated at that time. By the eighteenth century, anxiety had begun to play an increasing role in the developing symptom complex of nervous and mental disorders and of individual anxieties; these, until then primarily the concern of theologians, became the responsibility of psychological physicians (Clark, 1995:564). At that time emphasis was placed on the classification of phobic symptoms (Errera, 1962:328), and nosologists described sudden states of restlessness, worry, and panic (Berrios and Link, 1995:546). The surgeon Le Camus (1722–72) sought to classify phobias according to the sense most affected, and Boissier de Sauvages (1706–67), a botanist, classified his observations using symptomatology and identified vertigo as the most striking characteristic of phobias. The French alienist Philippe Pinel (1745–1826) was reluctant to replace the earlier Hippocratic system, preferring to elaborate on existing classifications. He included anxiety symptoms with epilepsy, melancholia, rabies, and the 'motility' neuroses (Pinel in Berrios and Link, 1995:547). Pinel's student Jean-Etienne Dominique Esquirol (1772–1840) introduced the term *monomanie* to refer to both patients with classical phobias and patients with more delusional fears (Errera, 1962:328–31).

The remarks of Edme Pierre Chauvot de Beauchêne (1748–1830), Ernst Wilhelm von Brücke (1819–92), and Moritz Benedikt (1835–1920), however, are especially striking because these physicians spoke most directly to what eventually became the diagnostic category known as 'agoraphobia.' First, de Beauchêne observed that for his patients the presence of a companion often relieved phobic symptoms (Errera, 1962:331); this characteristic would be reported throughout the case literature on the disease. Brücke described symptoms he observed as 'schwindel angst' (in Van Horn, 1886); and Benedikt, regarded by some as the first to describe agoraphobic symptoms (in 1870), used the term *platzschwindel* (dizziness of places) to describe a patient 'unable to cross wide streets or open spaces' (in Knapp and Schumacher, 1988:25).

But it was the German (Prussian) neurologist Carl Friedrich Otto Westphal's (1833–90) famous article 'Die Agoraphobie' (1871), published in the journal *Archiv für Psychiatrie und Nervenkrankheiten*, that really set things in motion. Westphal gave this pathology its permanent name, and his report led to the almost immediate publication of several responses by American practitioners. From this point on, the clinical discourse of agoraphobia has continued to expand, with increasing publication of medical case literature, trials, and studies, discussion papers, letters to the editors of journals, and entries in the *Diagnostic and Statistical Manual of Mental Disorders*. (A recent search on Medline turned up more than two thousand references published in the last thirty years alone.) Together these publications have provided a forum in which physicians can discuss the phenomenology, causation, and treatment of agoraphobia, and many cite Westphal's report even today.

Reinterpreting Agoraphobia: A Sociological Problematic

Alongside these medical accounts, I offer in this book a sociological reinterpretation of agoraphobia – a critical analysis and conceptual framework for making sense of the dynamics and cultural implications of agoraphobia and psychiatric diagnosis in particular, and of sociocultural categories in general, since the publication of Westphal's 'Die Agoraphobie.' Contained within the clinical discourse of this disease is what may be referred to as the 'psychiatric narrative.' Specifically, although the discourse of the disease describes very real physiological and emotional experiences of suffering, implicit in the narrative is a sociocultural account of society, social order, social *ordering*, and, of course, power relations. This study takes a Foucaultian genealogical approach to demonstrating the overlap between the psychiatric narrative of agoraphobia and sociocultural narratives of marginalization. I assume that disease concepts are socially complex, and, drawing on the English-language psychiatric literature published since the late nineteenth century,[4] I explore three themes in particular: a) agoraphobia in the context of gender, 'race,' and class; b) the shift in recent decades from an emphasis on biopsycho*social* explanations for mental diseases to an emphasis on strictly biogenic explanations; and c) the sociocultural process of embodiment (materialization of the body) as it occurs in and through the category agoraphobia. All these are interconnected and indicative of a link between the discourse of agoraphobia and a larger discourse of social order, or the process of social inclusion/exclusion as it is manifest in psychiatry, particularly in terms of this disease classification.

Historically, a central question underpinning psychiatric accounts of agoraphobia concerns what it has meant to be 'normal,' a question that derives from the more fundamental and normative question of what it means to have social order. Indeed, the psychosciences are (to borrow from Rose) 'profoundly social' (Rose, 1998:67). Yet only a few social scientists have taken any interest in this psychological, apparently antisocial, disorder (see Brown, 1986; Reeves and Austin, 1986; Seidenberg and DeCrow, 1983; Swaan, 1990), even though medical sociology and the sociology of health, illness, and medicine are among the biggest subfields in sociology. Perhaps agoraphobia has received so little attention from sociologists because at first glance it seems to be a problem for individuals and therefore more suited to psychological study. However, I contend that agoraphobia is a sociological problematic in several respects.

First, Durkheim demonstrated in 1897 that suicide – the behaviour that seems to encapsulate individual distress par excellence – is in fact a social phenomenon (Durkheim, 1951 [1897]). And, because agoraphobia was not always so prevalent among women – until the First World War more than 80 per cent of the cases were diagnosed in men – we must consider the question of how a disease could be gendered (prevalent among men) and then subsequently *re*-gendered (to become prevalent among women). The issues of 'race' and class can be factored in here as well, in that agoraphobia, like hysteria and neurasthenia, has largely been constructed as a white, middle-class phenomenon. It is also evident that the question of what it means to be 'normal' has been informed by the capitalist imperatives of production and consumption. Moreover, evidence suggests that agoraphobia developed in response to the changes brought by modernity, that modern urban *social* conditions gave rise to the individual(ist) need for self-preservation. The symbiotic relationship between sociology and modernity clearly lends itself to a sociological study of this decidedly modern disorder.

But apart from these arguments, the study of individual problems such as agoraphobia in sociological terms is fundamental to the sociological imagination itself. As C. Wright Mills has stated, accumulations of 'personal troubles ... must be understood as public issues.' Sociologists must know that 'the human meaning of public issues must be revealed by relating them to personal troubles – and to the problems of the individual life' (Mills, 1959:226). As Mills also wrote, 'without an historical sense of psychological matters, the social scientist cannot adequately state the kinds of problems that ought now to be the orienting points of his [sic] studies' (143).

Rigorous sociology thus depends upon the examination of individual 'biographies' in the context of larger histories and social issues. An implicit question asked by this book, then, is what it means to do history and sociology *together*. Following Michel Foucault, I examine the practical, epistemological, and discursive production and regulation of (embodied) medical subjects in the context of a history of psychiatric ideas. In an implicit critique of linear history, in this book I contest claims to fixed meaning and am sceptical of 'natural' categories of knowledge. I draw attention to the relations of power that order our lives, by demonstrating that agoraphobia is a shifting category of knowledge that has changed in conjunction with a shifting psychiatric gaze. I scrutinize the politics, contestations, and conditions of possibility in which this disorder has been embedded, and I highlight the very act of representing agoraphobia (and really the people who experience it) as a key constitutive component of its production as a meaningful and powerful psychiatric entity. I call into question the representation of agoraphobics as classifiable and deviating from the *normal* and the *orderly*.

Medicalizing Gender

Previous analyses appropriately acknowledge the sociality of agoraphobia and the need to consider the disease in sociological terms. But they emphasize its prevalence among women as a direct result of women's structural inequality with men, thereby foreclosing on an analysis of agoraphobia in all its sociological complexity. This approach is consistent with other feminist studies of medicalized conditions ascribed to women such as anorexia, premenstrual syndrome, pregnancy and childbirth, menses, menopause, sexuality, and even battering. But of chief concern to feminists engaged in these analyses was, of course, the diagnosis of hysteria. Given its alleged prevalence among women, its origins in the nineteenth century, and its shared and overlapping history with agoraphobia (especially within psychoanalysis), hysteria is an important point of reference for the present analysis.

Feminists, especially since the second wave, have been exceedingly concerned with the history of this disease category and of psychiatry generally, not least because of their historical implications for women's position within patriarchal society.[5] Feminist arguments generally have sought to provide an alternative to traditional accounts of psychiatry and hysteria (e.g., Ellenberger, 1970; Veith, 1965), which have tended towards a progressivist view of history and medicine and have operated on the assumption that physicians are somehow located outside culture and are therefore immune to its prejudices. They have called into question histories of medicine and psychiatry that emphasized the achievements of 'great doctors' and eschewed analyses of the experiences of their female patients (Micale, 1995:67). Feminists have also challenged the uncritical acceptance of both hysteria and differences between women and men as biological, fixed, and universal.

Among these earliest feminist critiques of medicine and psychiatry were such books as Betty Friedan's *The Feminine Mystique* (1963), Kate Millett's *Sexual Politics* (1970), and Germaine Greer's *The Female Eunuch* (1970). Each in its own way cautioned against the destructive influence of science and medicine on women's lives. Psychiatry and psychology, and especially psychoanalysis, were seen in these critiques as being at the root of intellectual justifications for women's subordination, as serving only the interests of a patriarchy that sought women's social control – especially the control of women who transgressed traditional gender role expectations. In calling for a woman-centred approach to medical history, these accounts hoped to mitigate the negative impact of psychiatry on women's lives.

By the early 1970s, English-language feminist analyses specifically of hysteria had begun to emerge. The best known of these were Phyllis Chesler's *Women and Madness* (1972), Ann Douglas Wood's '"The Fashionable Diseases": Women's Complaints and Their Treatment in Nineteenth-Century America' (1974), and Barbara Ehrenreich and Deidre English's *For Her Own Good* (1978). These indictments of medical misogyny collectively sought to demonstrate the plight of women in the hands of the medical establishment. Chesler, a psychologist, drew from the social control arguments being made by an emergent anti-psychiatry movement to observe that women, especially iconoclastic women, were more likely than men to be labelled as mentally ill; and Ehrenreich and English, a biologist and social worker respectively, argued that psychiatry and psychology promoted a limited view of women's abilities and denied women their independence and their place in medicine as healers in their own right. Wood's objective as a historian was similarly to reveal the sexism and victimization of women in past medical writings and practices.

The 'male-oppression model' (Hartman, 1974:vii) that informed these hysteria studies, with its emphasis on the malevolence of doctors and the psychiatric establishment, came under sharp criticism by other feminists, and the focus soon shifted to women's roles and the meaning of women's hysterical behaviour. The historian Carroll Smith-Rosenberg (1972), for example, argued that hysteria was the outcome of women's anxiety about the ideal of Victorian womanhood and a form of passive resistance to the existing sex/gender system. Smith-Rosenberg's essay was extremely influential, especially for having successfully navigated around the narrow woman-as-victim approach.

In time literary studies of hysteria began to emerge. Among these was Elaine Showalter's *The Female Malady: Women, Madness, and English Culture, 1830–1980* (1985), which examined representations of mad women in literary and visual texts and argued that hysteria was a kind of protofeminism, a form of early protest or reaction to male domination. French feminists also entered the debate, arguing against psychoanalysis as a phallocentric discourse of power, and in particular saw hysteria as a struggle against controlling imperatives of femininity (see, e.g., Cixous and Clément, 1986). In the United States, the deconstructionists, most notably those whose work was compiled in a key collection entitled *In Dora's Case* (Bernheimer and Kahane, 1985; see also Hunter, 1983), were similarly hostile to Freud, and collectively undertook a severe critique of his handling of his patient Dora's hysteria.

Though sophisticated theoretically, these literary studies were not particularly useful as histories and suffered from a tendency to conceptualize hysteria within the narrow victimization framework that since the early 1970s had been rejected by other feminists. Still, all the texts mentioned above have made important contributions to both feminism and feminist scholarship for drawing attention to women's subordination vis-à-vis the medicalization of femininity. This book builds on those previous arguments but seeks to go beyond them, by offering important conceptual and discipline-specific insight – that is, a socio-logical perspective that is missing from these analyses of hysteria undertaken mainly by historians and literary critics.

Aims of the Book

Certainly the subordination of women through psychiatric diagnosis provided the initial motivation for my investigation, as it did for the scholars of hysteria described above. But the reductionist femininity of agoraphobia is only one of several important aspects of the history of this disease. We must interrogate the disease's early and substantive history as a disease prevalent among men. It is also necessary for us to examine the epistemological shifts within psychiatry since agoraphobia was first 'discovered,' and the important implications of those shifts for how agoraphobia has been treated and understood over time. Finally, we must consider agoraphobia's variability – and instability – as a disease category and the implications of this instability for the process of embodiment. Existing accounts accept uncritically the disease category of agoraphobia as a uniform and stable disease concept, yet a close reading of the psychiatric literature reveals that, in fact, practitioners and researchers deploy this disease concept quite inconsistently, thereby suggesting that agoraphobia has been a disease with many ontologies. Not only has agoraphobia been a disease prevalent among men and women, but it has also been referred to by several different names, including panic, panic disorder, agoraphobia with or without panic, space phobia, claustrophobia, neurosis, and anxiety, and by several different descriptions, including a symptom, a syndrome, a disease, and a disorder. This variability has persisted despite the American Psychiatric Association's efforts to contain agoraphobia within its 'scientific' system of classification, set forth in the *Diagnostic and Statistical Manual of Mental Disorders*.

Accordingly, the central aim of this text, like that of previous feminist analyses of hysteria, is to examine critically the practices and assumptions of psychiatry. But this book specifically seeks to confront the gap between sociological and psychiatric conceptions of mental disease by examining the discourse of agoraphobia in terms of wider social processes. My hope is that, by extension, my analysis will demonstrate the usefulness of sociology for understanding the 'psychiatric narrative' of other medicalized conditions – not least hysteria – because this narrative is inextricable from a normative theory of social order that both informs and is informed by the process of gendered medicalization. Such an endeavour follows from Foucault's genealogical work in its emphasis on the fluid and shifting nature of psychiatric discourse.

Method and Methodology: Towards a Genealogy of Psychiatric Discourse

In his essay 'Genealogy and Social Criticism,' Foucault observes an 'increasing vulnerability' in recent years to 'criticism of things, institutions, practices, discourses.' He remarks that the 'inhibiting effect of global, *totalitarian theories*' has become evident, as well as a 'certain fragility' in 'the very bedrock of existence,' especially those 'aspects of it that are most familiar, most solid and most intimately related to our bodies and to our everyday behaviour' (Foucault, 1994b:40). Foucault's own work has contributed greatly to this 'insurrection of subjugated knowledges,' this emergent interest in 'historical contents that have been buried and disguised in a functionalist coherence or formal systematisation.' He offers a genealogy of knowledge, a history of the centralized production of theories within privileged regimes of thought (41).

Though he would not say he had a method per se, I follow Foucault's genealogical approach in assessing critically the totalizing role of psychiatric practices and discourses in the production of agoraphobia. What follows is a 'history of the present,' a 'perspectival genealogy' of one among many 'problem spaces, rationalities, authorities and technologies' of which the combined truth effect is to 'situate persons in particular relations of force' (Rose, 1994:53). My aim is to disrupt those aspects of this psychiatric disorder that are taken for granted, especially the stability and authority of psychiatric knowledge and the 'historical contents [that have been] buried and disguised' (Foucault, 1994b:41). As Foucault has put it, 'it's a matter of shaking this false self-evidence, of demonstrating its precariousness, of making visible not its arbitrariness, but its complex interconnection with a multiplicity of historical processes' (1991:75). By examining critically the apparent stability of psychiatric categories, we may challenge the physical reductionism of the medical model of disease, the alleged neutrality of medical-scientific ideas, and the dualistic assumption of a mind-body split.

Accordingly, I am interested in the processes by which social categories are naturalized within and by psychiatry, and my methodological objective is to trace and to problematize these extant categories as historical formations. Such a post-structuralist approach can reveal how dominant rationalities – such as psychiatry – are deployed as technologies of power: 'how forms of rationality inscribe themselves in practices or systems of practices, and what role they play within them' (Foucault, 1991:79; see also 1982:210). Central to my analysis are Foucault's concepts of 'biopolitics' and 'biopower.' He defines biopolitics as that 'endeavor, begun in the eighteenth century, to rationalize the problems presented to governmental practice by the phenomena characteristic of a group of living human beings constituted as a population: health, sanitation, birthrate, longevity, race ...' (1994a:73). Biopolitics embodies the 'methods by which human behavior is directed' (77) and 'the subjugation of bodies and the control of populations,' or biopower (1978:140), is exercised. Power in this sense constitutes individuals' subjectivity, and operates through its access to individuals' bodies, acts, attitudes, and modes of everyday actions (1994f:125).

I examine, therefore, the role of psychiatry – as one of the human sciences of which Foucault was so critical – in *governing* the population, that is, in exercising this complex form of power over the lives and conduct of people through their normative constitution as 'objects for rational management' (Rose, 1998 – see especially chap. 3; 2000; also Foucault, 1978; 1979; 1991). I examine in particular the *authority* of psychiatry, its 'capacity to speak truthfully about humans, their nature and their problems' (Rose, 2000:313). This psycho-scientific imperative is epitomized especially in the *DSM*, a 'technology' of subjectification that has, with each successive edition, helped make it 'possible to think of achieving desired objectives – contentment, productivity, sanity, intellectual ability – through the systematic government of the psychological domain' (Rose, 1990 in Rose, 1998:70).[6] I seek to illuminate the conditions of agoraphobia's continued possibility, asking 'on what basis knowledge and theory' about the disease 'became possible' (Foucault, 1970:xxi), how the category agoraphobia has been deployed, and how it became 'capable of being accepted at a certain moment' (Foucault, 1991:75). This illumination requires tracing the disorder's history since it was first named through to the present in its psychiatric and cultural context.

I am particularly interested in its mobilization in and through medical texts because these materials have always been a central venue for doctors' dialogues with one another about disease. They also constitute an essential site for exploring the processes that Foucault describes. I take these texts as empirically viable indicators of the material and discursive practices and social relations involved in the emergence of agoraphobic patients. Medical reports are indispensable historical artefacts, each with many possible stories to tell and very much a part of this pathology's history.

To this end, I examine psychiatric accounts of agoraphobia, taking them as representative of the ideas held about the disorder in terms of its symptoms, treatment, causation, and classifiability. Like Foucault, I ask not *what* but *how* cultural categories have been deployed through this history. I explore the cultural assumptions that inform psychiatric writing, such as dichotomous ideas about gender, and especially the question of what it means, both medically and culturally, to be 'normal' and 'pathological.'

The main source of data for this project, then, has been psychiatric writings about agoraphobia since the first cases published by Westphal in 1871. I restricted my search to English-language articles only, a restriction that largely has meant a focus on British and American psychiatry, though I include translated articles whenever possible. In the last two to three decades especially, the discourse of agoraphobia has become more international. It is important to note, however, that the discourse continues to be oriented particularly to American concerns and experiences and that most of the literature published today is in English.[7]

I began collecting article references by manually combing through the *Index Medicus*, a paper index to current published medical literature of the world. Its first volume, published in 1879, included the literature that followed Westphal's 'Die Agoraphobie' of 1871. I used the *Index* to find literature published from 1871 to 1965, looking under 'agoraphobia' and its related terms, including anxiety, fear, panic, phobia, neurosis, phobic disorders, diseases of the nervous system, claustrophobia, cenophobia, kenophobia, topophobia, neurasthenia, neurology, phobic disorders, and so forth. I found some additional references in the bibliographies of articles catalogued in the *Index*. I also collected dictionary definitions (the oldest is from 1882) in order to compare; they were not especially helpful, largely because over time they became extremely short. They did, however, provide me with synonyms (e.g., cenophobia, kenophobia) for the term agoraphobia that I otherwise would not have discovered. As it turned out, the practitioners did not use these synonyms, and I found no articles when I searched for the terms in the *Index*.

All told, I found approximately 130 relevant publications from the years 1871 to 1965. This number is necessarily approximate because it includes references to Freud's writings on agoraphobia, none of which was the main focus of any journal article, but which nonetheless were centrally important in this history and in the body of psychoanalytic literature that developed as a result. Conversely, though I discuss it extensively, I exclude the *Diagnostic and Statistical Manual of Mental Disorders* and its precursors from this number, simply to distinguish between it – a manual to 'all' mental illnesses – and the journal literature specifically on agoraphobia.

To locate articles published from 1966 to the present, I took a different approach. I stopped using the *Index Medicus* and took my search to Medline, an electronic index to medical literature from 1966.[8] A broad search through the National Library of Medicine's PubMed portal in October 2000, that is, simply for the term 'agoraphobia' with no limits other than language of publication, turned up 899 references, nearly all of which were published after 1980, the year that *DSM-III* was released. I repeated the search in March 2001, by which time the list had more than doubled, but by then it was evident that adding to the bibliography would not augment my reading of the literature in a significant way. Lag-time between publication date and indexing, perhaps the addition of new journals to the Medline index, and continual research and marketing of pharmaceuticals would help account for this huge jump in numbers.

Given the high number of references to literature published from 1980 to the present, I sorted the references thematically. The themes that surfaced included

- physiological and psychological characteristics
- drug therapy
- cognitive-behaviour therapy
- drugs and cognitive-behaviour therapy together
- agoraphobia, depression, and other conditions
- symptoms/diagnosis/aetiology/classification
- marriage and family relations
- heredity
- nursing
- children
- agoraphobia and other conditions

I then simply went through each grouping, choosing articles according to themes, relevance to my topic, and the law of diminishing returns. (For example, I did not need to read all the articles on the antidepressant imipramine to know that it has been widely used in the treatment of agoraphobia.)

Despite the obvious predominance of some themes (especially drugs, behaviour therapy, physiological and psychological characteristics, and symptoms, diagnosis, aetiology, and classification), managing the large amount of literature in this period (1980 to the present) was particularly complicated. Although a relationship between the release of *DSM-III* in 1980 and the scope, tone, and amount of literature published thereafter was evident, the task of sorting the articles was counter-intuitive to the strong sense I had already developed that the classification of agoraphobia was extremely problematic. Yet here I found myself with the need to classify (however loosely and inconsistently) the articles written about it in order to proceed with my research. Needless to say, the divisions I assigned to the literature were arbitrary; but knowing of no other way to manage the huge number of references, I continued sorting and summarizing the literature in terms of emergent themes.

Following this extensive analysis of the medical literature, I turned to the cultural literature in order to situate the medical literature in a more critical and sociological context. This literature also helped bridge the division I had inevitably created by choosing to approach my study thematically rather than strictly chronologically. That is to say, on some level I did set out to write a traditional history of agoraphobia from the time it was named until the present. Doing so permitted me an overview of the disease in the context of psychiatry as a professional discipline, with shifting emphases and allegiances. But I also wanted to write a more self-conscious history, looking not for the 'truth' of agoraphobia per se, but rather for answers to sociological questions about its cultural emergence and persistence, and about the extent to which social theories and medical theories have historically overlapped and interconnected.

To this end, I attempt to stay as close as possible to the actual words doctors have used. Since one of the main objectives of this work is to provide a sociological analysis of their texts, attention to language is necessary so that the *sociality* of the clinical discourse will become evident. Readers will notice in particular that I frequently use the term 'disease' in describing agoraphobia, thereby suggesting an implicit endorsement of the very discourse I seek to critique. My decision to follow this naming was deliberate, in that I believe the only alternative terms are 'disorder' and 'syndrome,' and I am not convinced that using these terms would represent any less of an endorsement, since they too invoke the 'normal' and 'pathological' binary. Moreover, I am concerned that a 'lesser' term could imply that I do not take agoraphobia seriously as a real problem for people, and I am reluctant to send that message.

'Disease' is not the only term I use in the text, however. I use a number of terms interchangeably, especially disease, disorder, syndrome, symptom, and pathology, as well as agoraphobia and panic, and I do so because the doctors do. That means, for example, that in one passage describing a particular article I may use one term, whereas in the next, if it concerns an article using a different term, I will follow a second usage. (As it turns out, many articles themselves use more than one term.) Although this interchangeability of terms may be confusing, it helps illustrate the extent to which agoraphobia has been, despite its relative consistency of symptoms, a remarkably unstable category.

At the risk of conflating the unique disciplines of psychiatric medicine, psychoanalysis, and psychology, I also often use the words 'doctor,' 'psychiatrist,' and 'medicine' to include psychologists, who frequently are themselves doctors of medicine but sometimes are not (see Rosenberg, 1992:246 for a useful definition of psychiatry along these lines). In addition, I consider their work *medical* (and psychiatric) to the extent that Medline catalogues it as such. My intention is not to obscure the distinct contribution by psychologists, but I have elected not to distinguish between psychologists and medical doctors wherever the point I wish to make allows for such glossing over. Similarly, I sometimes use 'clinician,' 'physician,' 'practitioner,' and 'doctor' when, technically speaking, I mean 'researcher' (the latter being a more relevant term in the most recent literature). Here as well I distinguish among these terms when it is necessary for my argument to do so; otherwise, I use terms interchangeably simply in order to avoid monotony in the text.

An important criticism that may be made of my methodology is that I approach this work only from the perspective of doctors' written words. Like the vast majority of the articles written by psychiatrists, the voices of patients do not emerge in any substantive way in this analysis. But, as we shall see later in the text, first-person accounts are rare in this discourse, and individual case reports (not unlike the one depicted in the movie scene that opens this chapter) become increasingly few and far between as psychiatry becomes neo-positivist, evidence-based, and genetically oriented. I contend that the absence of patients is actually quite telling – that their silence in this discourse 'opens a space in which meanings can proliferate' (Poovey, 1987:152). The exclusion of patients from the literature ostensibly written about them is critically important to the objective tone that scientific writing must project and says much about patients' positioning as subject-objects in relation to the practice of psychiatry. Although this methodology has mirrored (if not implicitly endorsed) the psychiatric literature in excluding patients' voices, it has been useful in three respects. First, it has made possible an exploration of the ways in which representational practices are indicative of (psychiatric) culture and cultural shifts. Second, it has permitted an understanding of how psychiatric claims become facts through practices of representation, namely, medical publication. And third, it has illuminated the ways in which knowledge about agoraphobia has been *made* and not simply *found*. In light of this, I cannot offer the last word on agoraphobia, but nor would I want to do so. I can only offer one interpretation of these psychiatric texts, and, as Clifford Geertz (1973) might say, it is a matter of 'thick description.' These texts are interpretations of normative concepts and structures – interpretations of interpretations of interpretations. The notion that one could get at the truth of agoraphobia is precisely what I take as my problematic.

It is a central assumption of this text, then, that psychiatry is shaped by factors beyond medicine. In the words of Arthur Kleinman, 'psychiatric concepts, research methodologies, and even data are embedded in *social systems* ... Through them, psychiatric diagnostic categories are constrained by history and culture as much as by biology' (Kleinman, 1988:3–4). Accordingly, I argue that from the outset of its recorded history, the discourse of agoraphobia has been more than simply descriptive of an individual biological disease phenomenon. On a certain level the concept of agoraphobia is a metaphor – a window into our culture and social relations. As Susan Bordo puts it, the 'psychopathologies that develop within a culture, far from being anomalies or aberrations,' are 'characteristic expressions' of it. They may even be 'the crystallisation of much that is wrong with it' (Bordo, 1993:141).

To the extent that psychiatric diagnoses bear a certain amount of social content, psychiatric thought would benefit from a more sociohistorically informed understanding not only of the pathologies with which it is concerned, but also of the context in which these patholo-gies exist. Social currents have shaped the trajectory that agoraphobia has taken within psychological medicine; reading the literature on ago-raphobia with that shaping in mind enables us to see psychiatric narra-tives in terms of cultural processes and to interrogate the assumptions that inform this body of writing. These assumptions include but are not limited to dichotomous and normative ideas about gender, 'race,' and class, and especially the question of what it means, both medically and culturally, to be 'normal' and 'pathological.' Psychiatric texts are an important arena where values, meanings, and identities are negoti-ated (Poovey, 1987:138), and I aim to situate these clinical representa-tions by emphasizing their deep sociality and illuminating how the continual reinvention of agoraphobia has, to borrow again from Mary Poovey, historically 'performed critical ideological work'(1988:2).

Thus, as my genealogical approach would suggest, I do not think that a coherent theory of agoraphobia – of disease – has been viable for all times and places. The disease, like everything else, has a complex sociology – which is not to say that agoraphobia is not real or that the experiences of its sufferers are illegitimate, but rather that this shifting disease concept has a social and historical context. It is not meaning-less, for example, that the *DSM* includes no anecdotal or historical information, but offers only checklists of decontextualized criteria that a given patient may or may not fit.

I sympathize with agoraphobics and recognize that their anxiety is genuine; my hope is that analysis of the disorder's historical-socio-logical underpinnings – understanding one's 'personal trouble' as a 'public issue' – could offer persons with agoraphobia and the profes-sionals who work with them an additional means of making sense of their experiences. In seeking to facilitate deeper insight into what it is to experience this disease, I am assuming that a fuller picture – one that is not constrained by rigid psychiatric concerns, but that is inclusive of sociological considerations – will enable sufferers to suffer less. As we will see, pharmaceuticals, followed by and often combined with behaviour and cognitive therapies, today constitute the most common approach to treating agoraphobia. Might there be room within this framework to consider the disease within a social and historical con-text? What might understanding its normative dimensions, its politics, and its shifting epistemology contribute to the existing psychiatric picture?

Plan of the Book

Narrating Social Order unfolds as follows: chapter 2 looks at the relationship between modernity, social change, and the emergence of agoraphobia in the nineteenth century. The disease is situated in its urban conditions of possibility and examined in the context of parallel discourses of social disorder and anxiety among physicians, classical theorists, and architects and city planners. This discussion is followed by an overview in chapter 3 of the different psychiatric approaches to understanding and treating agoraphobia since the late nineteenth century. These include turn-of-the-century biopsychiatry, psychoanalysis, behaviourism, and late-twentieth-century biopsychiatry with its emphasis on genetics, pharmaceuticals, evidence-based medicine, and the categories in the *Diagnostic and Statistical Manual of Mental Disorders*. In chapter 4, I examine agoraphobia in terms of gender, 'race,' and class and especially in terms of the normative question of social order upon which this diagnosis historically has been based. This question continues to inform the category of agoraphobia today; its classification in the *Diagnostic and Statistical Manual of Mental Disorders*, the rise of neopositivism, and the associated marginalization of biopsychosocial explanation for mental disease in the form of psychoanalysis are explored in chapter 5. The perception of science as a superior form of knowledge in all instances is especially challenged here; despite the American Psychiatric Association's tireless efforts to implement its system of standardized psychiatric classifications, in practice the category of agoraphobia has been patchy at best. The official criteria for the disorder change with each edition of the *DSM*, and practitioners and researchers consistently deploy them inconsistently. Despite the projection of scientific neutrality, this chapter tries to show that the *DSM* – as a 'technology of normalcy' (Gleason, 1999:9) – is actually embedded in the social. It follows that the definitions of and criteria for agoraphobia would be as variable as they are from one edition to the next. Finally, the book concludes with a discussion of agoraphobic embodiment as a process that unfolds in and through disease and cultural categories. My objective here is to transcend current theoretical debates that distinguish between material and discursive explanations of medical phenomena. By conceptualizing the body beyond Foucault's subject-object as an intra-action *between* the material and the discursive, I attempt to account for agoraphobia's variability in spite of its representation and deployment by experts as a monolithic disease concept.

2 Urban Modernity and Social Change: Diagnosing Alienation

This history of agoraphobia begins in the late nineteenth century. At that time, science, including medicine, was assuming a position of great social importance in an increasingly secular society in which medical professionals could reasonably aspire to higher status (Porter, 1997:348; also Lunbeck, 1994:27). The gap between lay and professional medical knowledge was also expanding, and sickness was increasingly defined as best left in 'credentialed hands.' Physicians' abilities were 'powerful and seductive' (Rosenberg, 1992:267–8), and in this era of self-improvement doctors working within a potentially lucrative medical market had an unprecedented degree of authority (Hansen, 1992:119; also Porter, 1997:305).

As the role of medicine in society expanded, so too did the division of medical labour. Many doctors tended towards specialization in psychological medicine, for which demand was also on the rise. Professional psychotherapy provided a 'vocabulary of troubles ... shaping lay definitions of everyday difficulties [and] moulding the presentation of individual complaints [into] problems suitable for professional treatment' (Swaan, 1990:139). Psychiatry was becoming a gatekeeper, its societal tasks being to 'persuade ... citizens to behave in accordance with certain norms' (Grob, 1985:267) and to police the boundaries between the sane and the insane, the normal and the pathological (Porter, 1997:513). The citizenry, including those who presented themselves for treatment, supported this new kind of moral work because medicine gave people a language and a framework for speaking about themselves, their everyday experiences, and, most important, their problems. In this context the medicalization of their deviant behaviours 'well might have appeared humanitarian and progressive' (Hansen, 1992:118).

It follows that patients and doctors collaborated in the construction of both the agoraphobic condition and the agoraphobic person who did not conform to 'normal' expectations. A new discourse was emerging about the agoraphobe as a social type, a process that unfolded through medical encounters with agoraphobic patients and subsequent medical and non-medical publications.[1] But, as Clark has shown, the delineation of anxiety and panic disorders 'required more than just the existence of an organized medical profession and psychiatric specialty and the presence of free-floating symptomatologies waiting to be appropriated and classified.' What was also required was enough of a change in one part of society to ensure that 'anxiety and panic no longer appeared as more or less continuous or recurrent features of common life, but rather as exceptional and to some extent avoidable disturbances to individual mental health and well-being' (Clark, 1995:567).

In other words, it was 'normal' in pre-modern and modern times to be anxious about such things as crop failure and famine, epidemic diseases, personal security, war, and so forth. But with the rise of industrial capitalism, urban existence began to take on a new – and allegedly unhealthy – character. Only in the modern industrial period have anxiety and panic become more 'exceptional' and more 'individualized.' Indeed, agoraphobic anxiety and panic could have been seen as individual *illnesses* only when 'normal' everyday background anxiety had been significantly reduced (see Clark, 1995:568). In a paper aptly entitled 'Do Our Present Ways of Living Tend to the Increase of Certain Forms of Nervous and Mental Disorder?' Dr Charles Atwood of New York wrote that 'our rapid and over strenuous life,' unaccompanied by sufficient rest, is the cause of the 'increase in nervous and mental derangement.' He saw mental strain as the result of the 'increased demands upon us, the increased number of sensory impressions and variety of ideas forced upon us by our increasing interests. There is scarcely time for the reception of impressions and no time at all for their proper assimilation ... The emotions are intensified by our present rapid methods of living, and drawn upon continually' (Atwood, 1903:1070–2).

The 'rapid methods of living' described by Atwood were particular to the modern urban context, in which there was no shortage of psychological issues on which early-twentieth-century psychiatrists could work. With its diversity of inhabitants and the myriad issues available for moral and sociological analysis, psychiatrists were eager to make the most of all the city had to offer their project of turning everyday life into the very lifeblood of their professional expertise (Lunbeck, 1994:4). But Atwood's remarks also reflect an emerging and expanding fear of the city evident in many physicians' writings. Anthony Vidler observes that 'agoraphobia was identified not simply as an affliction of the modern city dweller but as proof that contemporary cities were in their very form bad for health' (Vidler, 1991:35).[2] Dr Henry Sutherland, for example, maintained that some patients experienced agoraphobic feelings only in cities, as demonstrated by their ability 'to bear the sight of a wide green plain' (Sutherland, 1877:266). Sigmund Freud also expressed some concerns about city living, arguing that 'modern nervousness' was spreading rapidly. The tension between individual constitution in the nervous patient and the demands of modern civilization, between 'living in simple, healthy, country conditions,' as the 'forefathers' did, and living in 'the great cities,' was causing the '"increasing nervousness" of the present day and modern civilized life' (Freud, 1950b [1908]:77–8).'[3] Abnormal anxiety was on the rise, acquiring a 'higher medical, social, and cultural profile' among neurologists, psychiatrists, and surgeons throughout the industrialized world, who faced a growing number of patients with anxious expectations of incapacity following minor or imaginary injuries that 'proved self-fulfilling even in the absence of any physical damage.' By the turn of the century, anxiety in the form of neurasthenia, anxiety neuroses, and psychasthenia had come to be seen as reflective and symptomatic of the problems in society at large (Clark, 1995:564).

Echoing physicians' concerns, many architects and urban planners were also convinced that urban living was detrimental to citizens' physical and mental well-being.[4] Couched in the language of public health, a combination of 'spaces, persons, [and] techniques' emerged to problematize and act upon people's activities (Rose, 1994:51). Especially noteworthy was a tendency in this discourse to link disease with human character.

Nikolas Rose has argued, following Foucault, that human beings are 'subjects of freedom' who 'must be governed, and must govern themselves.' This kind of liberalism has origins in the nineteenth century; at that time there emerged the 'freedom' to act according to a certain code of civility – that is, within the constraints of norms and principles designed to shape and manage conduct (Rose, 1999:62, 69). Accordingly, there developed numerous programs for promoting a healthy *social* body through urban improvement, that is, for governing the citizenry *spatially* (cf. Rabinow, 1989). As Foucault observes, architecture became involved in problems of population, health, and the urban question (Foucault, 1980:148), and medicine (beginning in the eighteenth century) played an increasingly important role in the 'machinery of power' (Foucault, 1994d:100). The city had become a medicalizable object by this time, and the control of urban space in general – as the 'space that constitutes perhaps the most dangerous environment for the population' – became a focus of authoritarian medical-urban policy (99). Furthermore, space began to be used for economico-political ends: architectural and urban spaces were functions 'of the aims and techniques of the government of societies' (Foucault, 1984:239). At a time when massive numbers of migrants from the rural countryside were entering cities, and the need emerged to reorganize city space in order to facilitate industrial production and keep the economy of urbanism together, cities served as models for governmental rationality. Accordingly, new technologies of social and spatial control were developed alongside those of labour discipline (Soja, 2000:77). As Ed Soja has argued, 'hidden within the modernity that was taking shape was a profound "spatial fix." At every scale of life, from the global to the local, the spatial organization of society was being restructured to meet the urgent demands of capitalism in crisis – to open up new opportunities for super-profits, to find new ways to maintain social control, to stimulate increased production and consumption' (Soja, 1989:34).

Continuing Foucault's project, Rabinow demonstrates how techniques of social control that sought to combine the 'normalization of people' with the 'regularization of spaces' (Rabinow, 1989:82) were implemented through the reshaping of the physical and social environment. Urban space and architecture became central to the micropolitics of a specific and modern form of power (Rabinow, 1983:271) that included normative schemes intended to facilitate (and regulate) hygiene, civility, morality, health, and happiness. Architects and planners 'enact[ed] a medical vocation' of sorts by designing space so as to organize social relations and mitigate the ill effects of poor light and sanitation, a lack of air, overcrowding, and congested circulation (Vidler, 2000:51; 2002:2).[5] If the received wisdom was that disease '[was] produced in certain types of social space, circulated around social space, alighted upon those predisposed by character or habits to succumb and ran its course in them' (Rose, 1994:56), then through their interventions architects and planners helped to constitute society as a 'social body' liable to sickness (52). They deployed various spatial 'technologies of health,' including (class-based) zoning to separate work and residential areas, and cultural and commercial activities. They opened up public space to a variety of normative gazes; through urban planning and the 'calculated use of architecture,' they enabled a 'well-regulated liberty' (Rose, 1999:73). In effect, they were an arm of the liberal state, governing and normalizing the population through redefinition of and intervention into the physical and social environment, including the private space of home and family.

Thus, along with physicians, architects and planners were positioned to specify what constituted the normal and the pathological, though it should be noted that their objective was not to discipline specific individuals per se (Rose, 1999:74; also Osborne and Rose, 1999) but to 'bring both norms and forms into a common frame that would produce a healthy, efficient, and productive social order' (Rabinow, 1989:11). As Rabinow puts it in his analysis of French modernity, society in the nineteenth century was gradually and increasingly perceived as an object *sui generis*; if the individual's actions were a function of his place in the social whole, there was no point in intervening in the individual's actions without addressing her or his social milieu (1989:11).

A parallel discourse in response to modern social change also surfaced among some classical social theorists, who, through their writing, sought at least to explain, if not ameliorate, the developing social turmoil they perceived. As Vidler observes, estrangement – between individuals, between the individual and the self, of classes and workers from work – was a persistent theme in the writings of social critics, who perceived a rupture in cities 'too rapidly changing and enlarging to comprehend in traditional terms' (Vidler, 2000:64). Thinkers such as Karl Marx (1964 [1884]), Emile Durkheim (1933 [1893]), Max Weber (1958 [1904–5]), and Ferdinand Tönnies (1957 [1887]) each in his own way was concerned about the social problems associated with the changes brought by modernity, including the rise of mass production and the new division of labour. With the decline of small-scale craft production and its replacement with modern mass production, a new division of labour produced impersonal relations and a loss of individuality, even as the ideology of individualism continued to grow and have influence.

For example, Karl Marx's (1818–83) historical materialism, concerned as it was with the transformation of society from feudal to capitalist relations of production, turned on the concept of alienation and the idea that in capitalist society 'political economy conceals the estrangement inherent in the nature of labor by not considering the direct relationship between the worker (labor) and production,' and between the worker and the 'objects of his production.' Estrangement was manifested 'not only in the result but in the act of production, within the producing activity, itself.' Marx went on to ask, 'How could the worker come to face the product of his activity as a stranger, were it not that in the very act of production he was estranging himself from himself?' Human beings were estranged not only from their work, its products, and themselves, however. They were estranged also from their fellow human beings. As Marx wrote, 'an immediate consequence of the fact that man is estranged from the product of his labor, from his life activity, from his species being is the estrangement of man from man' (1964 [1884]:109–14).

Examining the shift from (pre-modern) mechanical to (modern) organic solidarity, Emile Durkheim (1858–1936) was troubled by the problem of 'anomie' or normlessness and the lack of certainty that was so common in modern social relations. He observed that in pre-modern societies, social integration came from the values and symbols belonging to tradition and homogeneity. Society was 'a more or less organized totality of beliefs and sentiments common to all the members of the group.' But in modern urban societies, the situation was 'quite otherwise' owing to 'the solidarity which the division of labor produces.' In this context, 'solidarity resembles that which we observe among the higher animals. Each organ, in effect, has its special physiognomy, its autonomy. And moreover, the unity of the organism is as great as the individuation of the parts is more marked.' Organic solidarity is possible 'only if each [individual] has a sphere of action which is peculiar to him' (Durkheim, 1933 [1893]:129–31).

Max Weber (1864–1920) was critical of the inevitable bureaucratization of society and the concomitant destruction of human creativity. He described modern capitalist society as a 'cage' of 'rational conduct,' which was 'one of the fundamental elements' of both 'modern capitalism' and 'all modern culture' (Weber, 1958 [1904–5]:180–3). He wrote that the 'most important opponent with which the spirit of capitalism ... has had to struggle is 'traditionalism' (59). Ferdinand Tönnies's (1858–1936) assessment was quite similar; he used the terms 'gemeinschaft' and 'gesellschaft' to capture the change from social relations based in 'community' to relations based in 'associations,' or the individualistic, impersonal, competitive, calculative, and contractual dealings endemic in the modern industrial context. 'Gesellschaft' suggested a 'mere coexistence of people independent of each other,' whereas 'all praise of rural life has pointed out that the Gemeinschaft among people is stronger there and more alive.' In a gemeinschaft the sense of community among people is greater; it is a 'lasting and genuine form of living together,' not one 'transitory and superficial,' as in a gesellschaft (Tönnies, 1957 [1887]:34–5).

But it was Georg Simmel (1858–1918) who especially focused on mental life and the metropolis or 'seat of the money economy,' where exchange value and consumption were the basis for social relations. Like the other theorists, Simmel perceived that modernity had brought with it a host of social problems, and he observed that life in the modern city, with all its 'nervous stimulation' – the crowds, the intensity, and the rampant individualism – produced the ideal conditions for the development of mental and emotional difficulties. The 'psychological conditions which the metropolis create[d]' were constituted, in Simmel's words, by the 'rapid crowding of changing images, the sharp discontinuity in the grasp of a single glance, and the unexpectedness of onrushing impressions ... The city sets up a deep contrast with small town and rural life with reference to the sensory foundations of psychic life.' He went on to say, 'The metropolis exacts from man as a discriminating creature a different amount of consciousness than does rural life' (Simmel, 1950:410–11).

The city (especially the capital city, because it was there that bourgeois culture tended to dominate) was a 'key [site] for the changing modes of experiencing modernity' owing to its transformations in work, housing, and, ultimately, social relations (Frisby, 1986:5 and 70; also Wolff, 1989:143). Life was so fragmented in this 'asphalt and stone wilderness' (Vidler, 1993:34) that people had to create an 'inner barrier' in order to protect their fragile psyches and a 'blasé attitude' just to be able to cope. This blasé attitude was the result of 'rapidly changing and closely compressed contrasting stimulations of the nerves.' In this context, one's nerves were agitated 'to their strongest reactivity for such a long time that they finally cease to react at all.' Similarly, 'harmless impressions force such violent responses, tearing the nerves so brutally hither and thither that their last reserves of strength are spent; and if one remains in the same milieu they have no time to gather new strength.' Eventually, one would become unable to 'react to new sensations with the appropriate energy' (Simmel, 1950:413–14), a state of affairs driving one to take social distance by developing 'an inner barrier.' This inner barrier was 'indispensable for the modern form of life.' Without such psychological distance, the metropolis, with all its 'jostling crowdedness,' would 'simply be unbearable' for the 'sensitive and modern individual.' Simmel also noted, 'Since contemporary urban culture, with its commercial, professional and social intercourse, forces us to be physically close to an enormous number of people, sensitive and nervous modern people would sink completely into despair if the objectification of social relationships did not bring with it an inner boundary and reserve' (in Frisby, 1986:73).

As Simmel's remarks demonstrate, people were alienated and estranged psychologically and spatially – from one another, from themselves, and from their work. Emotional withdrawal and retreat into the self was a way of coping with progress and the exigencies of modern existence. But the condition that best captured this 'emotional trait' of anxious reserve at its most acute, this 'pathological deformation,' was, as Simmel wrote, 'the so-called "agoraphobia": the fear of coming into too close a contact with objects, a consequence of hyperaesthesia, for which every direct and energetic disturbance causes pain' (Simmel, 1978 [1907]:474–5). For Simmel, then, psychological conditions resulted from living in too close proximity to too many others.

Yet even the isolation typical of agoraphobic behaviour was considered by Simmel to be essentially social, unlike the view of it taken by physicians who conceptualized agoraphobia as strictly antisocial and therefore pathological (such as Dr Sutherland, who wrote that his patient 'scarcely ever leaves the house, [and] never goes into society' [Sutherland, 1877:267–8]). As Simmel explained, the 'mere fact that an individual does not interact with others ... does [not] express the whole idea of isolation. For, isolation ... refers by no means to the absence of society.' Moreover, the feeling of isolation is never as intense as when one is a stranger among many who are physically close, as in a crowded city street. Association determines isolation; it 'attains its unequivocal, positive significance only as society's effect at a distance – whether as lingering on of past relations, as anticipation of future contacts, as nostalgia, or as an intentional turning away from society.' Isolation represents a very specific relation *to* society, and 'a given quantity and quality of social life creates a certain number of temporarily or chronically lonely existences' (Simmel, 1950:118–19). Simmel's words suggest that psychological conditions were an inevitable consequence of – or panacea for – the strains of modern urban life.

The private sphere was thus constructed by middle-class ideologues as a purified and aerated refuge from the filth and immorality that the lower classes produced in urban streets (Wilson, 1995:149). This separation of space greatly intrigued Walter Benjamin, who was a contemporary of Georg Simmel's son and who attended some of Simmel's lectures. Benjamin simultaneously loathed and praised the city – it was the site of bourgeois domination on the one hand, and the space of intoxication and intrigue, of excitement and distraction, on the other. Fascinated with public space and all its stimuli, the display of commodities in the shopping arcades, the changing 'structure of experience,' and the different types of people moving through the crowds, Benjamin saw the city as a source of pleasure and danger, shocks and nervous pressure. Like Simmel, he described how people developed a defensive urban consciousness as a protective barrier against too much stimulation. Whereas Simmel theorized the *inner* barrier that urban individuals developed, however, Benjamin emphasized the *outer* barrier – that is, the retreat of the bourgeoisie into the privacy of their homes. In a manner suggestive of both Freud's theory of the unconscious and Simmel's observation of the tendency in modern individuals to retreat into themselves, Benjamin focused on the bourgeois interiorization of private life and observed that although it was exciting, the city was also alienating and necessitated self-preservation. He recognized that 'consciousness' had to be on constant alert as a 'screen against stimuli,' and that 'the more efficiently it is so, the less do these [shock] impressions enter experience' (Benjamin, 1973:117). The shocks and stimuli of the urban environment were 'unassimilable by the consciousness of the individual, and ... parried or deflected into the realm of the unconscious where they remain[ed] embedded' (Gilloch, 1996:143). In this context, the bourgeois home became a sanctuary:

> For the private person, living space becomes, for the first time, antithetical to the place of work ... The private person who squares his accounts with reality in his office demands that the interior be maintained in his illusions ... From this springs the phantasmagorias of the interior. For the private individual the private environment represents the universe. (Benjamin and Demetz, 1978:154)

In addition to the inner psychological retreat that Simmel described, then, refuge in the private home provided a means of coping with the pressures of modern urban life.

In sum, we can see how physicians, architects, planners, and social theorists helped give social estrangement 'all the dimensions of a psychological complex' constructed from a range of new mental diseases, which seemed to be tied to the urban environment. Agoraphobia was at once diagnosis and metaphor: the pathology described symptoms of anxiety at the same time as it captured the alienation that individuals felt and experienced in modern society (Vidler, 1994:12). More important, the diagnosis gave agoraphobic individuals a medical framework through which to make sense of their experiences in the city, and of themselves as different from 'normal' others (cf. Hansen, 1992). It was in this context that physicians diagnosed their patients with the disorder and debated the various aspects of it. In the next chapter we look at the three main approaches they have taken, namely biopsychiatry, psychoanalysis, and behaviourism.

3 Explaining Agoraphobia: Three Frameworks

The surest road to health, say what you will,
Is never to suppose we shall be ill;
Most of those evils we poor mortals know,
From doctors and imagination flow.   (D.K. Henderson, 1941)

European and American physicians began to publish case reports on agoraphobia in the later decades of the nineteenth century. Although there was a relatively strong consensus on the symptoms of agoraphobia and the profile of patients presenting with it, as well as a tendency to treat the disease outside institutional settings,[1] the approaches varied. Chief among them were explanations that unfolded along the lines of biological (neurological) psychiatry, those that followed a Freudian psychoanalytic approach, and those that favoured behaviourist principles. Although these approaches coexisted and shared a commitment to biology to varying degrees, they also competed and differed in their empiricism. With their emphases on different aspects and treatments of mental illness, each has occupied centre stage at a different point during the history of the disease. In this chapter I provide an overview of each framework and its main proponents, drawing on representative examples from the psychiatric literature.

Biopsychiatry, Old and 'New'

As a fairly new specialization, late-nineteenth-century psychological medicine was fundamentally neurological in its approach, and it was in this context that the first article on agoraphobia, by the German physician Carl Westphal (1833–90), appeared. Working within a tradition of academic brain psychiatry that emphasized systematic observation, experimentation, and dissection, Westphal was already known for his monographs on diseases of the brain and spinal cord and for the first-ever published medical case report (1869) of sexual inversion (homosexuality). But he would also become famous for his ideas about and his naming of agoraphobia. His article 'Die Agoraphobie' (1871; trans. in Knapp and Schumacher, 1988) would become the most celebrated paper on the disease, even though his colleague, Moritz Benedikt, had described the problem of *platzschwindel* in 1870.

In 'Die Agoraphobie,' Westphal detailed the symptoms of three patients: 'Mr C.,' a 32-year-old commercial traveller; 'Mr N.,' a 24-year-old merchant; and 'Mr P.,' a 26-year-old engineer.[2] These men had much in common. They all resided in the city of Berlin, and their symptoms all turned on their difficulty in walking through open spaces, crossing streets and squares, and being in crowds and enclosed spaces. When they found themselves in these situations they felt unsafe and were overcome with fear and even trembling. They thought they would be unable to cross the 'monstrous' square, believing, while in this state of fear and confusion, that something terrible would happen. But the presence of an 'escort,' a 'vehicle going the same direction,' or 'seeing an open door in one of the houses located on abandoned streets' seemed to alleviate the anxiety and enabled the men to go where they needed (Knapp and Schumacher, 1988:74). All were embarrassed by their condition and worried about being perceived as insane. All had lived with the condition for a period of time before consulting a physician. None knew the reasons for his fear, and for each of them it seemed to come on without warning. Similarly, they could not explain why at times they might make it halfway across a street or square and then feel the need to turn back instead of pushing on to the other side. In addition, they all had, to some extent, developed anticipatory anxiety or a 'fear of fear' following the first episode, so they could no longer cross open spaces where they had previously experienced an agoraphobic attack.

A neurologist, Westphal attempted to understand the disease and determine the cause of the men's suffering by attending closely to anatomical details. His investigation included a thorough examination of the eyes and, in one case, extensive measurement of the patient's physical features. His conclusion was that agoraphobia may have been allied to but was not of itself vertigo, as had been first suggested by Dr

Benedikt in 1870. Westphal wrote that his patients did 'not speak of dizziness, but of anxiety which overcomes them' (76). The eye examinations he performed likewise revealed no link to impaired vision (78). Although his patients had had some experience with epileptic seizures, Westphal maintained that agoraphobia was not a form of epilepsy – epileptic symptoms were thought to be an element of many mental disorders. Still, he conceded that agoraphobia was not necessarily an exclusive condition but could appear as a component of another illness. But since agoraphobic fears were traceable to circumstances that could be avoided (namely, public spaces), then the notion of a 'chronic psychological disorder' could not, as far as Westphal was concerned, be supported. Rather, agoraphobia was different from any other condition he had seen. Declaring that agoraphobia differed 'fundamentally from psychological diseases in a narrow sense' (79), he defined the condition as 'neuropathic,' that is, as a disease of the nerves, despite acknowledging that patients feared avoidable aspects of their surroundings. Still, he went on to say, he was 'unable to find an analogy to other known conditions, and, of all those peculiar sufferings that I have become familiar with in lunatic asylums, this one is quite different' (80).

Westphal had no success in treating his patients,[3] but 'Die Agoraphobie' was path-breaking and far-reaching in its influence. The ideas of other physicians such as Moritz Benedikt (1870), E. Cordes (1872), and Henri Legrand du Saulle (1876) were also influential, but Westphal's report really set the tone for the discourse of agoraphobia that developed. Several of his contemporaries immediately followed up with their own reports of agoraphobic patients. Even today 'Die Agoraphobie' finds its way into many bibliographies of the published literature on the disease.

There was general agreement among the early physicians as to the symptoms of agoraphobia. Although the word 'panic' was not yet in use, Westphal and his colleagues clearly were describing panic attacks. As Dr Albert Blodgett of Boston wrote in 1887, these episodes were a thing 'painful to observe [that] once seen [is] not to be forgotten' (Blodgett, 1887). The typical agoraphobic was easily recognizable, according to Dr J. Headley Neale, a British physician practising out of the Leicester Infirmary and Fever House. Sometimes the individual would suddenly grab a railing or a wall when in the street. But an agoraphobic could also be distinguished by his [sic] never being without a stick or umbrella, 'which you will notice he will plant at each step at some distance from him, in order to increase his base line of support.'

In the clinic context, Headley Neale added, 'you will have occasion to ask him but few if any questions, so graphic and pathognomic will be his statement of his symptoms' (Headley Neale, 1898:1322–3). Patients with agoraphobic feelings also had in common a tendency to wait a long time before consulting a physician about the problem, and although some were of 'nervous temperament' prior to the initial attacks of agoraphobia, others, who were not, endured the agoraphobic symptoms for several years before seeking help. For instance, Dr R. Prosser White of Wigan, England, reported on a patient who had complained that for the previous five or six years he had suffered from attacks of a nervous light-headedness occurring about twice a week and brought on by the ideas of space, vastness, height, depth, eternity, and other such things (Prosser White, 1884). Dr H.W. Hermann, of the St Louis Polyclinic Department of Diseases of the Nervous System, described two patients who suffered for three and four years respectively (Hermann, 1889); and the Kansas City physician Dr B.F. Records's patient, who had suffered from nerves for eight years, had been having agoraphobic symptoms for three (Records, 1896).

The question of why patients waited to seek help finds its answer at least partially in a common concern among patients as to how others would perceive them. As Frederick T. Roberts explained in the definition of agoraphobia in the *Dictionary of Medicine Including General Pathology* of 1882, during the attacks patients want to cry out, but do not want to be considered insane (see also Jones, 1898). Perhaps the most revealing account of the stigma associated with agoraphobia is that of a writer known only as 'Vincent.' He wrote: 'No one knows the truth about my condition. It is one of the characteristics of the victim of the disease to conceal it most cunningly.' This graduate of Yale University went on to say, 'I have deliberately told lies to avoid embarrassing situations and have even changed my plans to have my lies "come true"' ('Vincent,' 1919:299). Yet once diagnosed, many patients expressed relief. Perhaps, as Charles Rosenberg observes, 'an individual might well prefer to regard his or her deviant behaviour as the product of ... disease process. It might well have offered more comfort than the traditional option of seeing oneself as a reprehensible and culpable actor' (Rosenberg, 1992:269).

Even more interesting than the typical patient's behaviours and the tendency to postpone seeking help is that those most prone to agoraphobia in the period from 1872 to the First World War were affluent men, most commonly married 'adult men of education,' as the Yellow

Creek, Illinois, physician A.K. Van Horn put it in 1886 (601). Agoraphobia 'seldom attack[ed] poor people,' as Dr J. Headley Neale noted, and, in his experience, 'professional men suffer[ed] most, clergymen in particular.' He noted that he had known merchant princes, commercial travellers, middle-aged spinsters, and even young married women caught in its toils,' but had opted to use 'the male pronoun for brevity' since 'the disorder [was] more common in males' (Headley Neale, 1898:1322–3).

Although there was general agreement among these neurologically oriented physicians as to who developed agoraphobia and what it was like, the clinical status of agoraphobia was not so clear, partly because at the end of the nineteenth century phobias and obsessions were not yet seen as distinct problems, and would not be until Freud's work in this area (see Berrios and Link, 1995:551). A key issue in the early days was whether or not agoraphobia was simply a form of vertigo, and, secondarily, whether agoraphobia was merely a symptom of something else or a disease in its own right. (The latter issue formed part of a larger discussion of psychiatric symptoms as being to some extent the result of brain lesions [Berrios and Link, 1995:548].)

Following Benedikt's assessment, Westphal had already declared that whereas agoraphobia was perhaps related to vertigo, it could not be reduced to it. Citing the case of a 42-year-old seaman and soldier, the Boston physician S.G. Webber, who was among the first to respond to Westphal's report in 1872, rejected the vertigo thesis (Webber, 1872a, 1872b). But, also writing in 1872, another American physician, Dr Edward T. Williams, disagreed and argued that a 'person attacked with vertigo naturally seizes hold of the nearest object for support; a person subject to such attacks loses confidence in his power to walk alone, and feels unsafe without something at hand to cling to in case of emergency.' This person would have the 'same feeling in crossing a square that other men do in standing on the edge of a precipice, there is danger of being run over; add to this a state of nervous irritability amounting almost to insanity, and the pathogenesis is clear' (Williams, 1872:353).

The question of whether or not agoraphobia was symptomatic of vertigo, or perhaps neurasthenia (Suckling, 1890), epilepsy (Jones, 1898), hysteria (Records, 1896), or melancholia (Prosser White, 1884), was not a concern for all doctors, and they tended to use the terms interchangeably. Nonetheless, the question of aetiology remained, and generally speaking there were three related theories that often appeared together in the reporting of a given case: 1) inherited predis-position; 2) weak morals; and 3) problems with the nervous system. In the rare cases of agoraphobia in women before the First World War, problems with (or more specifically because of) the female reproduc-tive system were usually cited as the main source of trouble.

First, for example, 'properly adjusted eyeglasses' were thought by Dr H.W. Hermann to help with this 'distressing symptom' in people with a predisposition to neuropathy (Hermann, 1889) and hence a faulty constitution. The idea of predisposition or 'taint' informed the tendency to note any family history of insanity and any qualities of 'peculiarity' and 'nervous temperament' (Jones, 1898) and was consis-tent with the increasingly popular belief that heredity was the princi-pal cause of mental degeneracy. Dr Charles Mercier, Physician for Mental Diseases at Charing Cross Hospital, extended the notion of pre-disposition through heredity much farther back in patients' histories: he argued that agoraphobia could be attributed to the 'revival of instincts which existed in full force, and had great biological value' when 'our ancestors were arboreal in habit,' leaping 'from bough to bough and from tree to tree' (Mercier, 1906:990). In the arboreal stage of existence, the 'ancestors had a very strong aversion to any extended excursion from their place of security and refuge,' so when away from trees they felt a well-founded dread. This state of mind was repro-duced in agoraphobia, he claimed, so the 'mental craving' of the 'sub-ject of this malady' was not necessarily to be near trees, but near any tall vertical structures. Dr E. McConnelly similarly asserted in 1926 that agoraphobic 'fear' conflicted with our 'herd instinct.'

In the final decades of the nineteenth century, problematic behav-iours previously conceptualized as sin were increasingly medicalized and deemed the responsibility of physicians rather than the clergy (and patients were thereby relieved of guilt and responsibility). But although the medical model was becoming dominant at this time, its dominance was not complete, and patients' weak morals, as defined by the social attitudes of the era (not least an ideology of temperance and sexual propriety), were often cited as a factor in the development of agoraphobia. Accordingly, several doctors attributed its aetiology to moral impairment that manifested as debauchery and immoral exces-sive behaviour. For example, echoing the controversial but still some-what popular ideas of phrenology and degeneracy developed by the Austrians Franz Joseph Gall and J.C. Spurzheim in the eighteenth cen-tury, Dr R. Jones, Medical Superintendent of the London County Asylum in Claybury, described his agoraphobic patient as a 'degenerate' whose head accorded 'with those unexpected measurements often found in the insane, being full and well shaped.' He classified his patient as neurotic but acknowledged that not all neurotics were immoral types, since 'their kindred ... are noted for high literary and intellectual attainments' (Jones, 1898:568–70). The British physician Henry Sutherland described a patient who suffered from agoraphobia owing to overwork, another who 'devoured ... three times as much meat at each meal as is usually taken by a healthy person,' and a third whose agoraphobia was precipitated by 'the habitual indulgence in sexual excitement ... unaccompanied by natural gratification.' The six glasses of sherry he drank each day and the nude models who regularly posed in his art studio exacerbated this man's agoraphobia. A fourth patient, a clergyman, was afraid to walk in the street three months after his marriage, and a fifth was 'scarcely able to "crawl" about the town, as he was so much reduced by the unusual calls made upon his *physique* during [the] first few days of married life.' A sixth patient, taking leave of his marriage and his home for days at a time and complicating the situation with the consumption of spirits, indulged in 'excessive and promiscuous sexual intercourse.' Indeed, 'after these debauches he was unable, through nervousness, to walk down the stairs of his office without leaning on the arm of a clerk' (Sutherland, 1877:267–8).

In taking patients' histories, doctors also considered masturbation, if not as a cause of agoraphobia then at least as a contributing factor; there was a sense that masturbation was a crime for which mental illness was the punishment. For example, Dr S.G. Webber noted that his patient, a 42-year-old sailor, 'practised masturbation till seven years previous to [his] seeing him' (Webber, 1872a:297). And, citing weak morals as a contributing factor, physicians fairly commonly encouraged their patients to develop will power and 'moral determination' as a means of lessening the severity of or even avoiding agoraphobic symptoms altogether. As with 'sexual inversion,' though, a 'growing secularism paralleled and lent emotional plausibility to this framing in medical terms of matters that had been previously construed as essentially moral' (Hansen, 1992:125).

Finally, on the rare occasion that a woman was diagnosed with agoraphobia, the origin of the disease was believed to be her reproductive system. In one woman's case, for example, agoraphobia was thought to have resulted from excessive lactation and frequent childbearing.

Her physician, Dr C.W. Suckling, of the Queen's Hospital in Birmingham, was 'struck by the marked potency of childbearing as a cause of agoraphobia and allied morbid fears' (Suckling, 1890:478). Along similar lines, another woman's agoraphobia was alleged to be the result of, or at least exacerbated by, a 'laceration on the cervix'; her agoraphobic problem was always much worse in the week prior to her menstrual period. After Dr L.T. Potter 'made local applications,' however, this Chicago patient was still unable to travel without trepidation, so she took matters into her own hands. As the doctor reported, a 'bottle of valerianate of ammonia, and a flask well filled with brandy, were always her constant companions when undertaking a journey by rail.' Whenever this patient travelled, 'invariably' she sat 'with a brandy flask in the right hand, and her Bible in the left; presumably the one counteracting the influence of the other' (Potter, 1882:474).

In contrast, diagnoses in men were usually linked to problems of the nervous system. This diagnostic bent was consistent with the tendency (first demonstrated among American physicians but increasingly common in Europe) to include all the symptoms of anxiety and panic disorder within the concept of neurasthenia, a disease concept that 'had become so large ... it was threatening to engulf most of the "neurotic" states' (Berrios and Link, 1995:552). Even though most of the earliest patients were men, 'from the outset' these mental problems 'were assigned a definite place in the gendering of metropolitan psychopathology ... and thought of as fundamentally "female" in character' (Vidler, 1993:35). As Nancy Theriot observes, in the nineteenth century, women's nervous systems were thought to be more honed than men's; indeed, nerves themselves were thought to be feminine. Medical illustrations depicted the nervous system as female (as opposed to the muscular system, normally represented as male), as rendering women 'inherently prone to nervousness and to manic, depressive, or hysterical responses to life's difficulties' (Theriot, 1997:165).

If nerves were seen as essentially feminine, then even though men were being diagnosed with agoraphobia, they were in effect being diagnosed with a feminine (feminized) disorder. Dr Prosser White wrote in 1884, for example, that agoraphobia represented a 'curious phase of nervous phenomenon.' He went on to describe the symptoms in a 30-year-old professional man with no family history of nervous disorders but who 'suffered from a nervous kind of light-headedness ... brought on by the ideas of space' (Prosser White, 1884:1140). Dr Webber wrote that at 'the foundation of these sensations of anxiety lies one common ... corporeal cause' occurring 'in a certain pathological group, including what may be expressed by the name nervous irritability, crethism, irritable weakness.' He maintained that in this 'pathological group the entire nervous system ... may be thrown into extreme commotion' (Webber, 1872b:446).

Whereas questions of heredity persist in the contemporary biopsychiatric discourse of agoraphobia, the themes of morality, nerves, and the female reproductive system do not. In more recent times the discourse of agoraphobia has largely prioritized research (rather than case reporting). In turn, with the *Diagnostic and Statistical Manual of Mental Disorders* securely established as the 'bible' of contemporary psychiatry (Kutchins and Kirk, 1997), mental health research has largely been driven by interconnected concerns, namely, the signs and symptoms (phenomenology) of agoraphobia, its treatment, and its causation (aetiology). These emphases are not unique to contemporary medicine/psychiatry; rather, they have become amplified in today's context of hyper-empiricist evidence-based medicine and expanded to include epidemiological, pathophysiological, prognostic, and genetic investigations.

The concern with treatment reflects the desire of clinicians to be able to alleviate human suffering. Studies that test the efficacy of various treatments, such as cognitive-behavioural methods or drug therapies, seek to determine what treatments do and do not work to relieve certain disease states. In order to target and test the right treatments, however, there is a more fundamental need to understand the phenomenology of disease, meaning its observed and associated symptoms and features that form the basis for the disease's classification (although it should be noted that non-medical professionals [psychologists] are less concerned with differential diagnosis than are medical professionals [psychiatrists], who can and do prescribe drugs). Studies that describe the various characteristics of agoraphobia strive to establish a set of symptoms and related signs that practitioners can then treat. In other words, clinicians need to understand what a given disease looks like – its physiological and psychological markers – in order to rule out certain conditions and determine a suitable treatment modality, as well as to classify the disease appropriately (and delineate comorbid conditions).

To this end, agoraphobia researchers study the functioning of the endocrine system, for example, including the thyroid, the hypothalamus, the pituitary, the adrenals, and related hormones. They also investigate the heart, including heart rates and heart conditions such as mitral valve prolapse; the skin, especially skin conductance of electricity; the inner ear, especially balance and otoneurological and audio-vestibular abnormalities; the eyes and the processing of visual stimuli; the brain, especially the activity level of the right versus the left side, the electric signals emitted by the brain (electroencephalography), brain blood flow, and brain morphology; and the respiratory system, especially the problem of hyperventilation in panic. MAO (monoamine oxidase) and serotonin activity and levels are also examined (presumably for the purpose of MAOI and SSRI drug development). Finally, researchers also examine non-specific physiological markers, such as chronic pain.

Epidemiological research provides data that measure the incidence, distribution, treatment, and prevention of disease. They relate the distribution of disease to various factors affecting the population, and through their 'understanding [of] the magnitude of a disorder and the patterns of risk for the occurrence of a disorder (risk factors),' they may obtain 'clues as to what alterations might lead to prevention of the disorder.' This type of information 'is important for understanding [the] full clinical picture, who is at risk for being ill, and who may need treatment' (Weissman, 1990a:3).

Unlike the concern with symptoms and treatment, the concern with aetiology is an implicit one, however. Although there may be explicit interest in issues of aetiology in the basic science literature, there is very little direct discussion in the psychiatric literature of the aetiology of agoraphobia per se. But given the biopsychiatric orientation of the doctors and researchers involved, it is a fair generalization to say that, following a biomedical model of disease, they locate agoraphobia fundamentally in genetic predisposition and/or biological malfunctioning. To this end, there is a clear preference for pharmaceutically based treatment (often in conjunction with cognitive-behaviour therapies). That said, the use of a particular type of treatment can be taken only as a sign of what a practitioner's theory of causation might be, and, in fact, theories of causation are often not developed until *after* a particular treatment does or does not work. Treatments only point to theories – theories rooted in a biological versus a psychosocial framework. There is plenty of 'aetiological confusion' (*Lancet*, 1990:1314) and, moreover, no certain correlation between what are believed to be the causes of mental disease and the prescribed treatments.[4]

To be sure, though, biological explanations and treatment have clearly been favoured since the closing decades of the twentieth century. As one group of psychiatrists wrote in 1981, there is a strong prevailing sense that 'biological factors are preeminent' and are seen within mainstream psychiatry to 'outweigh psychosocial factors' in the aetiology of this condition (Sheehan et al., 1981). However, as we shall see in chapter 5, the renewed biopsychiatric framework is not simply a matter of returning to past paradigms. For one thing, late-nineteenth-century biopsychiatry did not so much disappear as become overshadowed by psychoanalysis, which was the mainstream psychiatric approach until relatively recently. But more important, although reductionist biopsychiatry in the late twentieth and early twenty-first centuries has re-emerged as mainstream, it has been recast based on a new technical, genetic, and pharmacological conception of the normal and pathological, and even of 'nature,' 'culture,' and 'society' (see Franklin, 2001a:3; 2001b:2; Rabinow, 1996 [1992]). As Healy put it in 2000, 'the psychobabble prevalent during much of the century has begun to give ground to a newly minted biobabble' (Healy, 2000:21). With vitalism on its deathbed (Healy, 2002:6) and the very meaning of life itself changing through biotechnological interventions, the line between 'interventions targeting susceptibility to illness or frailty' and 'interventions aimed at the enhancement of capacities' is increasingly difficult to distinguish (Rose, 2001b:20–1). This has been particularly evident in the discourse of agoraphobia in recent decades, with the proliferation of biotechnological fixes (and an accompanying counterintuitive preoccupation with the genetics of disease).

Consequently there is enormous interest in the efficacy of pharmaceuticals for interventions into agoraphobia. Although its history as a major component of medical practice begins as early as the nineteenth century (see Liebenau, 1987; Silverman and Lee, 1974), without question the pharmaceutical industry has had a significant and lucrative involvement in the treatment – and arguably the biopsychiatric (re)construction – of agoraphobia in the last thirty years. It is important to consider this involvement in two respects.

The first concerns the particular classes of drugs predominantly used to treat this disease, namely, antidepressants and minor tranquillizers, and the question of who prescribes them to whom.[5] The use of antidepressants to treat agoraphobia is particularly interesting in light of the long-standing debate in psychiatry over the question of whether or not depression and anxiety are related conditions.[6] For those clinicians who see them as linked and who opt for a pharmaceutical approach to treating agoraphobia, however, the most popular class of antidepressants has been the tricyclics (e.g., imipramine [Tofranil]),[7] in spite of evidence supporting the greater efficacy of the more recently developed (and heavily marketed) selective serotonin reuptake inhibitors, or SSRIs as they are more commonly known (such as Prozac and Paxil). Heavily studied and marketed, the SSRIs not only are considered effective as antidepressants but are described as having many applications within psychiatry, especially in the treatment of anxiety (Lopez-Munoz et al., 2003). Despite the popularization of SSRIs as the 'first-line treatment for panic disorder' (Bandelow et al., 2002) on the basis of their superiority to tricyclics such as imipramine (Verster and Volkerts, 2004), minor tranquillizers (benzodiazepines) have continued (as of 2002) to be the most commonly used medication for panic disorder (Bruce et al., 2003). These anxiolytics are still valued for their efficacy in blocking anticipatory anxiety or the fear of the physical symptoms of panic so often described by sufferers.[8] The study and use of alprazolam (Xanax), for example, has been especially widespread. Other minor tranquillizers, too, have been used to treat agoraphobia and panic.

The second issue is how the profit motive and pharmaceutical research interconnect. With the transformation in recent decades to a psychiatry that is, like the rest of medicine, much more evidence-driven, the relationship among controlled trials, drug prescription, drug marketing, and (a need for) the construction/invention of relevant disorders cannot be underestimated. The pharmaceutical industry reports and recommends treatments according to its own business interests. The elevation of SSRIs, therefore, needs to be understood in context. As Healy has demonstrated (1997), pharmaceutical companies are increasingly marketing diseases in order to sell their products, so the allegedly greater efficacy of SSRIs for treating anxiety disorders may say more about the skills and ingenuity of a given pharmaceutical company's marketing team than anything else.[9]

Finally, the question of which drug offers the better treatment has long been debated, but it may simply be a matter of which drug company is more forthcoming with research funding. It is clear, however, that pharmacotherapy, in conjunction with some cognitive-behaviour therapy, is seen as the best approach to treating agoraphobia today (see Bakker et al., 1998; Pecknold, 1987; Sakai and Takeichi, 1996; Telch et al., 1983). (This endorsement of cognitive-behaviour therapy is not insignificant and will be taken up below.) As we shall see later, by the end of the 1970s, psychoanalytic therapy, 'once the mainstay of treatment, [had] largely become an adjunctive procedure' (Rohs and Noyes, 1978:701) to the dominant biopsychiatry. It is to the psychoanalytic approach that we turn next.

Sigmund Freud and Psychoanalysts after Him

Although he may or may not have been motivated to do so by his own personal experiences with agoraphobia (Reik, 1948:15),[10] Sigmund Freud, the father of psychoanalysis, wrote extensively on the subject of anxiety neurosis, which as far as he was concerned was a disease in its own right separate from neurasthenia and hysteria and having symptoms that included phobias. Two of his cases – that of 'Little Hans' (Freud, 1925 [1909]), a 5-year-old boy with a phobia of horses, and that of 'Wolf Man' (Freud, 1955c [1918]), given this moniker for a dream the patient had had about wolves sitting in a tree outside his window – are perhaps his best-known works on the topic of phobias, but the only case literature he published on agoraphobia per se was actually relegated to a footnote in his translation of a lecture by the neurologist and psychiatrist Jean-Martin Charcot. At the time of translating, Freud already suspected that 'forgotten' trauma and sexual experiences and impulses played a part in the development of this hysterical symptom.

Describing a woman who suffered from 'anxiety neurosis (agoraphobia, attacks of fear of death, etc.),' Freud wrote that she was reluctant to admit 'that she had acquired these troubles in her married life.' Through analysis he discovered that the 'forgotten experience' was the deaths of two girls in her childhood town, which were 'retained in the patient's memory even when they seem[ed] to be forgotten' (Freud, 1955b [1893]:112–14 n2). In this analysis, along with a letter Freud wrote to his colleague and supporter Wilhelm Fliess at about the same time, in which he suggested that neurotic difficulties were rooted in undischarged libido, we begin to see the origins of Freud's theory of repression. He wrote: 'Things become more and more complicated as confirmation comes in. Yesterday, for instance, I saw four new cases whose aetiology, as shown by the chronological data, could only be coitus interruptus' (Freud, 1966b [1893]:184–5). Contra Charcot's assertion that hysterical attacks, vertigo, and agoraphobia were caused by heredity, Freud went on to say that 'the more frequent cause of agoraphobia as well as of most other phobias lies not in heredity but in abnormalities of sexual life. It is even possible to specify the form of abuse of the sexual function involved. Such disorders can be *acquired* in any degree of intensity; naturally they occur more intensely, with the same aetiology, in individuals with a hereditary disposition' (Freud, 1966a [1892–4]:139). In an effort to distance himself also from the then popular view of hysteria as degeneracy, Freud collaborated with the highly respected Viennese internist Josef Breuer to establish hysteria as a form of illness. He contended that phobias, like hysteria, were the result of traumas, but that whereas 'psychical factors ... may account for the *choice* of ... phobias, [they] cannot explain their *persistence*' (Freud, 1955a [1893]:88). Their persistence was the result of 'aktual' neurosis, or the development of symptoms as a result of disturbances in the 'sexual economy,' that is to say, obstacles to the gratification of instinctual sexual needs.

In an 1894 essay on 'defence neuropsychoses,' Freud distinguished among three classes of phobia: 1) the purely hysterical, 2) the typical, and 3) the obsessional (Freud, 1924 [1894]). Agoraphobia belonged to the last category, but Freud also distinguished between obsessions and phobias because in phobias the associated emotional state 'is always one of "anxiety," while in true obsessions other emotional states, such as doubt, remorse, or anger, may occur just as well' (Freud, 1962a [1894]). Moreover, whereas obsessions were varied and individualized, phobias were 'monotonous' and 'typical,' and divisible into two groups: the common phobias that are simply 'an exaggerated fear of things' ordinarily feared by everyone (such as snakes, night, death, illnesses, solitude), and specific contingent phobias – phobias of 'special conditions that inspire no fear in the normal man.' As an example he cited agoraphobia and 'other phobias of locomotion' that are based in the *recollection* of a state of anxiety, whereby the 'emotional state appears in their instance only under special conditions which the patient carefully avoids.' As Freud put it, 'what the patient actually fears is the occurrence of such an attack under the special conditions in which he believes he cannot escape it' (Freud, 1962a [1894]:74–81). The 'anxiety attack' thus feared is characterized by 'disturbance of the heart action' and of 'respiration,' as well as by 'sweating,' 'tremor and shivering,' 'ravenous hunger,' 'diarrhoea,' 'vertigo,' 'congestions,' 'paraesthesias.' Agoraphobia itself is frequently 'based on an attack of vertigo that has preceded it,' but not always. In some cases vertigo occurs without anxiety, permitting 'locomotion' to continue, but when anxiety occurs with vertigo under certain conditions 'such as being alone or in a narrow street ... locomotion breaks down' (Freud, 1962b [1894]:94–6).

For Freud, this type of specific 'contingent phobia' was a symptom and psychical manifestation of anxiety neurosis caused by the sexual tension 'extremely frequent in modern society' (Freud, 1962a [1894]: 80–1). In 1895 he illustrated this 'special constellation in the sexual sphere' with an anecdote about a patient named Emma who was unable to go into shops alone.[11] She remembered that at the age of 12 she 'went into a shop to buy something, saw the two shop-assistants (one of whom she can remember) laughing together, and ran away in some kind of *affect of fright.*' They were 'laughing at her clothes and ... one of them had pleased her sexually.' Then she had a second memory that 'when she was a child of eight she had gone into a small shop to buy some sweets, and the shopkeeper had grabbed at her genitals through her clothes.' Although this had happened, she went to the shop a second time, reproaching herself for having done so, 'as though she had wanted in that way to provoke the assault.' Freud surmised that Emma's state of '"oppressive bad conscience" is to be traced back to this experience' (Freud, 1966c [1895]:353–4). (Freud also included a visual representation – a map – of Emma's problem with the shops, which is significant because it sets him apart from practitioners both then and now. Visual representations have always been a crucial medium for medical knowledge, yet, historically, agoraphobia has been anomalous in having no visual representations apart from this one map drawn by Freud.)

As in his analysis of Emma, in letters to Fliess written between 1896 and 1899, Freud theorized that phobias or 'anxiety symptoms' were derived from fantasies, which are an 'unconscious combination of things experienced and heard, according to certain tendencies.' He wrote that 'if such a fantasy increases to a point at which it would be bound to force its way into consciousness,' the fantasy is repressed and a symptom is generated through a process of 'pushing the fantasy back to its constituent memories' (Freud, 1985 [1889]:247). Phobias have a 'more complicated structure than purely somatic anxiety attacks' and are 'linked to a definite ideational or perceptual content.' Still, it is clear that the disruption of sexual instinct is fundamental for Freud. As he stated in a reply to his critics (of which there were many): 'The main thing about the problem of the phobias seems to me to be that *when the vita sexualis is normal* – when the specific condition, a dis- turbance of sexual life in the sense of a deflection of the somatic from the psychical is not fulfilled – *phobias do not appear at all'* (Freud, 1962c [1895]:134). Marshalling the concept of desire to explain agoraphobia, something no one had yet done, Freud would eventually make a link between agoraphobia and 'the sexual nature of pleasure in movement' (Freud, 1953 [1905, 1910]:122 [original: 1905; footnote added 1910]) and the idea that the street was the site of forbidden sexual seduction (Freud, 1954a [1911]:360–2; 1954b [1911]:362–4), with agoraphobia the 'frontier fortification against the anxiety' so generated (1954c:581).

By 1900 Freud had established the psychoanalytic method of treatment based on his 'discovery' of infantile sexuality, the Oedipus complex, the unconscious, the dynamic nature of mental processes, and the dominance of the pleasure principle (the mechanism for reducing psychic tension arising from the drives). With the case of 'Little Hans' in 1909, he introduced the term 'anxiety-hysteria' to represent the psychic processes of phobias and other problems explicable through the Oedipus story. Freud described anxiety-hysteria as the most common of all psychoneurotic disorders and one that tends to develop into a phobia. On the basis of his analysis of Little Hans, Freud concluded that phobias were not 'converted,' that is to say, diverted from the mental sphere into a somatic form. Rather, they were 'set free in the shape of *anxiety.*' If phobias were not converted, then Freud's next task was to explain the nature and *process* of a phobia. As he stated, anxiety-hysteria developed into a phobia as the consequence of ridding oneself of anxiety. That is, the patient pays a 'price of subjecting himself [*sic*] to all kinds of inhibition and restrictions ... Nothing is left for [the mind] but to cut off access to every possible occasion that might lead to the development of anxiety, by erecting mental barriers in the nature of precautions, inhibitions, or prohibitions.' These are 'defensive structures' that take the form of phobias and are the 'essence of the disease' (Freud, 1950a [1909]:257–8).

Unlike the biopsychiatric methods, which, in Freud's opinion, were not successful, a certain amount of psychoanalytic work can succeed in uncovering the 'actual content' of a phobia. In such manifestations of anxiety-hysteria, repression has 'descended upon the unconscious complexes,' and is 'continually attacking their derivatives,' obscuring the 'products of the disease itself.' The analyst's role, he argued, was to help the disease by 'procuring it its due of attention.' That is, those who misunderstood the nature of psychoanalysis would think it would cause harm rather than help, but Freud maintained that 'you must catch your thief before you can hang him,' and for this the analyst needs to 'get securely hold of the pathological structures at the destruction of which the treatment is aimed' (1950a [1909]: 265–6).

In 1917, Freud included all phobic syndromes under the rubric of 'anxiety-hysteria,' distinguishing between phobic anxiety and 'free floating expectant anxiety' (Freud, 1963 [1916–17]:400). He also observed two phases of the neurotic process – repression and the transformation of libido into anxiety, and then the 'erection of all the precautions and guarantees by means of which any contact can be avoided with this danger, treated as it is like an external thing.' Accordingly, a phobia may be compared to an 'entrenchment against an external danger which now represents the dreaded libido' (410). Anxiety was thus not inherently pathological, but rather a mechanism developed by the ego in response to a perceived danger. Hence the term 'defence neuroses' (Compton, 1992a:219).

Interestingly, in 1918 Freud proposed a slight modification of his analytic method of treating phobias – a modification that would become the cornerstone of behavioural treatment, namely, the need for exposure. He wrote: 'One can hardly master a phobia if one waits till the patient lets the analysis influence him to give it up ... Take the example of agoraphobia; there are two classes of it, one mild, the other severe.' He went on to say, 'Patients belonging to the first class suffer from anxiety when they go into the street by themselves, but they have not yet given up going out alone on that account; the others protect themselves from the anxiety by altogether ceasing to go about alone.' Successful treatment is realized only when 'phobic patients of the first class ... go into the street and ... struggle with their anxiety while they make the attempt.' Freud continued by saying that it is only when the phobia has been moderated that 'the associations and memories come into the patient's mind which enable the phobia to be resolved' (Freud, 1955d [1918]:165–6).

By this time, other physicians were well aware of Freud's ideas, and a debate had arisen over the validity, utility, and scientific merit of psychoanalysis. As Elizabeth Lunbeck observes in her history of early twentieth-century American psychiatry, it was more than just differences in intellectual style that distinguished Freud's ideas from those of his biopsychiatric colleagues (albeit those working in institutions). For them, 'the mind's topography was flat, its workings unproblematically evident in behavior.' For Freud and his followers, however, the mind was conceived 'in terms of mechanisms and drives, and ... a portion or a function of the mind – the unconscious – was in normal circumstances altogether inaccessible, beyond individuals' conscious control.' Accordingly, the two subdisciplines of psychological medicine conceptualized the 'normal' quite differently, at least until they were merged into a 'peculiarly American dynamic psychiatry' in the 1920s (Lunbeck, 1994:24).

Some of Freud's supporters made key contributions to the discourse of agoraphobia. His colleague Karl Abraham, for example, took up the question of why some neuroses manifest in this particular way, that is, as agoraphobia or what he called 'street' or 'locomotor anxiety' (Abraham, 1973 [1913]). Abraham asserted that in individuals with agoraphobic symptoms there must have been a specific factor present in their sexual constitution that was not present in that of other neurotics. He surmised that this factor was a failure to repress the pleasure derived from movement when in the company of one's object of childhood desire. To support his argument, Abraham described patients who experienced pleasure when walking. In one case this pleasure was demonstrated by the 'pollution dreams' of dancing of a male patient. For this patient, walking outside with his mother was like dancing, and both activities offered a viable substitute for the sexual gratification otherwise denied him. In another patient, the pleasure in movement was derived from walking with her father, which symbolically fulfilled her incest wish and prevented her from being able to walk with anyone else. In short, these individuals derived 'locomotor pleasure' only when with particular companions, apart from whose company the pleasure in movement was transformed into a fear of movement and related street anxiety.

Not all Freud's colleagues were as receptive as Abraham to his ideas, however, and the articles that followed Abraham's demonstrate the contested early relationship of psychoanalysis with the medical establishment. The remarks – and actions – of Freud's critics are indicative of the resilience of the earlier biopsychiatric ideas. For example, in 1911, after the Freudian David Eder presented a case of hysteria to the neurological section of the British Medical Association, the 'entire audience, including the chairman, rose and walked out in icy silence' (Porter, 1997:518). Dr Charles Mercier (who, as we may recall, attributed agoraphobia to an arboreal instinct), declared in 1916 that 'psychoanalysis is past its perihelion, and is rapidly retreating in to the dark and silent depths from which it emerged. It is well that it should be systematically described before it goes to join pounded toads and sour milk in the limbo of discarded remedies' (in Porter, 1997:518).

Dr Hugh T. Patrick, Clinical Professor of Nervous and Mental Diseases at Northwestern University Medical School in Chicago, was somewhat ambiguous in his opinion of psychoanalysis. In a 1916 presentation to the American Medical Association, he noted that there were a number of factors other than repressed sexual desire or undischarged libido involved in the aetiology of this disease, including food, tobacco, and alcohol poisoning; dizziness or loss of consciousness due to overheated or overcrowded rooms; weakness from typhoid or other acute illness, surgery, or confinement; heat stroke; excessive eating; rheumatism; aural vertigo; tinnitus; syphilis; nocturnal emissions; the shock and haemorrhage of initial coitus; cerebral thrombosis; migraine; indigestion; uremic convulsions (urine in the blood); night numbness or night palsy; and predormal shocks. He stated that the remedies most frequently prescribed were absolutely futile. As he put it, 'how can "tonics" or "sedatives," change of climate, a vacation, tacking up a floating kidney, lifting a prolapsed uterus or rest in bed and massage eradicate fear? Would a winter in Florida, a trip around the world, an operation for haemorrhoids, or strychnin pills make a sinner less afraid of eternal punishment?' (Patrick, 1916:183).

Yet Patrick also went on to say that with this type of nervous disorder patients did not realize they had a fear per se. Rather, they were dominated by an idea, and the problems they experienced arose from temperament. The key to overcoming their problem was to recognize the mechanism of the fear by going back to the first appearance of the symptoms and its circumstances. Patrick asserted that the patient had usually experienced some sort of trauma and that the only logical treatment was 'analysis' and re-education through gradual exposure to the object of fear. He was careful to qualify his remarks, however, by emphasizing that by 'analysis' he did not mean that of the Freudian variety. Each patient was an individual and not a machine, not something out of a mould, he said. He wrote, 'We can scarcely be said to treat a psychoneurosis; we are working with the individual who has it.' But in spite of his concern to distance himself from Freud's ideas, Patrick maintained that the key to discovering the cause of agoraphobic symptoms was to trace the patient's history to a traumatic event that could be redefined through re-education. With this argument he was effectively drawing on Freud's earliest thesis and simultaneously creating an opening for a cognitive-behaviourist approach. Interestingly, in his response to discussants he added that the object of treatment was not to give the patient the true explanation of the symptoms, but to provide an explanation that would satisfy him, that would appeal to his mentality and harmonize with his viewpoint, his past, his education, and his environment: 'some of the successes of the freud-ians [sic] have been attained not because they have found the truth, but because they have done something which begot confidence, which presented to the patient what for him was an adequate explana-tion'(Patrick, 1916:186).

The discussion section of Patrick's paper was rather extensive, and the views offered were split. Dr Charles R. Ball of St Paul asserted that Freudian 'doctrine' may have some elements of truth, but there was a biological factor to consider: there was 'something which brings about those conditions in addition to ideas' (Ball, 1916:185). The other remarks were more explicitly for or against, with one St Louis physi-cian, Dr David S. Booth, expressing sarcastically or seriously – it is not clear which – his wish to have a Freudian explain to him his own fear of snakes and lizards (Booth, 1916:185). The Springfield, Illinois, dis-cussant Dr Frank Parsons Norbury stated that Freudian theory was crucial in this question, that it was 'the freudian wish on which is involved the essential determining factor of life itself' (Norbury, 1916:184). Opposing views included that of Dr Francis Rhodes of St Louis, who argued that there was no place in the practice of medicine and psychiatry for 'the freudian intrusion in any serious sense,' because with phobias it 'does not do to remind the patient too soon that his trouble is psychic' (Rhodes, 1916:185). Dr Foster Kennedy, a discussant from New York, stated that Freud's symbolic theories were used as mechanically as a set of chemical analytic tables, and that 'this has led not to the careful detailed personalized examination of the individual under consideration, but to a request for symptoms and their automatic pigeon-holing on a basis of preconceived data of purely pontifical character' (Kennedy, 1916:185). Dr Tom A. Williams, Lecturer on Nervous and Mental Diseases at Harvard University, insisted that 'the only explanatory analysis is not freudian analysis. People were cured of these troubles long before that doctrine was known' (Williams, 1916:184).

There is no evidence to suggest that Freud was involved in or even aware of this particular debate, but he did go on to publish more on the subject of neuroses after it took place. Freud's interest was in determin-ing how it was possible for the familiar to become unfamiliar and terri-fying, and this question was significant for his subsequent accounts of the ego. In his essay 'The Uncanny' – which would become one of his most famous – he defined the uncanny as being at once homely, familiar, agreeable, and intimate, *and* unfamiliar, frightening, and kept out of sight. Freud theorized that if every affect is transformed into anxiety – if it is repressed – then 'among instances of frightening things there must be one class in which the frightening element can be shown to be something repressed which *recurs*.' This would 'constitute the uncanny; and it must be a matter of indifference whether what is uncanny was itself originally frightening or whether it carried some *other* affect' (Freud, 1955e [1919]:241).

Freud's concept of the uncanny helps to account for how the street and open spaces can become unfamiliar to a person by explaining how that which is repressed can come to the surface and manifest in these ambivalent terms. Soldiers returning from the front, for example, found, both psychically and literally, that that which was familiar to them before they left home was quite unfamiliar and frightening upon their return, and their experience gave rise to what Freud described as war neurosis (see Freud, 1955f [1919]).

By 1925, Freud had modified his theory of anxiety and phobia formation to include (in addition to sexual impulses) the role of aggression in the aetiology of neurotic disorders. In effect he recanted his earlier theory when he said that anxiety 'never arises from repressed libido. If I had contented myself earlier with saying that after the occurrence of repression a certain amount of anxiety appeared in place of the manifestation of libido that was to be expected, I should have nothing to retract to-day.' He continued: 'I must admit that I thought I was giving more than a mere description. I believed I had put my finger on a metapsychological process of direct transformation of libido into anxiety. I can now no longer maintain this view' (Freud, 1959 [1925]:109). Freud held that his theory about disrupted sexual impulses was 'still ... good.' But he asked, 'How can we reconcile this conclusion with our other conclusion that the anxiety felt in phobias is an ego anxiety and arises in the ego, and that it does not proceed out of repression but, on the contrary, sets repression in motion?' (110). With this second theory of neurosis he held that where sexual impulses were perceived to lead to danger – that is, when desire for one's mother ultimately leads to castration by one's father – an unconscious and self-protective displacement occurs. In conflict with the ego, the id impulses are sublimated, or shifted to a substitute activity or object that is considered appropriate and not dangerous. Accordingly, in agoraphobia the fear of the street masks the fear of sexual temptation (109).

An ego-derived fear of the substitute object thus manifests in consciousness, in place of the fantasies of danger and desire. And as long as neurotic patients avoid the substituted fear-objects, they avoid the anxiety associated with them. Anxiety therefore is a 'reaction to a situation of danger' that is 'obviated by the ego's doing something to avoid that situation or to withdraw from it.' In other words, 'symptoms are created' in order to 'avoid a *danger-situation* whose presence has been signalled by the generation of anxiety [, such as] the danger of castration or of something traceable back to castration' (Freud, 1959 [1925]:128–9). Anxiety is no longer the *result* of a defence against ungratified sexual impulses, then, but now *activates* a defence against the repercussions of acting on those impulses – anxiety is a reaction of the ego to danger. Phobia sets in after a first anxiety attack in 'specific circumstances, such as in the street or in a train or in solitude.' Whenever the 'protective condition cannot be fulfilled,' the phobic mechanism 'does good service as a means of defence' (128). Developing the symptom of agoraphobia following an attack of anxiety in the street may therefore be 'described as an inhibition, a restriction of the ego's functioning' by which the agoraphobic patient 'spares himself anxiety attacks' (Freud, 1964 [1932–6]:83).

Notwithstanding the shift in Freud's thinking on neurosis (a shift that ultimately represented not much of a departure from his earlier perspective), it is evident that he offered a clear alternative to the theories of phobia that had been developed by physicians more narrowly oriented towards strictly biological accounts of mental diseases. Conceiving of phobia as a neurotic symptom deriving from psychosocial and family-relational factors meant that (agora)phobia (and other mental disturbances) was a social process set in motion by personal historical events.

Though it took until well into the second decade of the twentieth century for psychoanalysis to gain much purchase in the United States, by the 1930s the dominance of psychoanalysis in psychiatry was well established. Nearly all the physicians writing on agoraphobia after 1930 and until roughly the 1970s took a psychoanalytic approach consistent with Freud's ideas. His influence is evident to the extent that they formulated their analyses around the premise that phobias developed as a protection from danger, and that the street was a source of sexual temptation (Freud, 1985 [1897]:248). Later analysts built on many other aspects of Freud's framework as well.

The Viennese analyst Helene Deutsch, for example, took up the thoughts on exhibitionism that Freud had communicated to Fliess, noting that with one of her patients agoraphobia was at first associated only with a certain part of her route from home, a path where she often saw men urinating. She stated: 'My reason for emphasising this is that I have received the impression that exhibitionistic tendencies play an important (though subordinate) part in the determination of street-perils' (Deutsch, 1929:60). Anny Katan of Cleveland agreed, and also asserted the importance of exhibitionistic desires in this aetiology. Her patient was 'very exhibitionistic,' and this tendency was traceable to her asking as a child to be put on the toilet by her father, whom she called to her bed late at night when she had her nocturnal anxiety attacks. The manoeuvre had the effect of disrupting relations between her parents: 'this exhibition while urinating served the purpose of seducing her father' (Katan, 1951 [1937]:49).

Several analysts also observed fantasies of prostitution in their patients, a finding Freud had remarked upon to Fliess. Dr Edoardo Weiss of Rome argued that in female patients who suffered from agoraphobia and had fantasies of prostitution, the fantasies were an 'utterance of the destructive instinct, announcing itself through the medium of the super-ego ... an aggressive qualification on its part' (Weiss, 1935:80). In all successful repression, he continued, there was a conflict between libidinal impulse and self-destructive tendency (the unconscious desire for punishment). Identification with their emotional rivals led patients to turn the aggression they felt inward, as with the Viennese analyst Edmund Bergler's patient who wished death for her mother (Bergler, 1935:401). This patient became engaged to a man suffering from tuberculosis but broke off relations with him once he had recovered, only to become engaged to another man with tuberculosis. Bergler theorized that putting herself in the position of caregiver in relation to these men was a means of bringing to fruition her need for punishment for the libidinous feelings she had for her father.

In another case it was clarified that redirection of repressed desires towards strangers in the street served to protect the ego from the more dangerous Oedipal desires (Katan, 1951 [1937]). This process of redirection was what Freud called 'displacement,' referring again to the mechanism whereby desires are displaced from the incestuous object onto other new objects (in this case the street). Anny Katan asserted that this displacement was a component of adolescent development that normally occurred once in a person's life, and that only when this process failed did objects become cathected pathologically, with agoraphobia the result. In the 'process of normal puberal development ... [the result is] successful relinquishment of the old infantile object relationships' (45). Agoraphobic patients, hostile to their drive and to their object of desire, successfully replace the dangerous incestuous object and retain the direction of the displacement, but the instinctual energy has still not been engaged – hence the fantasies of prostitution.

The superego acted as the gatekeeper of the desires that informed such fantasies, and, in the context of agoraphobia, the superego was said to reside out of doors. Dr Emanuel Miller put it as follows in a paper read before the Medical Section of the British Psychological Society in 1927:

> The external world contain[s] all those persons who can administer censure ... the world at large. Our external world is built up by inter-subjective intercourse and the moral order finds its social expression in the opinion of people outside – in the agora – or market-place. However much we speak of the moral law within us, we are always projecting into the external world the physical manifestation of its force ... And thus the agoraphobe at the level of sociality sees in the external world the mentor of all offences against the moral law which has gone to make up the super-ego against which it has offended. (Miller, 1930:265–6)

Miller's patient had a conflicted relationship with her mother, whom she both desired and hated. Her desire was represented by a fascination with mouths (an oral fixation), and her hatred stemmed from the access her mother had to her father, whom she herself desired. Relations between mother and child were cold, and, to compensate, the patient engaged in secret sexual play with a nephew and other boys. This play also included cunnilingus with a younger girl behind half-closed bathroom doors, and eventually gave rise to a claustrophobia that was closely related to her agoraphobic fear of open spaces (266–7). In another case involving a superego conflict, the patient had a mother who did not allow her to go out alone when she was young; when this patient grew up and had her own daughter, she maintained the condition of being watched by means of an inability, as an adult, to go out alone. The only person she would accept as a companion was her daughter, whose role was to ensure that she did not succumb to instinctual impulses. In effect, she assumed the role of her mother's superego, 'the vigilant faculty, the guardian who forbids and menaces – the role which was formerly filled by the patient's mother' (Deutsch, 1929:59).

In another case, a middle-aged Berlin woman with three children was unable to go out into the street and experienced a horrible murderous obsession that destroyed her nightly rest. Her analyst, Dr Franz Gabriel Alexander, reported that she worried she might get up in the night and strangle her children in their sleep (Alexander, 1930:60). To compensate for these death wishes against her children (which were versions of her childhood death wishes against her brother and stepsister), the woman developed a severe superego that would keep her murderous impulses in check. She adopted an unusually self-sacrificing way of life so as to remove her sense of guilt and in her married life was ascetic and dutiful, allowing herself no pleasure, sexual or otherwise. Her children stood in the way of pleasure between her and her husband, just as her siblings had obstructed her relations with her father.

The theme of the ascetic mother appeared in other cases too, and Dr Ralph R. Greenschpoon of Los Angeles surmised that this kind of self-sacrifice actually represented the Janus-faced relation of hatred and love. In describing a patient who claimed to live for her daughter, he said, 'When we hear such words we must always think of the bipolarity (ambivalence) of feelings' (Greenschpoon, 1936:390). Exaggerated love was, in his view, overcompensation for repressed hate, and this patient's dreams did indeed reflect the death wishes she harboured against her daughter.

What is striking about all these cases is that the agoraphobia in the patients did not always manifest in an inability to go out; in some cases it appeared as an inability to handle the object of desire's going out. Deutsch's patient, for example, could not stay home without her mother, but nor could she handle her mother's going out without her. She worried that something might happen to her mother if the mother went out alone, yet she also worried that her mother might 'bestow her love on the father' if she left the mother alone at home with him (Deutsch, 1929:54). Similarly, a patient of Katan's, a young boy, experienced anxiety whenever his mother left the house without him. He became anxious whenever he knew she was going to use a means of public transport, fearing that the men who directed traffic would harm her, and he was convinced that only he could protect her. He was not reassured when his father accompanied his mother into the street; rather his anxiety increased. Katan concluded that the boy felt compelled to play the masculine aggressive and protective role in order to defend himself against his feminine desires towards his father, and against the corresponding death wishes he harboured against his mother, whom he saw as his competitor. At the time of Katan's writing, this patient was not considered an agoraphobic per se, though elements of his case indicated that he was well on the way to becoming one. He avoided going into the street so as to avoid anxiety, and similarly forbade his mother to go out (Katan, 1951 [1937]; see also Bergler, 1935:393 n1).

The notion of penis envy was another factor in several cases. Dr Weiss, for example, had one patient for whom large open squares were the main source of anxiety. This patient dreamed that her analyst (Weiss) had to have sex with her, but had no penis, just an 'empty space' where the penis 'should have been.' The analyst was transformed into her mother, for whom it was normal not to have 'the desired organ,' and Weiss concluded that this dream showed 'that *open places*, from the dread of which term *agoraphobia* is derived, [signified] *the castrated mother.* Probably some inner urge prompts us to put a statue, an obelisk and, especially, a fountain in the middle of squares' (Weiss, 1935:67). Desire for the male organ was even clearer in Greenschpoon's patient, apparently, because 'Frau Gina' had a 'very strong homosexual fixation' (Greenschpoon, 1936:391).

As in some cases we saw in the previous section, masturbation continued to play a central role in that it constituted a significant source of the guilt felt by psychoanalytic patients. One woman who boarded at a convent school as a child lived there in a constant state of fear because the nuns, in an effort to curtail masturbation, told the students the devil lived in the washroom. The patient did not recall masturbating as a child but admitted to doing so in puberty and felt 'murderously guilty' for it (Bergler, 1935:396). Another patient understood anxiety as a punishment for engaging in masturbation. Believing that an admission of symptoms was as good as an admission of having practised masturbation, she waited twenty-seven years before seeking psychiatric help (Katan, 1951 [1937]:45; also Fenichel, 1944). In 1951, Dr Walter Schmideberg of New York described a young female patient whose agoraphobia derived from her having witnessed her parents' intercourse when she was a child (Schmideberg, 1951:347). 'Ruth' had masturbation and related sadistic fantasies; she believed herself to be a menace who infected everything she touched or possessed because her hand had been in contact with her genital organs (346).

A confused sense of morality, or, more specifically, a failed superego, was a common theme by the middle of the century, but there was also a developing interest in incest and sexual abuse, and the role played by these experiences in patients' problems. For example, one analyst, Dr Martin J. Wangh, wrote about an agoraphobic patient, 'Diane,' whose father regularly exhibited himself before his children and was seductive towards her: 'Definitely he was not a figure who gave Diane a sense of moral strength. He confused her with respect to what was and was not permissible' (Wangh, 1959:680). Diane's older brother was similarly abusive; they had sexual relations until her brother turned his attentions to their younger sister. Hurt by the rejection, Diane competed with him for the younger girl's attentions, and her efforts culminated in a sexual relationship between the two girls for many years. And though not directly related to the issue of sexual abuse, Diane's nurse and mother also contributed to her failed superego by behaving cruelly towards the 'Negro' servants. This cruelty resulted in Diane's agoraphobic fear – an apprehension about meeting Jews and Puerto Ricans, 'little black people,' downtown (681, 684). Whether or not the racism was a factor in the development of her phobia, it did provide Diane with an object on which to displace her fear.

The New York analyst Dr B. Ruddick described a similar scenario in 1961. His patient's agoraphobia also was related to the failure to incorporate a functioning superego, in that her older brother, from the time she was 5 until she was 12, had sexually abused her. Their parents, along with her brother, failed to act as 'acceptable superego figures' (Ruddick, 1961:539). The abuse, coupled with unresolved feelings of desire for her father, caused her to regard the street as representing dangerous heterosexuality, and eventually she became a lesbian.

Whereas these analysts described situations in which parents were effectively guilty of under-parenting, others had concerns about the opposite problem. One case of over-parenting was described by the Washington, D.C., analyst Dr Louis London, whose patient, a 25-year-old male and an orthodox Jew, struggled with deep cultural conflicts as well as an inability to go against his mother's plans for him. His doctor noted, 'The patient on the couch who talks of his agoraphobia is a person in whom more than fear of the "open spaces" is involved' (London, 1963:607). This man battled against a compulsion to masturbate, homosexual desire, religious doubts, and an overbearing mother who wanted him to marry the woman of her choice. Her efforts to sequester him from the world, along with his religious upbringing, led him to fight for the preservation and development of a free ego, but at a cost. He feared that he would exhibit himself, and developed guilty feelings about any relationship with women, however casual, and these feelings manifested as agoraphobia. According to his psychiatrist, this patient demonstrated a kind of immaturity, a difficulty that another practitioner, Dr Walter I. Tucker of Boston, found in seventy-seven other patients. Among almost all of them there was a problem of unhealthy dependence on the mother; it ranged from complete dependence on a wholly dominant mother to a fear of doing something of which she might not approve. Unhealthy marital attitudes were frequently cited as an inheritance from the mother in these cases, and manifested in the rejection of sexual activity, fear of childbirth, a 'martyr' attitude towards the role of wife and mother, and resentment towards men. Tucker's patients accordingly had 'difficulty adjusting to the duties and responsibilities of [being a] wife and mother' and needed to change their relationships to their own frequently neurotic, demanding, critical, and overprotective mothers (Tucker, 1956:827). In one case, the patient was able to modify her attitudes – 'resulting in a better acceptance of the female role and a better adjustment to her husband and child' (825).[12] Gender role expectations played an important part in accounting for women's agoraphobia as far as Tucker was concerned.

In the more recent psychoanalytic discourse of agoraphobia, an emphasis on narcissism and on separation-individuation issues has emerged.[13] For example, the analyst Dr J.L. Stamm of Brooklyn argued that there was a specific relationship between heightened narcissistic vulnerability and the development of agoraphobia. Specifically, sexual and non-sexual childhood traumas led to the development of a 'narcissistic character structure' (Stamm, 1972:267). Drs Allen Frances and Peter Dunn (1975) of New York, working from an object-relations perspective to illustrate the issue of separation-individuation, argued that just as the child's attitude towards the outside and unknown territory beyond his [sic] mother depended on her ability to tolerate the child's explorations of it, so did the agoraphobic person fear the outside owing to its inherent uncertainty. They theorized that agoraphobia acted as a substitute for the dependent relationship of early childhood and symbolized the attachment-autonomy conflict that comes with separation-individuation.

Dr M. Donald Coleman, also of New York, attributed the anxiety experienced by his patient, a 'sweet' and 'somewhat shy, retiring' 40-year-old mother of two, to the 'maternal overprotection she experienced as a child' (Coleman, 1982:539). 'R.' could function only when another person was present, looking after things for her as her mother had done. '[Her] mother supervised every aspect of her life, with the overt premise that she was a weak, sickly child who might at any moment be carried away by a fatal illness,' even though 'there were no major illnesses to account for this.' R. was not allowed as an adolescent to perform the 'simplest tasks' such as picking up shoes from the shoemaker, or other minor errands 'that most parents would encourage or require.' In short, she was 'not allowed to exercise her judgement.' Accordingly, she came to learn that 'the outside world was ... a terrifying place, full of disasters that the patient could not possibly cope with alone.' Suffering from mild diarrhoea and the fear that she would lose sphincter control in unfamiliar situations, R. 'lived a life of "quiet desperation,"' with no close friends and a husband who, like her mother, had 'doll-like expectations of her' (539–40). In consequence of the denial of her autonomy, R.'s ego was weak and underdeveloped, and it was not until her husband died of a sudden illness in the third year of therapy that R. became 'much more resourceful,' with more of an 'anxiety-free ego than was apparent at the beginning of ... therapy' (547).

Psychoanalysis of late has increasingly emphasized theory and technique. Another theme that emerges is that psychoanalytic principles (without its method) can be a helpful complement to non-analytic psychotherapy. With the proliferation of other forms of psychotherapy and psychiatric medications in the decades since Freud's death, as well as the tendency towards *DSM*-based mental health care, psychoanalysis proper has lost its near monopolistic hold on psychiatry. Yet psychoanalysis has also expanded its influence in a way, in that most of the non-psychoanalytic psychotherapies available employ classical and contemporary psychoanalytic concepts quite frequently. Object-relations and self-psychology theories have especially influenced cognitive and behaviour psychotherapy.

For example, one article (published in a non-psychoanalytic journal) illustrates the advantages of drawing on object-relations theory when implementing exposure treatment for agoraphobia. The author attempted to transcend the 'unnecessary dichotomy' between analysis and behaviour therapy that was 'based upon mutual suspicions of methodology and basic assumptions as well as ignorance of recent developments' (Friedman, 1985:525).

Steven Friedman, Professor of Psychiatry and Director of the Phobia Clinic in Brooklyn, New York, observed that, although it has been a long-standing theme in the history of psychotherapy, integrating psychotherapeutic approaches has not always been well received (Friedman, 1985:525). He maintained, however, that though the cognitive-behaviourist model offered many useful clinical strategies, it did not address the predisposition to the disorder. Nor did it provide a framework for conceptualizing the patient-therapist relationship, the nature of which may have implications for treatment outcome (527). This gap, he insisted, illuminated the need to consider object-relations interpretations of agoraphobia. Rather than focusing on the symbolic dangers of proscribed territory as Freud did, Friedman emphasized the home and companion of the patient, thereby permitting a connection to early failures in the separation-individuation phase, as seen in the cases described above. Separation, when not 'normal,' can be either too harsh or too insufficient, and send the message that independence is not desirable or even safe.

To illustrate this last point, Dr Friedman describes his patient 'M.G.,' a 29-year-old woman who was overprotected by her mother as a child. She developed a fear of travelling alone when she became engaged to marry, but initially was not diagnosed with agoraphobia because she would often travel long distances alone. She had a pattern of staying home for several days and then becoming furious, 'and in a frenzy of activity [she would] go outside in spite of her panic attacks' (Friedman, 1985:529, 533). Her 'activity level would heighten, until she would become exhausted and collapse and return to her housebound state' (534). Her therapist drew on object-relations psychoanalytic theory by resisting M.G.'s efforts at premature independence through attempts to master greater and greater levels of exposure to anxiety-provoking stimuli. M.G. was told that 'at appropriate times she would be encouraged to try harder assignments.' At other times, when M.G. felt, in her words, 'sick and unable to go on,' the therapist would offer encouragement and empathy (534). But the process of therapy, like the parent-child relationship, does not always go so well. As Friedman noted, therapists often either try too hard to cure the patient or give up when they do not get the desired results, both of which responses replicate a failed separation: 'the therapist, like the family, can then be seen as either a safety-producing companion or a spokesman "pushing" for a traumatic degree of separation' (535).

The psychoanalytic cases reflect how methodological and theoretical frameworks may guide clinical practice and psychotherapeutic interpretation. There is another methodological consideration that surfaces in these reports, however, and it has deeper disciplinary and professional implications. Specifically, it concerns the lack of scientific rigour in psychoanalysis and the jeopardized professional standing of psychoanalysis within the field of mental health care (of which the lack of psychoanalytic literature on agoraphobia may be a strong indicator).

A subtle reference to this weakness is made in an article lauding the elaboration of the unconscious through mathematical concepts of symmetrical and asymmetrical thinking, as outlined by Ignacio Matte Blanco, an Italian psychoanalyst (Fink, 1989; also Blanco, 1989). Briefly, according to Matte Blanco's theory of the unconscious and the 'logical laws' by which it is governed, the unconscious treats all relations as symmetrical, as without a difference between the part and the whole, and as without recourse to the existence of space and time. In other words, 'traumatic events of the past are not only seen in the unconscious as ever present and permanently happening but also about to happen, hence the need or compulsion [à la Freud] to repeat the defensive behaviour' (Fink, 1989:482–3). The self and object cannot be differentiated, given that both occupy the same places and the whole and its parts are interchangeable (483). This means that conscious thoughts are asymmetrical, and the purpose of analysis is to enable the patient to understand the transference that occurs with a move from symmetry to asymmetry (483). Two cases illustrate this thinking.

In the first, 'Peter' was a 32-year-old dentist of German descent, married and the father of three children. He had developed his agoraphobic symptoms during his youth following the Second World War, but when his family emigrated to Britain and he was faced with a new language, a new school, and a new environment, his symptoms disappeared. After he underwent some emergency surgery at the age of 15, however, the symptoms reappeared and Peter was unable to go anywhere alone. He consulted a psychoanalyst and then a psychiatrist, to no avail. When he went to university he found another psychoanalyst, whom he saw for five years, until the analyst left the country. He switched to a new analyst, with whom he also remained in therapy for five years, until this analyst too moved away. Peter made no advance in these ten-plus years.

Eventually Peter began therapy with the London analyst Klaus P. Fink, but he frequently missed sessions and so dragged out the treatment. Only when Fink imposed a termination date and declared that he would tolerate no more absences did Peter begin to make real progress.[14] Setting a deadline and a boundary on missed sessions 'made time appear in the analysis; it stopped it being a timeless affair and caused some part of it to shift from the unconscious to the conscious level of his mind ... [which made] possible the introduction of other asymmetrical factors into his thinking' (Fink, 1989:485). Peter used timelessness to deceive himself about the non-passing of time, with endless, unsuccessful analysis as the result (485). In addition to setting these limits, Fink challenged Peter about not letting go of his agoraphobia, about using it as an identity – 'as if on his visiting card he had put his name and underneath "Agoraphobic" instead of "Dentist."' With this challenge Fink introduced the problem of space into Peter's analysis: 'When Peter realized his space factor symptoms, his agoraphobia could not function any further as a symptom or, as I put it previously, as a cathected object-symptom, that is, as an identity; the acceptance of it on a conscious level in terms of asymmetry allowed him to decathect it, to give it up' (485–6). Peter thereby 'gained access to a large portion of his ego that had finally emerged from the chaos of symmetric thinking ... into the conscious world of asymmetric thinking' (486). Evidently, it is not only external, public space that is implicated in agoraphobia – but unfortunately this point remains unexamined in the literature.

Conversely, another patient, 'Caroline,' was unable to make the transition from symmetrical to asymmetrical thinking. She was born prematurely – 'a colossal deviation from normality' (Blanco, 1989:496) – and remained in an incubator for several months, where she was subjected to all sorts of 'medical tortures' (497). 'She was in a confined space with transparent walls permanently lit up, observed at all times by the hospital staff, connected to tubes, handled only with great care by doctors and nurses wearing sterile gloves, and so on' (Fink, 1989:486). Like Peter, she suffered from agoraphobia, which was becoming a significant problem with respect to her employment. She was also 'sexually naïve' and could not tolerate the idea of intercourse, though the thought of being slapped on her bare buttocks was quite exciting to her. Unfortunately, unlike Peter, analysis did not help her at all. Fink reported:

> Nothing she or I said would make any difference to her state of feelings, she felt a prisoner of her symptoms and felt desperate because time was passing and she was getting nowhere, feeling more and more inadequate ... Caroline's basic problems never changed. She continued for two and a half years to attend her sessions ... [but] nothing ever touched her inner self. After five and a half years of analysis we fixed an ending date a few months ahead. (486–7)

The question becomes, why did setting a deadline not have the same positive effect for Caroline as it did for Peter? The answer is that she 'never acquired a normal capacity for asymmetric thinking ... her ego remained incomplete' (487). Her concept of space was defective, owing to the early post-natal trauma of being confined to an incubator when she should still have been a foetus. Moreover, having to undergo endless medical interventions and penetrations (needles) symbolically left her with a resistance to sexual intercourse (Blanco, 1989:497, 499; Fink, 1989:487). Unlike Peter, for whom the concept of time was the main obstacle, Caroline's issues were with space: 'I think Caroline never really left the incubator, she is still inside it. Her fear of leaving it constitutes, to a large extent, her agoraphobia' (Fink, 1989:487). Unfortunately for Caroline, traditional psychoanalysis was ill equipped to deal with early post-natal trauma. Consequently, Fink proposed developing 'wider concepts' that could 'explain more phenomena in a unitary way.' Fink credits Matte Blanco with attempting to address this problem through making a theory of the unconscious 'into an exact science by using the most exact of sciences, mathematics.' He urges colleagues to consider that 'only when we gain new scientific knowledge will we be able to introduce new methods and only if the new facts warrant it. I believe psychoanalysis has been, is and always will be in a state of development which is the only way in which a science remains young, potent and alive' (488).

To sum up, ultimately the goal of all these psychoanalysts was to achieve transference. Transference enabled the analyst to get at the repressed emotions residing in the patient's unconscious and shift them from important figures, such as parents and siblings, to the analyst. In spite of its success and popularity by the 1960s and 1970s, however, psychoanalysis gradually found itself on a downward slope, as the American Psychiatric Association worked its way back to a more strictly biological orientation. While Frances and Dunn's object-relations approach signified the 'branching out' of psychoanalysis, on the whole it was forced increasingly to share its foremost position on the clinical landscape with the behaviourists, to whose ideas we turn next. Although it took the behaviourist approach some time to become widespread, its ideas are important because, in the final decades of the twentieth century, behaviourism (along with pharmaceuticals) came to overshadow the psychoanalytic approach to treating agoraphobia. Behaviourism did not particularly emphasize the biological, but it was more open to it than psychoanalysis was, and the American Psychiatric Association eventually endorsed behaviourism over psychoanalysis owing to its quick results. Moreover, the behaviourists were much more willing than the psychoanalysts to package their ideas (research) in a form that met the APA's growing requirement that psychiatry be evidence-based.

Behaviourism

The scientific origins of behaviourism and cognitive therapies may be traced back to the early twentieth century, if not earlier. There was, for example, Ivan Petrovich Pavlov's famous experiment with dogs, in which he showed that the secretion of saliva could be stimulated by the ringing of a bell, which the dogs associated with being fed. There was also the classic 1920 experiment by the American psychologists J.B. Watson (who coined the term 'behaviourism' in 1913) and his romantic partner, R. Raynore, on an eleven-month-old infant named Albert. Viewing behaviour as determined by a combination of genetic and environmental factors, they performed an experiment on Albert that enabled them to show how a phobia could be created (and resolved) through conditioning (Birk, 1978:433).

Drawing on these sorts of ideas, the handful of early practitioners oriented more towards behavioural and cognitive psychology took as their first assumption that behaviour (and thought) could be reshaped back to normality; anxiety, accordingly, could be reconditioned through rationalization, re-education, and persuasion. The cause of agoraphobic anxiety was the habituation of wrong ways of thinking; as with Pavlov's dogs, 'the reflex action itself, like other reflex actions, is a physiological phenomenon ... attended by conscious sensations,' in the words of Dr T.H. Thomas of Bristol (1922:129). We may recall Dr Hugh T. Patrick, for example, who argued in 1916 that precipitating traumatic events could be redefined through re-education. His colleague Dr Tom A. Williams similarly claimed to be able to remove his patient's 'disturbance' in one week. He contended that there were two types of phobias. One was the sort that manifested from an 'emotional predisposition ... inherent in the constitution of [the] organism,' and the other the sort that is 'readily removable by present psychotherapeutic methods' (Williams, 1919:181). The first type was incurable, but the second, which included agoraphobia and the genesis and mechanism of which were different from those of the first type, could, as with Pavlov's dogs, be reconditioned. Williams believed that once the mechanism of origin was determined, the patient, 'comprehend[ing] the real nature of his [sic] condition,' could view his reactions rationally and then 'forestall them.' The patient could face these terrifying situations 'with a clear and open mind' and 'by analyzing his own relationship to the situation' each time it arose, so that the situation would 'rapidly' become 'shorn of its emotional aspect' (182). The key, then, was to effect a change in the meaning the patient attached to the fear-provoking situation, since the problem of agoraphobia was due ultimately to a 'faulty attitude of mind or way of looking at the situation' (185). The removal of such a phobia was a purely intellectual process of re-learning and cognitive adjustment.

As one might expect, some behaviourists were, like the biopsychiatrists, critical of the psychoanalytic approach, and especially the notion that repression or inhibition was a necessary factor in the production of fear or anxiety (Thomas, 1922:129). As the Yale psychiatry professor Dr William B. Terhune put it, the concept of repression did not offer a convincing explanation because phobias were simply the outcome of a 'soft' upbringing (Terhune, 1949). The cause of phobia was better explained by the notion of 'physiological disharmony' with the patient's environment. Agoraphobic fear was seen as a conditioned emotional reaction to the complexities of 'our modern business world [, where there is a] struggle for existence, especially in large congested monetary centres.' Dr L.V. Lopez argued in a paper read before the Louisiana State Medical Society in 1925 that in this context 'contagion now and then breaks out in fright, which imperils the fortune and lives of individuals or a people's financial stability; just as a country's cause is sometimes lost through panic striking its armies in battle' (Lopez, 1926:424–5). The Northwestern University Medical School professor Dr Lewis J. Pollock similarly argued that 'it would be impossible to bring every patient suffering with a neurosis characterized by fear to a psychiatrist or to a psychoanalyst who, by virtue of the great time required for analysis, could see but a very limited number of patients' (Pollock, 1928:44–5). Removing agoraphobia through re-education was much easier and quicker than tackling the patient's character, as the psychoanalysts did: 'the exercise of ordinary homely horse sense and advice frequently suffices' (46–7). For a number of doctors, the trick therefore was to get the patient to 'adopt a different attitude towards the facts' (Williams, 1930:436) through explanation, because the anxiety was simply a matter of misinterpretation (Pollock, 1928:43–4). But the other component of treatment was 'exposure' – having the patient face those situations that were frightening:

If he is afraid to walk alone, the first day he may be accompanied in one direction for two blocks and instructed to walk back alone. Daily this is increased until finally within a short time he is ordered to walk alone, then to ride on street cars, then to enter into all the activities that a normal individual would encounter, despite his feelings. (46)

In spite of their overall rejection of Freud, these early doctors still drew on certain concepts and ideas that resonated with those of psychoanalysis. For example, Dr Thomas (1922) drew on Freud's concept of the id to argue that agoraphobic fear resulted from the inhibition of 'instinct.' Dr Williams was interested in his patient's dreams and asked her to write an account of the way in which she viewed her own psychology – as she fell asleep, this woman had visions of 'a rough, brutal, very large skulking negro under the bedclothes' – he took such dreams as the point of departure for many associations and questions. He referred to psychoanalysis as the 'Freudian cult' yet advised this patient that 'the satisfaction of her repressed impulse might be secured by the co-operation of her husband' (Williams, 1930:438).

Dr Ernest Snowden, a lecturer on psychotherapy at the West London Hospital Post-Graduate College, observed that phobias were produced when the mental picture of an original, terrifying experience was forgotten. Specifically, if the recalling of a terrifying memory meant the reappearance of the painful sensation of terror in the body, then gradually all those things associated with the original experience were avoided until it was completely forgotten and surrounded by a barrier or guard of forbidden activities (Snowden, 1934:318). All terrifying experiences had the potential to become phobias through the process of 'forgetting,' he maintained. Dr J.A. Hadfield stated in his 1929 address to a Joint Meeting of the Royal Society of Medicine (Psychiatric Section) and the British Psychological Society (Medical Section) that the difference between normal fear and anxiety was in the 'damming back' of the normal expression of fear so that it failed to discharge itself normally and instead discharged itself in activities connected with the autonomic nervous system. Anxiety remained chronic owing to the persistent conflict between sexual or egoistic impulses, and the fear associated with the need to protect the ego. He maintained, however, that repressed libido as an explanation was not the only game in town; indeed, anything threatening the ego was cause enough for the creation of a protective anxiety (Hadfield, 1929). The influence of psychoanalysis was evident, but behaviourism was emerging as a counter-therapy in its own right. To return briefly to Dr Williams, his belief was, again, that a phobia could be 'reconditioned' and that a patient could learn to view his fear scientifically (Williams, 1919:182). As he put it, the 'same signal which at one time provoked fear can be later utilized to provoke pleasure if the dog is reeducated by accustoming him to associate with this signal a pleasurable experience, whereby there is a gradual disappearance of the painful or fearful association' (183).

Although there were quite a few of these 'counter-therapists' around as Freud and his ideas gained prominence in the psychiatric landscape, it was not until after the 1950s (and really the 1970s) that the ideas and methods of behaviourism and cognitive therapy truly began to impact on the discourse of agoraphobia. As a result of the influential research contributions made by such individuals as J. Wolpe, A. Lazarus, and S. Rachman (all of whom originated in South Africa and then moved to the United States), by the American B.F. Skinner and his followers, and, finally, by the British practitioners M.B. Shapiro and Isaac Marks (the latter of whom published extensively on agoraphobia; his work contributed to the eventual merging of behaviour and cognitive therapies),[15] the behaviourist-cognitivist approach was fully recognized within psychiatry by the 1960s, and an American Psychiatric Association task force appointed to evaluate the therapeutic potential of behaviourism gave it very favourable reviews. In 1973, behaviourism received its official endorsement from the APA, which declared its therapies 'brief and economical' and recommended them wholeheartedly for use with psychiatric patients. Though it developed very much in the background of psychoanalysis, the two psychiatries were similar in that they pertained to feelings and thoughts. They differed epistemologically, however, in that behaviourism was based in the experimental scientific method. Behaviour psychotherapy insisted on the observability of phenomena, as opposed to psychodynamic therapies, which were satisfied with inferences of psychic processes. Probably the most important – and influential – difference between psychoanalysis and behavioural methods, though, was the clearer, more practical orientation of behaviourism towards patients' immediate problems and its concomitant ability to bring quicker results than lengthy psychoanalysis. As a result of these differences, behaviourism would come to be seen as the more efficient treatment option (Birk, 1978:434).

For example, one patient's previous resistance to other forms of therapy and her 'reduced economic circumstances,' in her therapist's words, 'necessitated selection of a method which held at least some promise of relatively quick results.' As M.G. Gelder and I.M. Marks, both of the Maudsley Hospital in London, put it, 'if behaviour therapy must be carried out more than three times a week it is no longer a brief and economical treatment' (Gelder and Marks, 1966:318). The benefits of behaviour therapy could be maximized through group therapy, which meant 'a considerable time-saving for the therapists' (Emmelkamp and Emmelkamp-Benner, 1975). In contrast, psychoanalysis had never been either cheap or quick (see Gay, 1998:296–7). To 'ensure continuity and intensity,' most of Freud's patients were seen by him as many as six times a week, and the arrangement could go on for years. Behaviour therapy, on the other hand, claimed to produce results in a matter of weeks (see Pinto, 1972).[16]

Although they may describe the treatment technique differently, behaviour therapies tend to be variations on a theme. In any behavioural treatment, be it 'breathing retraining,' 'systematic desensitization,' 'successive approximation,' 'flooding' *in vivo* and in the imagination (both alone and in groups), 'self-observation,' 'group therapy,' 'relaxation,' 'modelling' through video, 'reinforced graded practice,' 'stress inoculation,' or 'behavioural counselling,' *exposure* in some form to the anxiety-provoking stimulus is the most crucial ingredient.[17] The assumption behind these therapies is that the patient has experienced frightening stimuli together with neutral stimuli, so that his or her subsequent exposure to neutral stimuli provokes anxiety as if the exposure were to the frightening stimuli. In other words, the patient has become conditioned to the previously neutral stimuli, in this case public open spaces, and the conditioning leads to avoidance behaviour. Exposure therapies seek to reduce the anxiety and the avoidance by *de*conditioning the patients through exposure to stimuli that are objectively harmless yet anxiety-producing (Young, 1995:177).

There is also strong emphasis on cognitive therapy, including such techniques as 'assertiveness training,' 'self-statement training,' 'guided mastery,' and 'paradoxical intention.' Cognitive therapy seeks to effect recovery by focusing on patients' understandings of their circumstances and the meanings and labels they attach to their feelings and to the anxiety-provoking stimuli. Seeking to 'modify the internal dialogue' (Biran, 1987:127), cognitive therapies provide patients with skills for 'cognitive restructuring,' that is, for correcting distorted perceptions; they can also be a means of improving patients' sense of self-efficacy, or the idea patients often have that they cannot cope effectively with their phobia. For example, 'self-statement training' takes negative thoughts, such as 'I'll never be able to handle shopping in malls' or 'I'll certainly make a fool of myself if I go shopping in a mall and faint,' and replaces them with alternatives, such as 'I'll be able to cope with the situation even though I may not feel perfectly relaxed; it won't be impossible to handle,' or 'Even though I may experience some anxiety, it certainly is no worse than the discomfort I experience in other situations, and I am able to handle those situations all right.' Thus self-statement training seeks to address 'preparing,' 'confronting,' 'coping,' and 'reinforcing.'[18]

Examples of these methods in action include the 'gradual exposure' used by the University College London physician Dr Nicolas Malleson in 1959. He had his patient go increasing distances from his front door and stay there until 'he had felt all the fear possible there – and [could] not feel more, so bored of it ha[d] he become' (Malleson, 1959:226). Dr D.F. Clark, of the Towers Hospital in Humberstone, Leicester, used a method called 'reciprocal inhibition' with his patient, who experienced spasms in the jaw muscles whenever she had to go out. She was trained in progressive relaxation and exposure: when a spasm started she was to smile widely in order to inhibit the tension of the jaw muscles (Clark, 1963:246). She was also to go increasing distances into the garden and return to the house as soon as she felt any apprehension; eventually she was able to travel to the stores a motorcycle ride away. Dr V. Meyer, Lecturer in Psychology at the Medical School of Middlesex Hospital, and his colleague M.G. Gelder had a somewhat different objective in their use of both reciprocal inhibition and graded exposure with their five patients. They sought to determine whether or not behaviour therapy would be effective in all phobic patients, and what effect the successful treatment of one symptom or a group of symptoms would have on other untreated symptoms. Theirs signalled the beginning of an important trend within behaviourist accounts of agoraphobia: the study of groups of agoraphobic patients' (or rather 'subjects'') responses to behavioural treatment methods, as opposed to single case study (Meyer and Gelder, 1963).

Finally, 're-education' or 'reconditioning,' as used by Terhune, was aimed at reprogramming the habituated response to the underlying problem. Terhune's approach was significant for its emphasis on cognition and would develop into a major area of study closely connected with behaviourist approaches. We may recall that Terhune sought to 're-educate' his patient and to facilitate 'emotional maturation.' All these patients needed, he felt, was to understand that 'neurosis is the income tax of civilization and that reeducation reduces that tax' (Terhune, 1959:768). His approach, though focused on cognitions, still involved exposure in that the re-education he proposed would occur in a hospital setting, where the patient could socialize with other patients and practise walking increasing distances outside. Although therapists disagree as to patients' likelihood of recovery, the success of behavioural-cognitive treatment is usually measured not only by the status of the patient's symptoms immediately following treatment, but also according to whether or not the patient remains free of symptoms after months and even years have passed.

By the 1960s and 1970s, diagnoses of agoraphobia had significantly increased, and disproportionately so among women (Hawkrigg, 1975a: 1280; Weekes, 1973:469). The increased presence of behaviour therapy, combined with a 'waning asylum era' and a 'new social psychiatry' that by this time had begun to see mental illness as 'part of normal variability' (Porter, 1997:521), signalled a higher likelihood that agoraphobia treatment would take place in a day-hospital setting rather than in an analyst's office. Agoraphobic patients had never been confined to asylums to any great extent, but the decline of the asylums was felt throughout the field of mental health, including in the treatment of agoraphobia. Roy Porter observes that as 'emphasis tilted from institutional provision *per se* to the clinical needs of the patient, it pointed in the direction of the "unlocked door," prompting a growth in outpatients' clinics, psychiatric day hospitals and regular visiting, and encouraging treatments which emphasized discharge' (521).

The ascendance of behaviourism contributed to the late-twentieth-century shift towards the experimental and, more specifically, towards the rise of evidence-based psychiatry; single-authored case reports decreased, and multi-authored reports on the efficacy of various behavioural methods began to increase. The behaviourists' real moment, however, came only after the 1980 publication of the third edition of the *Diagnostic and Statistical Manual of Mental Disorders* (*DSM*) by the American Psychiatric Association (see chapter 5). Drug therapies – on their own and in conjunction with behaviour therapies – were also studied to some extent, but like the behaviour therapies, much more so after publication of *DSM-III*. So the shift in psychiatry towards positivism is not limited to biological investigations, as positivist 'packaging' is the standard in the cognitive-behavioural reports as well. Concerned primarily with the psychology of agoraphobia, these articles describe such things as agoraphobics' cognitions, including their understanding of their symptoms (Liddell and Acton, 1988); their irrational beliefs (Warren et al., 1989); the types of thoughts they have during panic attacks and frightening tasks (Williams et al., 1997; Zucker et al., 1989); their tendency to catastrophize (Ahmad et al., 1992; Khawaja and Oei, 1998); the cues to and anticipations of panic (Andrews et al., 1994; Cox et al., 1995; Street et al., 1989); information processing (Hayward et al., 1994); their interpretations of the environment (Jones et al., 1996); and their interpretations of their bodily sensations (Chambless et al., 2000; Kamieniecki et al., 1997). They also examine agoraphobics' self-consciousness and embarrassment, their interaction with others, and their willingness to discuss symptoms (Lundh et al., 1997, 1998; Neidhardt and Florin, 1999; Nunn et al., 1984; Pickles and van den Broek, 1988); their memory bias, especially in relation to phobic content, their social roles, and their interpersonal style (Shean and Uchenwa, 1990); and their avoidant personality, coping strategies, and escape/safety-seeking behaviour (Cox et al., 1991; Hoffart and Martinsen, 1992, 1993; Hughes et al., 1999; Mavissakalian, 1990; Salkovskis et al., 1999).

From the work of the behaviourists, whose methods became most popular roughly a century after agoraphobia was 'discovered,' we can make the following observations. First, the disease by this time was clearly an issue more for women than for men. Second, psychoanalysis was on the decline, and consequently, reports on individual cases were becoming less fashionable whereas research reports on large trials and studies were increasing. In many respects these shifts set the stage for what was to come next, namely, a shift from understanding agoraphobia in terms of individuals with particular problems to an understanding of agoraphobia as an object for hypothesis testing. I shall return to this point in chapter 5, when I discuss the development of the *DSM* and the far-reaching effects of that development on psychiatry in general and on agoraphobia in particular. A consideration of the history of the classification of agoraphobia will make apparent the need to call into question the implicit authority, objectivity, and ostensible asociality of psychiatric knowledge. For now, I turn to agoraphobia in terms of gender, 'race,' and class.

4 The Prerogative of Being 'Normal': Gender, 'Race,' and Class

Alongside discussions of the perils of social change and the problem of over-stimulation in fast-paced cities, the individual characters of patients figured prominently in literature on the aetiology of agoraphobia. As we saw in the previous chapter, mental disorders were often equated with moral depravity and personal weakness; as one American neurologist wrote, 'mental disorder, in neurotic individuals, [could bring] about a moral epidemic or even [threaten] to change the structure of society and unity of the household' (Atwood, 1903:1072). Recall Dr Sutherland (chapter 2), for example, who concluded that the agoraphobia in his patients was the result of excess and debauchery. His theory was consistent with a notion popular among doctors of the period, who believed that as the Birmingham physician Dr S.W. Agar put it, diseases 'followed in the wake of excesses of all kinds' (Agar, 1886:3) and 'deficiencies in the way a patient lived' (Warner, 1986:86). As another physician, F.W. Van Dyke of Oregon, observed, 'with the majority of men who begin [drinking alcohol] in moderation, the immoderate use becomes the rule, and with this a decline of mental and physical power' (Van Dyke, 1908:178). Alongside the perilous social changes of modernity, then, individuals' mental disorders threatened to usher in a broad moral and social collapse.

But if the thesis put forth by Georg Simmel, by physicians, and by architects and urban planners – that the stresses people experienced in the metropolis led some individuals to develop agoraphobia – was correct, then the question becomes, why for the first fifty years of its history were most of these more vulnerable (and apparently immoral) individuals men? Were not both sexes exposed to the stresses of modern urban life? Why did the tendency to diagnose the disorder mainly in men become a tendency to diagnose it in women after the First World War? In this chapter I explore the masculine gendering and the subsequent feminine re-gendering of agoraphobia. My objective is to demonstrate the inextricability of this psychiatric category from the normative social-cultural category of gender. I argue that agoraphobia is more than an individual disease phenomenon or a benign psychiatric category; rather, contained within the discourse of this disease is a conception of patriarchal, that is, male-dominated, capitalist social order that turns on normative imperatives of gender, class, and 'race.'

As we saw in the previous chapter, in the late nineteenth and early twentieth centuries, (bourgeois) women were considered especially susceptible to nervous diseases. Indeed, nerves and nervous problems were seen as essentially feminine (Theriot, 1997), so one way or another, regardless of whether it was women or men who were diagnosed with it, agoraphobia, like other modern urban mental diseases, was conceptualized in essentially feminine terms (Vidler, 1993). Excess and debauchery was a popular explanation for this essentially 'feminine' illness, but also central to the looming 'moral epidemic' were strong ideas about gender roles and private and public spaces.

The era placed restrictions on women's movement in public space designed to exclude them from public life, albeit restrictions that were bound up with highly contradictory messages. As Wilson writes, 'just as nineteenth-century society was trying to deepen and secure the boundary between public and private, industrial capitalism was erasing it' (Wilson, 1995:149). A woman's social status hinged in part on her and her husband's material possessions and ability to consume (Wolff, 1989), the result being an increasing and seductive market consumerism that included exhibitions, department stores, refreshment rooms, rest rooms, and reading rooms – all places where bourgeois women could go unchaperoned.

Yet alongside this tendency to encourage bourgeois women to consume and move about in public space was a perhaps stronger desire to control them. This desire, the ideology of separate spheres, is evident in nineteenth-century 'ladies'' deportment manuals, for example, in which a woman's role was declared to be primarily that of wife and mother. As Barbara Welter has shown, prescriptive guides to True Womanhood (such as the aptly entitled *The Young Lady's Book: A Manual of Elegant Recreations, Exercises, and Pursuits* and *Woman As She Was, Is, and Should Be* [Welter, 1966:152 nn6–7]) promoted a clear and definite boundary between women of refinement and those of the dangerous lower classes. In keeping with the middle-class notion that a 'lady's' place was in the home, and the reformers' unease about women's sexual and intellectual independence, women unaccompanied in city streets were seen as a moral problem (see Wilson, 1992:5-6; also Strange, 1995). In this context, staying home may well have signified normality for a bourgeois woman – agoraphobic or not – in that it was consistent with what was deemed proper and moral middle-class feminine behaviour. In fact, by the nineteenth century, physicians had begun to conceptualize class itself as a natural, biological distinction, albeit one that often applied only to white males of Western European descent (see Fee, 1994:13).

Accordingly, the early historiography on separate spheres, which included Welter's work, was based on two contested assumptions. The first was that nervous diseases, which would have included agoraphobia, were 'a kind of pathological by-product of middle-class Victorian and Wilhelminian society' (Micale, 1995:156). But historians have established convincingly that these problems have manifested in lower-class populations since well before the nineteenth century. That such problems were evident among the lower classes suggests not that they were rare, but rather that they were 'simply unrecognized, untreated, and unreported.' Citing Charles Rosenberg, Micale observes that in the later decades of the nineteenth century, health care services administering to and increasingly used by the working classes were created. Until the early twentieth century, however, the bourgeoisie and the aristocracy were much more likely than people of the lower classes to consult doctors and to be treated by the professionals doing the sort of medical writing we have been examining here (Micale, 1995:155–7; also Rosenberg, 1974).

The early historiography also assumed congruence between the prescriptions of deportment literature and bourgeois women's real, lived experiences – this is the second contested assumption. Although there were restrictions on women's presence in the streets alone, scholars have questioned the extent to which women occupied a truly separate sphere (Davidoff and Hall, 1987; Kerber, 1988; Vickery, 1993). Evidence suggests that the metaphor of separate spheres oversimplified the 'real' situation of women in the second half of the nineteenth century, that the rhetoric – the ideology – represented a departure from the reality. While there was something to the metaphor, women's lives were more complex, more varied by class, region, degree and type of industrialization, and numerous other factors (Wolff, 1989:153) including the participation of men in domestic life, than the notion of separate spheres would suggest (Davidoff and Hall, 1987). And certainly working-class women would have been more concerned about subsistence than about the imperative of domesticity. As August (1994) has demonstrated in his study of lower-class and poor women's employment in late-nineteenth-century London, notwithstanding the middle-class notion that married women worked only when the household was in financial crisis, it was common for single, married, and widowed poor women to work hard throughout their lives.

While clearly the symptoms of agoraphobia mapped directly onto what was expected of bourgeois women, then, it is arguable that prior to the shift in diagnosis after the First World War their staying home had gone unacknowledged as pathological. Perhaps their staying home 'passed' as appropriate feminine behaviour rather than making them candidates for psychiatric diagnosis like their male counterparts[1] precisely because the symptoms were consistent with the criteria for 'normal' femininity.[2]

Yet the domesticity that previously had been considered normal bourgeois feminine behaviour did eventually come to be seen as pathological and agoraphobic, and I propose that there are several possible explanations for this change in perception. First, affluent (white) women's experiences of public space were changing, and the change points to a possible relationship between the increasing tendency to diagnose women with agoraphobia after the First World War and women's increasing participation in the public sphere. During the war and in the absence of their male relatives, women achieved a measure of independence, but the independence came with greater public responsibilities that not all women necessarily wanted to assume. As Kohler Riessman has demonstrated in her study of the medicalization of childbirth and reproductive control, 'women have simultaneously *gained and lost* with the medicalization of their life problems.' In fact, women have 'actively participated in the construction of the new medical definitions ... Women were not simply passive victims of medical ascendancy [, and to] cast them solely in a passive role is to perpetuate the very kinds of assumptions about women that feminists have been trying to challenge' (Kohler Riessman, 1998:47). As an extrapolation from this argument, it is conceivable that with modern urban life apparently presenting so much difficulty for everyone, not all women could face their own emancipation, and agoraphobia may have provided a legitimate means to avoid gender politics. In other words, in line with Smith-Rosenberg's influential argument that hysteria served as 'an alternate role option for particular women incapable of accepting their life situation' (Smith-Rosenberg, 1972:655), the agoraphobic 'sick role' similarly may have provided a means for women to circumvent the gap between the ideal and the reality of wartime and post-war independence.

Second (and conversely), although the doctrine of separate spheres was on some level a matter of rhetoric, the 'invention' of agoraphobia provided the added advantage of social control: given the social authority medicine had secured for itself by this time, perhaps reinforcing the imperative of True Womanhood in the language of disease was a way of thwarting the expansion of (bourgeois) women's rights. As an American psychiatrist, Abraham Myerson, put it in one of the several essays he wrote on the tyranny of domesticity, 'the neurotic woman, a chronic invalid for housework, may do a dragon's work for Woman Suffrage' (Myerson, 1929 [1920]:71–2).

Myerson's support of feminism was exceptional, however, and despite a substantial number of women practitioners, early-twentieth-century psychiatry, in its 'aggressive masculinism' (Lunbeck, 1994: 35–6), was unmistakably a man's field. Accordingly, the literature on agoraphobia was written predominantly by men, and left little room for the possibility that the disease could be something other than a peculiarly feminine problem the subtext of which was a narrative about proper (normal) gender behaviour. As Lunbeck observes, in the early twentieth century, American psychiatry shifted its focus from insanity to the normal, that is, the 'realm of everyday concerns – sex, marriage, womanhood, and manhood' and so forth, 'weaving a psychiatric point of view into its many aspects' (47). The shift in the prevalence of agoraphobia from men to women may well reflect psychiatry's overall shift to an emphasis on normative gender roles.

Third, 'war neurosis' or shell shock had also emerged in the psychiatric landscape by this time. As Allan Young documents, by the war's end the Royal Army Medical Corps, for example, had treated 80,000 cases of the disorder, and 30,000 troops diagnosed with nervous trauma had been evacuated to British hospitals (Young, 1995:42). In fact, this diagnosis rather than the diagnosis of agoraphobia was frequently invoked in doctors' reports of men's anxieties – whether or not they had been anywhere near an exploding shell (Shephard, 2001:31).[3] With 200,000 ex-servicemen in receipt of pensions for nervous disorders (Stone, 1988:249), the war produced 'large numbers of men who acted like women,' that is, 'strangely hysterical.' Psychiatrists had no choice but to reconceptualize hysteria as *not* a strictly female problem (Lunbeck, 1994:252). And, since the conceptual separation of hysteria and agoraphobia did not become widespread until Freud's ideas did – that is, not until well into the 1920s – arguably agoraphobia was included in psychiatrists' rethinking about what they meant exactly by hysteria, especially in relation to men, before and after the war.

Finally, given its resonance with the ideals of True Womanhood and the perceived essential femininity of nervous disease, a diagnosis of agoraphobia would have called into question male patients' masculinity, unlike the more heroic war neurosis. Of course, diagnosing men with shell shock would not necessarily have saved them from stigma or disgrace, but the point is that agoraphobia served the important purpose of demarcating feminine gender identity. As the writer known only as 'Vincent' lamented in 1919, 'Can I ever take my place in the world unhandicapped as other men are, and enjoy a single day undepressed by dark dread? If I could be as other men, it seems to me that my usefulness should be increased a hundredfold' ('Vincent,' 1919:299). The following passage from *Regeneration*, Pat Barker's fictionalized account of the attempts by the (real) British medical psychologist William Rivers to treat soldiers with shell shock, vividly captures the type of distress 'Vincent' describes. Rivers observes that

> in leading his patients to understand that breakdown was nothing to be ashamed of, that horror and fear were inevitable responses to the trauma of war and were better acknowledged than suppressed, that feelings of tenderness for other men were natural and right, that tears were an acceptable and helpful part of grieving, he was setting himself against the whole tenor of their upbringing. They'd been trained to identify emotional repression, as the essence of manliness. Men who broke down, or cried, or admitted to feeling fear, were sissies, weaklings, failures. Not *men*. (Barker, 1991:48)[4]

Rivers's words echo those of one physician who wrote of his own suffering from agoraphobia; he told his own physician, Dr John D. Jackson of Kentucky, that he 'tried manfully to brave off the spells' of agoraphobia, but, he said, 'Each time I permitted myself to be alone, I suffered terrible agony' (Jackson, 1872:61).

In juxtaposing these three excerpts I mean to demonstrate, first, that the men referred to here invoked and measured themselves against a cultural ideal of manliness; as Lunbeck argues, the man 'who did not measure up as a man' was perceived as mentally unhinged (Lunbeck, 1994:238). Although more difficult to prove, it may be that the diagnosis of agoraphobia in men, who especially during and after the war were expected *as men* to keep a 'stiff upper lip,' suggests resistance on their part to an imperative of masculinity that they could not fulfil – resistance that was subsequently pathologized. Second, physicians' concerns were not strictly 'medical' in that they both reinforced and were clearly embedded in ideas about sex and gender roles, with implicit (sometimes explicit) assumptions about a gendered (and classed and raced) social order and the role of psychiatry in its negotiation.[5]

This tendency towards gendered psychiatric thinking was not limited to the early cases of agoraphobia, however. For example, in 1964, gendered expectations informed a report on five female patients, all of whom were 'coping adequately with routine home duties,' as its author, Dr Roberts, wrote (Roberts, 1964:195). Dr B.C. Bignold described ten women he treated at the Mental Hospital of Claremont in Western Australia as opportunists for whom 'the symptom was personally useful' as a way of avoiding scrubbing the kitchen floor, controlling family outings, and, in once case, 'bring[ing] pressure to bear on [a] husband' who refused to capitulate to his wife's wish to move to Holland. 'When the symptom served a useful purpose, it was refractory to treatment. The possessive mother features in several histories. Dominant dames have diffident daughters' (Bignold, 1960:333).

The description of two patients in another report published as recently as 1996 is also provocative. The first patient is described as a '33 year old woman living with her husband and three children, who were aged between 2 and 12 years'; she came to the authors' clinic in 1986 complaining of panic attacks after the birth of her third child. The authors wrote, 'No other stress was evident.' The second patient is described as a '23 year old single male patient ... referred to [the] clinic in ... 1991' who 'worked for the sales department of a company in a technologically advanced industry for 1 year following his graduation from college. He worked hard but reported that his working conditions were stressful.' His agoraphobic avoidance began after a panic attack while he was out on business with the company car (Sakai and Takeichi, 1996:335). Interestingly, the male patient is defined by his education and paid work, whereas the female patient is defined by her role as wife and mother – this definition is problematic because neither aspect of her life is perceived as a source of stress or, for that matter, as *work*.

These contrasting descriptions reflect the seemingly benign criteria listed in *DSM-IV*, released in 1994, when it was already clear that most diagnoses of agoraphobia were in women: 'Individuals' avoidance of situations may impair their ability to travel to work *or carry out homemaking responsibilities* (e.g., grocery shopping, taking children to the doctor)' (APA, 1994:396; my emphasis). Jarring for its having been *added* to the 1994 edition, this wording is reminiscent of the sociologist Talcott Parsons's assertion that a wife's 'primary function' was housekeeping and the care of children (Parsons, 1954:187–9). An extension of gender ideology, contemporary psychiatry's message to women has been double-edged. It has presented the stereotypic feminine role – staying at home, being anxious and non-functional, depending on a significant other – as unacceptable for modern women, yet maintained that family responsibilities must remain women's priority or they risk being pathologized. So women 'are expected to be "out there" in the world and still put their families first' (Fodor, 1992:201).

Behaviour therapy programs, which are developed according to *DSM* criteria, tend to build upon this gendered conception of agoraphobia. Specifically, although notably few cases of agoraphobia in men were being reported by the time behaviour therapies entered the picture, there is a tendency in men's treatment to gear the program towards getting them back to paid work. In contrast, women's treatment tends to emphasize getting them back into the stores, the implication being that *not* shopping (and, by extension, not being good, i.e., feminine, homemakers) is abnormal. This observation is by no means intended to disparage homemaking, nor should it be taken to suggest that agoraphobia is not really a disabling condition. But it is significant that, for example, one clinical trial of the drug imipramine included a 'test walk' through a shopping mall (Roth et al., 1988), and that another study examined whether agoraphobics interpret the environment in large shops and supermarkets differently from the way 'general' (read, 'normal') shoppers do (Jones et al., 1996). As Kupers observes, since 'the explosive growth of consumerism in the 1920s, newer, milder, diagnoses are needed for those who are capable of working, who buy into the promise of ad campaigns that the purchase of one commodity after another will lead to happiness, and yet are unable to attain the kind of happiness portrayed in advertisements and films.' They must be 'neurotic; perhaps they need psychoanalysis, psychotherapy, a tranquilizer or an antidepressant' (Kupers, 1995:70). What could be more problematic than a disease that disables some individuals from even entering stores?

For example, in the case of one patient, 'Mrs Griffiths,' the 'furthest she could venture alone was to the two shops about 50 yards from her house' (Stantworth, 1982:400). Although she resented having been 'tied to the house for 14 years' and forced into 'the role of wife and mother' (403), she depended almost completely on her husband, 'who had to carry out for or with her many of the normal day to day tasks of a housewife' (400). Eventually, however, she achieved her goal of entering the local shops on her own, a challenge Mrs Griffiths's therapist planned for a day on which she normally bought meat so that she would have 'a good incentive to succeed or the family would be hungry' (402). For 'Holly,' a 'pleasant, tubby 46-year-old woman,' problems arose on the first day of her program, when she started to walk with her nurse therapist to the shops (Wondrak, 1980:43). On the way she became very anxious, sweaty, and faint, but with encouragement was able to walk a bit farther until the shops were in sight, at which point she and her therapist returned to the hospital. The next day Holly's success was even greater – Holly made it *all the way* to the shops. 'Mrs A' similarly wanted to make it to a dress shop in the mall near her house. She knew the store and 'was able to imagine herself going through the process of getting to the store, entering it, looking at dresses, going into the changing rooms, standing at a sales counter, paying for her selection, leaving the store and going home' (Pyke and Longdon, 1985:21). During the previous three years, Mrs A had not ventured beyond a three-block radius of her home, and had increasingly avoided anxiety-producing situations and places, including shopping malls, movie theatres, banks, hairdressers, and dentists. Like the others, 'Mrs Manton,' an 'extremely obese woman,' had difficulty shopping and was unable to use public transport or visit friends and relatives (Brooker, 1980). For another woman, shopping and other domestic errands had to be done by her teenage daughter, who frequently missed school in order to accomplish everything her mother required (Liffiton, 1992:33). One therapist, whose patient, 'Helen,' also suffered from an inability to shop for groceries, had Helen visit the supermarket twice a week, including busy Saturday mornings, and remain there for at least an hour (Garland, 1992:26).

In striking contrast is a patient, 'Mr Prince,' who had difficulty walking certain distances and riding on a bus, which made it impossible for him to get to his workplace. As part of his therapy, Mr Prince was 'encouraged to go on short walks by himself and to increase the distances gradually.' By the end of the third week of his treatment from home, he was to come on his own for an appointment at the clinic, and to the nurse therapist's great surprise and delight Mr Prince was successful. From this achievement the patient graduated to public transportation: 'His next step would be to ... take the bus to the city where he worked ... and find his way to his [place of employment].' With his career at a large international bank in jeopardy, Mr Prince was determined to return to his job after five months away, and achieving that goal was a major accomplishment. He was 'very pleased with himself [and] grateful ... that we had helped him retain his work and with it his dignity and self-respect ... If he had lost his job he would have been utterly demoralised' (Lim, 1985:19).

The extent to which Mr Prince's 'dignity and self-respect' – his identity, really – were tied to his (in)ability to get to his place of employment makes his case stand in stark contrast to many of the others, mostly concerning women, for whom the central goal of treatment was to overcome their inability to shop. Although it is possible that the gendered nature of the treatment programs may simply reflect a gendering in the types of agoraphobic situations reported by the male and female patients involved, and although it is also true that in cities one must shop for (as opposed to grow) one's food, it is significant that in the reports this particular activity – shopping – is associated only with women. Put differently, it is curious that Mr Prince's anxiety was associated with going to work; surely he also required groceries and the occasional item of new clothing. But there is an added political economic component of this gendered imperative that we must consider, too.

Specifically, production and consumption are being cited in these reports (and the *DSM*) as criteria for 'normal' behaviour. That is, when doctors incorporate shopping into treatment, they transmit an ideological cultural imperative to their patients, one that reflects a dominant ideal linking normal femininity with consumption and, in Mr Prince's case, normal masculinity with paid work. Edlund (1990) has demonstrated convincingly that agoraphobia is bad for the economy, so, although some may consider not working (for pay) ideal feminine behaviour, the general implication is that an economic assumption colours the lens through which psychiatrists gaze at their patients and pathologizes living outside the framework of patriarchal capitalism.

But nowhere are interested economics more evident than in the area of pharmaceuticals. In the last two to three decades, the pharmacological approach to treating agoraphobia, as we saw in chapter 3, has mainly involved antidepressants and tranquillizers, an approach that makes the disproportionate diagnosis of agoraphobia in women alarming. In 1977, Waldron observed that coinciding with the rapid growth in the use of minor tranquillizers in the 1970s and a rise in social problems, including suicide, homicide, and alcoholism, was a tendency to focus attention on individual malfunction rather than on problems as having social causes. The result was that 'social and economic problems' were 'dealt with in the framework of a medical model of relief of individual distress rather than in a social and political context of cooperative efforts for societal change.' Accordingly, the 'medico-pharmaceutical complex' has shifted its focus from the discovery of treatments for major diseases to the medicalization of the human condition (Healy, 2002:2), thereby reducing the 'pressures for social change' – a shift that is increasingly 'advantageous from the point of view of those who profit from the existing economic and political order' (Waldron, 1977:43).

So one must wonder, is it merely a coincidence that both the prevalence of agoraphobia and the prescription of antidepressants and minor tranquillizers to women increased at a time in history when women's participation in the paid labour force increased as well? As Kupers asks in a discussion of gender bias in the psychiatric diagnosis of PMS, 'is it merely coincidental that just when middle-class women are entering the workplace in record numbers, premenstrual syndrome is declared a form of mental disorder?' (Kupers, 1995:69). The important social changes of the last few decades undoubtedly have introduced new stressors for women, but the medicalization of these stressors (not to mention the medicalization of the women themselves) that takes place when the response is to prescribe benzodiazepines (minor tranquillizers) such as alprazolam (Xanax) may have proved a very effective means of gendered social control. For instance, it is well documented that benzodiazepines – alprazolam and others – are addictive (Hallfors and Saxe, 1993; *Medical Letter*, 1981, 1982, 1988; Pecknold and Swinson, 1986; Salzman, 1993). As of the late 1990s, they were also the most widely prescribed and possibly *over*prescribed anti-anxiety medications (Botts, 1997; Swinson et al., 1992), if not one of the most widely prescribed of all medications (Evans et al., 1988; Freeman et al., 1993; Salzman, 1993). There is also ample evidence that stopping alprazolam (and the antidepressant imipramine) too soon or too abruptly can lead to a recurrence of symptoms (National Institute of Health, 1993; Verster and Volkerts, 2004) – a feature of the drug that is very good for the pharmaceutical business. As Orr observes, the 'story of panic disorder' is one 'told by a medical/corporate model of biological illness' that reproduces 'women-bodies as a secure, because we're panicked, site for pharmaceutical profits. The effect of women's panic when experienced within this discourse is to speed up the theoretical and technological machinery of transnational corporate capital' (Orr, 1990:483).

The addictive properties of benzodiazepines may help explain why one patient described in a 1979 case report, 'Anna,' was for ten years able to 'carry out normal daily activities' only with 'out-patient support supplemented by diazepam (Valium) and Chlordiazepoxide (Librium)' (King, 1981; also Stantworth, 1982). Yet Anna's story has implications on a much larger scale. It is undeniable that these drugs help reduce the number of patients in mental hospitals (Silverman and Lee, 1974:12) and that they have had positive effects for some patients in enabling them to function 'normally' in their day-to-day lives. The positive effects *must* be contextualized, however; these drugs serve as a tool in the management of agoraphobia and panic experiences, but they must also be understood in the context of a patriarchal capitalist social system.

In other words, analysis of the role of pharmaceuticals in the history of agoraphobia requires that in addition to looking at the reinforcing (addictive) properties of the drugs themselves, we question the gendered pharmacoepidemiology – the gendered patterns of drug use – and the relationship among 'pills, profits and politics' (Silverman and Lee, 1974). Indeed, as Metzl and Angel have demonstrated in their study of popular notions of women's depression and the expansion of categories of women's mental illness with the introduction and increasing prescription of SSRIs, 'the seemingly "normal" states that become medicalized are neither random nor happenstance, but instead depend on prevailing cultural stereotypes and assumptions about matters such as gender, race, or mental illness' (Metzl and Angel, 2004:583). That is, as SSRI sales and use have grown, so too has the number of conditions they are used to treat, to the point of encompassing a range of events previously considered as normal in women's lives, such as menstruation and childbirth (577); and this parallel growth reinforces the important link between the medicalization of gender and the capitalist imperatives of consumption and profit.

But it is important to recognize that along with gendered and patriarchal capitalist concerns, racialism too, however tacitly, has informed the psychiatric gaze. The affluent (white) medical subject has persisted as normative in the discourse of agoraphobia, a tendency that is evident even in the earliest literature on the disease. Recall Abraham Myerson, for example, who in 1920 linked women's troubles with their inequality. He insisted that the forces of social life were mainly responsible for mental problems, but he also believed that women were ultimately predisposed to such problems by overemotionality. Although Myerson, a Jew, was alert to racism (Lunbeck, 1994:33), he noted that a predisposition to overemotionality was especially true of Jewish women, because the 'Jewish home reverberates with emotionality and largely through this the attitude of the Jewish housewife' (Myerson, 1929 [1920]:59–60). In fact the notion that Jews were especially prone to nervous disease was quite widespread; as Sander Gilman observes, the 'face of the Jew was as much a sign of the pathological as was the face of the hysteric,' and the notion that Eastern European Jewish men were most at risk for hysteria was a 'truism of medical science' for decades (Gilman, 1991:63). The American physician Charles E. Atwood wrote in 1903, for example, that in 80 per cent of the cases of neurasthenia he saw while working in the Department for Nervous Diseases of the Vanderbilt Clinic in New York the patients were foreign-born, and mostly Russian Jews (Atwood, 1903:1072).

But the pathological Jewish psyche was not strictly about Jewishness per se. Early-twentieth-century psychiatry was generally 'shot through with racial concerns' (Lunbeck, 1994:122), and, in America at least, these concerns were inextricable from a widespread discourse of anti-immigration and growing fears of 'race-suicide.' Dr Atwood deduced that most at risk for nervous disease was the immigrant, especially in large cities, 'partly owing to some inherent racial peculiarities, partly to neurotic heredity, or tendencies, partly to deprivation, partly to competition, and partly to the fact that the sordid processes of evolution are before him.' Problems of 'degeneracy, physical stigmata, perversions, mental enfeeblement, neurasthenia, insanity and criminals' were commonly found 'in this imported foreign population,' a finding that made the issue of immigration 'of exceeding importance' in the prevention of nervous disease (Atwood, 1903:1702).

Atwood's remarks are revealing, but it should be noted that his concern was with neurasthenia in particular, and the xenophobia informing his remarks has never appeared in the literature on agoraphobia proper. In fact, agoraphobic patients are rarely described in 'racial' terms at all, even though historically many mental diseases have been racialized and the use of racial categories by psychiatrists has been commonplace. As Grob states, early psychiatry was not 'immune from the racial and ethnic divisions of the larger society. Many believed that susceptibility toward mental illness was in part determined by race' (Grob, 1985:269). Historically, 'race' has been important in psychiatry because 'it accounted for peculiarities that were otherwise attributable only to pathology' (Lunbeck, 1994:125). It is unusual, therefore, that the discourse of agoraphobia has been decidedly 'race-less.' It suggests that, historically, the typical agoraphobic patient has been white, since in Western discourse, medical and otherwise, whiteness tends not to require qualification or even articulation. Whiteness is taken for granted and tacitly normalized in its position as the privileged signifier (see Dyer, 2002; also McIntosh, 2003).

The racial classification system contained in the *Statistical Manual for the Use of Institutions for the Insane*, first published in 1918 by the American Medico-Psychological Association and a precursor to the *Diagnostic and Statistical Manual of Mental Disorders* used today, corroborates this assumption. As a standardized manual compiling statistical data to be used by mental institutions, it set out various criteria for classifying incoming patients, including classification by 'race.' The criteria were taken from *The Dictionary of Races or Peoples*, a report of the United States government's Immigration Service (directed by Senator William Paul Dillingham) published in 1911.

There, the 'Negro, Negroid, African, Black, Ethiopian, or Austrafrican' is distinguished 'by ... *its* black color and, generally speaking, by ... *its* woolly hair.' 'Negroes' are 'alike in inhabiting hot countries and in belonging to the lowest division of mankind from an evolutionary standpoint' (Dillingham, 1911:100; my emphasis). Notably, they are presented as differing from the 'English,' who constitute 'the principal race' and whose higher evolutionary status is self-evident: 'Of course there is no necessity in this dictionary for discussion of a subject so well understood by all as the character, social institutions, and other qualities of the English as an immigrant people' (54).

To the extent that this system of racial classification derived from notions of evolutionary progress, it follows that the normalization of whiteness, evident in both this *Dictionary* and the *Statistical Manual*, can also be linked to Social Darwinist ideas about civilization and modernity and related assumptions about the frailty of affluent white women's bodies. Indeed, the attribution of disease to overcivilization was fairly common. As Atwood wrote in his 1903 article, for example, 'General paresis has been called a product of civilisation and syphilization' (Atwood, 1903:1073). Recall as well his remark that immigrants were especially vulnerable to mental diseases because they still had the 'sordid processes of evolution' before them. Sir Philip Gibbs, a British novelist invited to speak at the Annual General Meeting of the Tavistock Square Clinic for Functional Nervous Disorders, echoed Atwood's assessment. He declared that 'nerves' are the 'disease of civilization ... We are less brutal, less cruel, less ignorant, but we are more sensitive, more highly-strung, and therefore more quick to suffer. We have to pay the price for divorcing ourselves from the old earth, and from flowers and trees, and bodily labour, and handicraft ... This city life, cost[s] a great price in nervous strain' (Gibbs, 1929:468).

Because nervousness was characterized as a problem of 'overcivilization,' as Laura Briggs has demonstrated in her historical examination of hysteria, its diagnosis was as much about 'race' as about class and gender, in that hysterical illness 'was the provenance almost exclusively of ... white women of a certain class' (Briggs, 2000:246). Their nervous weakness, popularized by such famous American neurologists as Silas Weir Mitchell (best known for his 'rest cure') and George Miller Beard, resulted from 'the frantic pressures of advanced civilization (Porter, 1997:511). Beard wrote, 'Nervous disease ... scarcely exists among savages or barbarians, or semi-barbarians or partially civilized people' (Beard, 1881:92–3). He went on to say that 'functional nervous disease' results only when 'civilization prepare[s] the way.' Civilization is 'the one constant factor, the foundation of all these neuroses, wherever they exist' (171).

The notion that only civilized (white and affluent) people were candidates for hysteria is particularly significant if we recall the collective concerns about modern social change expressed by social theorists (chapter 2). They too were preoccupied essentially with evolution and (the dangers of) civilization, and implicitly drew a distinction between the civilized and the uncivilized. Similar to those deplored by physicians, the changes these social theorists lamented implied a standard of evolution against which the dominant class (and 'race') could measure their own progress. Given the belief in 'the differences between country and city ... the edenic, innocent pastoral as against the vexations of industrialization, the nostalgic against the modern' (Briggs, 2000:249), along with the historical connection between the categories of hysteria and agoraphobia, I contend that agoraphobia was, at least tacitly, also constructed as a nervous 'disease of overcivilization' and as such was an option available only to privileged whites.

In other words, the racialism of agoraphobia was present by implication; white middle- and upper-class people were the privileged subject of medicine because, as civilized subjects, only they qualified for 'normality,' and only the 'normal' had the prerogative of being pathological. Accordingly, there was no need to articulate any 'racial' criteria or characteristics in the psychiatric literature because in a social context fraught with supremacist ideology and even violent assertions of whites' superiority, patients' normative whiteness was tacitly understood. Herzig's observation that in the history of hypertrichosis (2000) the distinction between normal and abnormal bodies was inextricable from that between white and non-white bodies may help to illustrate.

In the discourse of hypertrichosis, body hair was invested with the weight of evolutionary progress (or rather its absence) in a way that directly signified racial difference. Herzig contends that 'even when acknowledging cultural variation in perceptions of beauty and normalcy, physicians were quick to mark some bodies as fundamentally "deficient" or "excessive" in secondary hair growth ... At stake in the diagnosis of hypertrichosis, then, was the very meaning of racialized manliness and womanliness themselves' (Herzig, 2000:n.p.). The desire to appear feminine, that is, not excessively and unnaturally hairy, 'made sense only against the backdrop of an already-presumed distinction between normal [read, white] and abnormal [read, non-white] bodies, since only the normal body could become ill with hypertrichosis. Other bodies were presumed to be [merely] expressing their characteristic racial difference.' Accordingly, 'Caucasian' bodies were the sole candidates for this pathology because they were the only bodies that qualified for 'normality.' 'Mongolian' and 'Negro' bodies were excluded from both the normal and the pathological. They were simply 'deficient' – a separate category altogether. In other words, their hairiness (or hairlessness) was simply an expression of their 'race.' In fact, whiteness, for all intents and purposes, though superior, did not really even constitute a 'race' in the sense that blackness and other characteristics did. The term 'coloured' captures this negative relation well, the assumption behind it being that white was and is not a colour at all.[6] If we borrow again from Herzig, we can see that, as with hirsutism, it is arguable that 'only the normal [white] body could become ill with [agoraphobia], while other bodies [the non-white ones] were presumed to be expressing their characteristic racial difference.'

Evidently the affluent, by virtue of being the right (read, normal) 'race,' also had the prerogative of suffering from a socially sanctioned disease. Yet civilization and its privileges came at a cost. The affluent were less hardy and more prone to illness than their uncivilized counterparts, but, given their more evolved social status, that was to be expected. Accordingly, white middle- and upper-class people were the privileged subject of medicine – and social theory – because as civilized subjects they alone qualified for 'normality.'[7] With the well-heeled English as the normative standard against which all the other so-called races were measured, it seems that only white affluent people were regarded as viable candidates for these kinds of problems. In fact, the literature on agoraphobia, all published out of the developed West, historically has reflected – through its silence on race – a (normative) predominance of agoraphobia among married, educated, middle-class white women (Reuter, 2001).

In this context the findings of a relatively recent American epidemiological study on agoraphobia (Boyd et al., 1990; Weissman, 1990a) are especially striking. In this community study of five major American cities, the researchers discovered that the incidence of agoraphobia (and other phobias) was greater among African American women with the lowest socioeconomic status than among groups of white women (Boyd et al., 1990).[8] The newness of this finding can be accounted for in part by the fact that most of the psychiatric literature on agoraphobia is based on clinical populations consisting of the most severely disabled phobics (as opposed to community populations consisting of individuals who tend not to seek treatment). For historical and economic reasons, in these clinical populations there is over-representation by middle-class 'whites.' The historical reasons include a long-standing legacy of distrust among African Americans that prevents them from consulting doctors with their problems (see Gamble, 1993, 1997a, 1997b). This distrust stems largely from the well-known Tuskegee, Alabama, Syphilis Study. Briefly, the United States government funded a forty-year syphilis study (1932–72) designed to document the disease's natural course. The research subjects were 399 poor African American men, from whom the physicians conducting the research deliberately withheld treatment, and on whom they conducted other procedures, deceiving them into thinking they were being treated for 'bad blood.'

Unfortunately, despite public disclosure of the experiment and subsequent implementation of the 1974 National Research Act, designed to protect human subjects of experimentation, questionable research continues. As recently as 1989, the Centers for Disease Control and Prevention were involved in a study to test an experimental measles vaccine, a trial of which the research protocol was not disclosed until 1996. By 1991, most of the approximately nine hundred infants to whom the drug had been administered were of African and Latin descent. Their parents were not told that the vaccine was not yet licensed in the United States, or that it was linked to increased death rates in Africa (Gamble, 1997b:1776–7).

In short, medical racism and the continued exploitation of 'minority' communities for the purposes of research ensure a virulent level of scepticism on the part of patients of colour (Gamble, 1997b:1776–7). This type of exploitation has much earlier origins, however, in various gruelling antebellum experiments as well as in a substantial folklore about 'night-doctors' and the threat to African Americans of being taken away for the purpose of dissection.[9] There is evidence that African Americans were terrified by the possibility of being bled and dismembered, and their fear prompted many of them, until the 1930s at least, to stay out of the vicinity of hospitals during the daytime and to avoid night travel and even certain cities altogether (Fry, 1975:210–11).

These examples go a long way to illustrate why African Americans would be resistant to medical interventions. They also help to explain why, in recent history, African Americans have declined for the most part to participate in clinical trials and organ donation, and why many believe the HIV virus to be synthetic, and a deliberate attempt at genocide against them (Gamble, 1997b:1773–5). But the most compelling illustration comes from the 'night-doctors' folklore, which chillingly demonstrates that, just as affluent white women 'passed' as True Women rather than agoraphobic, so African Americans' anxieties about being out in white-dominated racist and dangerous public space may have 'passed' unnoticed – that is, as something other than agoraphobia.

There are important economic reasons for the over-representation of whites in the agoraphobia literature as well. In 1984 (roughly when the epidemiological data were collected) the median annual family income of whites in the United States was significantly higher, at $27,686 (USD), than that of African Americans, which averaged only $15,432 (USD). This inequality corresponds with disparities in health insurance coverage and state and county mental hospital admissions (see United States Department of Health and Human Services, 1986:14 and 74),[10] as well as with whites' greater economic access to private therapy (United States Census Bureau, 2000; United States Department of Health and Human Services, 1986, 1987). This greater access means that whites appear more often in the clinical literature; it is well known, moreover, that not only do African Americans visit physicians less frequently than whites, but they do not receive the same quality of care (United States Census Bureau, 1999, 2000; United States Department of Health and Human Services, 1986, 1987; also Geiger, 1997: 1766).[11] In the light of these data, it should come as no surprise that poor, urban African American women do not present for treatment, so are generally not reflected in clinical articles and emerge only in community studies. The fact that African Americans do not receive the same quality of care as do white Americans demonstrates that poor access is an important obstacle to health and has negative implications for health outcomes (Geiger, 1997:1766).

The findings of this epidemiological study also reflect the possibility that agoraphobia may have gone undetected in poor African American women because the official criteria for this diagnosis, derived from the *DSM*, are based on a normative white, middle-class urban experience that excludes racism as a possible (and legitimate) reason for not going out into public spaces. Though not explicitly about 'race,' two cases reported from the volatile context of Northern Ireland are instructive here. As one therapist reported, 'Mrs. James had never been in the city for any length of time since the outbreak of violence, [so] she had to be prepared for the security arrangements and what to do during a bomb scare, all of which were new to her' (Bradley, 1975:967). Another therapist, also Irish, described a similar situation involving an agoraphobic-claustrophobic woman. 'Cynthia,' his patient, decided to pursue treatment even though 'everyday somewhere in Belfast buses were being hi-jacked. Everyday there was the possibility of being injured in bomb blasts. People were being shot. There were security checks to pass through which meant waiting to be searched. And not long ago, a shopping centre, similar to the one she [wanted] to go to, had been wrecked in a car bomb which had resulted in three deaths and many injuries' (Williamson, 1974:1843–4).

There is no reason to think that poor African American women, living most likely in the inner city, would not have had parallel concerns. In fact, contrary to the usual characterization of agoraphobic fear in the literature, these examples underscore the possibility that it could represent a completely rational response to the pressures of urban public space. That does not mean that African American women do not really experience the distress of agoraphobia, but it may account in part for why their agoraphobia previously had gone unnoticed. Once again, just as affluent white women 'passed' as True Women rather than as agoraphobic at the beginning of the twentieth century, so contemporary African American women fearful of venturing out may have also 'passed' as something other than agoraphobic – the epidemiological findings point to the possibility that racism informs such women's fear. As Carol Brooks Gardner (1994) has shown, agoraphobic and non-agoraphobic women who fear being accosted in public spaces engage in remarkably similar behaviours. Clearly 'non-whites,' too, have had to cope with the frenetic pace and the perils of modern urban life, but their experience of it has also been infused by the realities of racism.

Until recently most researchers 'have used white men as the standard or norm from which to extrapolate data to the rest of the population.' Young white men were presumed to make up 'a homogeneous population that had fewer confounding factors.' Members of minority groups, along with women, were frequently excluded from clinical studies (Gamble, 1993:37) and really studied only in order to measure degrees of racial difference (Fee, 1994:16). Since the discovery of 'race' (along with gender), there has been some recognition that the body is not always that of a seventy-kilogram white male. Perhaps agoraphobic whites are reported on more frequently by clinicians because they are the ones who seek help, but it may also be true that once race and gender were 'invented' as research variables, researchers needed only to look to be able to find them.[12] And, as Fee writes, it is 'critical to read these omissions [of women and men of colour] as evidence of a logic of difference rather than as an assumption of similarity' (Fee, 1994:16).

For example, the interviews conducted for the 1980s American epidemiological study were based on a schedule (the 'DIS') defined by the criteria of *DSM-III*. If the revised *DSM-III-R* schedule (the 'SCID') is any indication, it is likely that the DIS was also based on normative white experiences and did not address issues of racism. Indeed, as Knowles has demonstrated in her insightful analysis of the interconnections between 'administrative' and 'existential' racism, 'psychiatry contains a series of powerful, racialized narratives which dictate the terms on which certain lives will be lived and judged' (Knowles, 1996:56). Moreover, racism in psychiatric narratives has important psychological (and political) consequences, and can feature in both the narratives' silences and their explicit statements. This is highly significant: the African American women 'discovered' through community (as opposed to clinical) research may have 'qualified' as agoraphobics simply because researchers did not ask the right questions, that is, questions that might have opened up the possibility that racism and the women's fear of crime and violence, rather than irrational fear, are what, quite reasonably, deter these African American women from venturing into public places.

All that said, we must also ask how and why this finding of prevalence among African American women came to light when it did. We must problematize the concept of 'race' as it is used in contemporary epidemiological research in spite of its unviability as a biological concept. A social and historical construct, the purpose behind its use as a biological concept has been to give meaning to human variation based on the notion that different 'packages of genes' exist from one human group to another. This notion is false, however, because the boundaries between racialized groups are indistinct, and because, even though individuals within groups may share certain external features such as skin colour, they are heterogeneous in most other genetic respects. But the primacy given to such visible characteristics is ultimately arbitrary, and a single trait represents an inadequate ground on which to characterize human diversity (Cooper, 1984:716). Rather, as Sandra Harding states, 'race is not a thing ... but a relationship between groups,' and racializing is 'a consequence of the symbolic meanings and structural relations of races, not the reverse' (as reported by Freeman, 1998:223).

Despite all the evidence and arguments against it, and despite the fact that there is still no international agreement on racial classification, the concept is still routinely used, not least in epidemiological research. References to race have steadily increased in recent decades, as one group of researchers found by examining the various volumes of two epidemiology journals published between 1921 and 1990, in which 79 per cent of the 124 American studies contained references to race. The researchers also found a growing trend towards the explicit exclusion of 'non-white' subjects, despite the National Institute of Health's requirement that all groups be included in studies unless there is compelling scientific evidence justifying the exclusion of some (Jones et al., 1991).

This kind of research must also be examined critically in the light of three factors. First, there is a lack of continuity among data collection agencies as to how to count/classify/categorize by race and ethnicity, and miscounting and misclassification by race occur frequently. Second, individual subjects' self-reporting of race and ethnic identity varies according to different indicators, surveys, and times, and perhaps even different subjective understandings of the criteria. Third, the concept of race itself is untenable. Statistics generated on the basis of an inherently unsustainable biological concept of race may not be accurate or meaningful, although gathering such information is necessary for the redressing of excess morbidity and mortality among 'minority' populations. But it is arguably more important to explore how race relations and discrimination have health consequences, rather than how race explains racial differences in health (Freeman, 1998:223–4).

In sum, the subjects of the 1980s epidemiological study came from the community rather than from private clinics (as is usually the case in the agoraphobia literature), with implications for the study's findings. But the question of *why* poor African American women supposedly suffer from agoraphobia more than whites was not explored substantively by the authors. Cooper's analysis of the prevalence of heart disease among African Americans in the United States is instructive here: 'Black people in this society are imprisoned by institutional racism; this is the attribute of blackness which at bottom determines their health status ... The epidemiology of [coronary heart disease] among [them] has ... been determined by ... social conditions.' Cooper goes on to say: 'Greater cigarette use, relative exclusion from preventive campaigns, bad nutrition, excess hypertension, and obesity are all important attributes of the contemporary experience of black Americans. Higher rates of [coronary heart disease] are to be anticipated' (Cooper, 1984:722). Racial and gender discrimination, then, may harm cardiovascular health (Krieger, 1990; Krieger and Sidney, 1996); it is equally plausible that racism may prevent African Americans both from leaving their houses and, owing to their fear of medical professionals, from seeking help. Their sudden appearance on the epidemiologists' radar, where they stand in spite of a discourse of agoraphobia in which they did not even exist, is at once counter-intuitive and entirely predictable.

In the next chapter I explore further the connection between the psychiatric and the social-cultural, with a focus on the formal classification of agoraphobia in the *Diagnostic and Statistical Manual of Mental Disorders* and its re-embedding in the discourse of neo-positivist biology in recent decades.

5 The *DSM* and the Decline of the Social

There is no such thing as a psychiatry that is too biological.

(S.B. Guze, 1989)

An affect such as anxiety must resist unequivocal and precise definition, for the emotions merge insensibly with one another in mental life, and cannot be expected to have sharp boundaries. The boundaries are artificial, created to reduce the task of investigating affective states to manageable proportion.

(M. Roth and N. Argyle, 1988)

Patients are not concerned with how we classify them, they only want to get better.

(M.A. Jenike et al., 1987)

In this chapter I describe the development of the *Diagnostic and Statistical Manual of Mental Disorders* (*DSM*) and discuss its implications for both psychoanalysis and agoraphobia. As we have seen, with the practice of early-twentieth-century psychiatry increasingly dominated by Sigmund Freud's psychoanalytic approach, by the 1930s agoraphobia had emerged as a symptom of 'neurosis,' as a biopsychosocial reaction to unresolved early childhood and family difficulties. This view, at least within the United States, endured for several decades, but relatively recently mainstream American psychiatry reoriented itself towards its earlier reductionist biological and positivist tendencies, in a shift to a neo-positivist paradigm more compatible with the medical model of health and disease,[1] albeit one rather concerned to enhance and manipulate life than merely to restore the body to its normative healthy state. This reorientation coincides with the 1980 publication of

DSM-III, the third edition of the American Psychiatric Association's (APA) *Diagnostic and Statistical Manual of Mental Disorders.*

DSM-III had several precursors, however. The American Medico-Psychological Association (AMPA) produced its first *Statistical Manual for the Use of Institutions for the Insane* in 1918. Both state and private hospitals widely approved of the *Statistical Manual,* and demand for it was so great that the supply of the first edition was nearly depleted, necessitating a second edition, which was published in 1920. This second version was essentially the same as the first, but with a few minor modifications, including expanded instructions, the addition of some new items, and adjustment of terms and categories to conform to current usage (AMPA, 1920:4). From 1918 to 1942, the manual went through ten editions. Not only was the system it set forth used by the Census Bureau and practically all the hospitals throughout the country, but the United States Public Health Service, the United States Army, and the Veterans' Bureau also adopted it for use (see sample below).

18. **Psychoneuroses and neuroses**
   (a) Hysterical type
   (b) Psychasthenic type
   (c) Neurasthenic type
   (d) Anxiety neuroses

The psychoneurosis group includes those disorders in which mental forces or ideas of which the subject is either aware (conscious) or unaware (unconscious) bring about various mental and physical symptoms; in other words, these disorders are essentially psychogenic in nature.

The term neurosis is now generally used synonymously with psychoneurosis, although it has been applied to certain disorders in which, while the symptoms are both mental and physical, the primary cause is thought to be essentially physical. In most instances, however, both psychogenic and physical causes are operative and we can assign only a relative weight to the one or the other.

The following types are sufficiently well defined clinically to be specified:

(a) Hysterical type: Episodic mental attacks in the form of

delirium, stupor or dream states during which repressed wishes, mental conflicts or emotional experiences detached from ordinary consciousness break through, and temporarily dominate the mind. The attack is followed by partial or complete amnesia. Various physical disturbances (sensory and motor) occur in hysteria, and these represent a conversion of the affect of the repressed disturbing complexes into bodily symptoms or, according to another formulation, there is a dissociation of consciousness relating to some physical function.

(b) Psychasthenic type: This includes the compulsive and obsessional neuroses of some writers. The main clinical characteristics are phobias, obsessions, morbid doubts and impulsions, feelings of insufficiency, nervous tension and anxiety. Episodes of marked depression and agitation may occur. There is no disturbance of consciousness or amnesia as in hysteria.

(c) Neurasthenic type: This should designate the fatigue neuroses in which physical as well as mental causes evidently figure; characterized essentially by mental and motor fatigability and irritability; also various hyperaesthesias and parasthesias; hypochondriasis and varying degrees of depression.

(d) Anxiety neuroses: A clinical type in which morbid anxiety or fear is the most prominent feature. A general nervous irritability (or excitability) is regularly associated with the anxious expectation or dread; in addition there are numerous physical symptoms which may be regarded as the bodily accompaniments of fear; particularly cardiac and vasomotor disturbances: the heart's action is increased, often there is irregularity and palpitation; there may be sweating, nausea, vomiting, diarrhea, suffocative feelings, dizziness, trembling, shaking, difficulty in locomotion, etc. Fluctuations occur in the intensity of the symptoms, the acute exacerbations constituting the 'anxiety attack.'

Source: 'Classification of Mental Diseases,' *Statistical Manual for the Use of Institutions for the Insane* (1918), pp. 14 and 26–7.

Meanwhile, in 1928, the New York Academy of Medicine held a conference on the nomenclature of disease attended by representatives of many organizations, including medical, government, military, and life insurance bodies, all of whom had, until then, devised and used their own classification systems. The American Medical Association sought consistency across the board, however, with the result the publication in 1933 of the first *Standard Classified Nomenclature of Disease* (*SCM*). The *SCM* was intended as a 'central guiding influence' in the face of a 'confusing multiplicity of effort' and was to include 'every disease which can be recognised clinically' in order to 'avoid repetition and overlapping' and to 'classify the diseases in a logical manner' (Logie, 1933:xi–xii). It was also intended as a reference work for clinicians, public health officials, and clerks. In 1935 a second edition of the *SCM* was published, and it 'found its way' into nearly five hundred hospitals in Canada and the United States (Emerson and Baehr in Logie, 1935:xi). By 1942, with the release of a third edition, the *SCM* included surgical operations. In all its editions, the classification system was based upon two organizing principles: the location of pathology (topographical classification) and causation (aetiological classification).

TOPOGRAPHICAL CLASSIFICATION

SYSTEM 0

0 *Diseases of the body as a whole (including diseases of the psyche, and of the body generally); and those not affecting a particular system exclusively*

00 PSYCHO-BIOLOGICAL UNIT
000   Generally and unspecified
001   Psyche
002 ⎫
003 ⎪
004 ⎬
005   Nervous system, generally and psyche
006
007
008
009   Somatic structures and psyche
00x   Endocrine system and psyche

Source: *A Standard Classified Nomenclature of Disease* (1933), p. 14.

00-X Diseases without clearly defined tangible cause or structural manifestations, including such due to heredity (constitutional psychoses)

000-x00	Psychoneuroses and neuroses *(87b)*
000-x01	Hysterical type *(87b)*
000-x02	Psychasthenic type
000-x04	Neurasthenic type *(87b)*
000-x0Y||	Other types of psychoenurosis *(87b)*
001-x10	Manic-depressive psychoses *(84)*
001-x11	Manic type *(84)*
001-x12	Depressive type *(84)*
001-x1Y||	Other types *(84)*
001-x20	Dementia praecox (schizophrenia) *(84)*
001-x21	Paranoid type *(84)*
001-x22	Catatonic type *(84)*
001-x23	Hebephrenic type *(84)*
001-x24	Simple type *(84)*
001-x2Y||	Other types *(84)*
001-x30	Paranoia and paranoid conditions *(84)*
001-x40	Psychoses with psychopathic personality *(84)*
001-x50	Psychoses with mental deficiency *(84)*
009-xY0||	Delirium of unknown origin *(200a)*

Y\|\| signifies an incomplete diagnosis. It is to be replaced, whenever possible, by a code digit signifying specific diagnosis.

Source: *A Standard Classified Nomenclature of Disease* (1933), p. 88.

DETAILED CLASSIFICATION OF PSYCHONEUROSES, NEUROSES, MALADJUSTMENT, AND ALLIED STATES
(Approved by the American Neurological Association)

000-x00	Psychoneuroses and neuroses *(87b)*
000-x01	Hysteria *(87b)*
000-x011	Anxiety hysteria *(87b)*
	Conversion hysteria. [...]

000-x012	Dissociated states (fugues, amnesia, somnambulism, catalepsy, trance, dual personality, etc.) *(87b)*
000-x013	Tics *(87b)*
000-x02	Simple depression
000-x03	Anxiety state
000-x04	Neurasthenia *(87b)*
000-x05	Hypochondriasis *(84)*
000-x06	Compulsive states
000-x061	Obsession
000-x062	Mania (kleptomania, pyromania, trichitillomania, etc.)
000-x063	Phobias (agoraphobia, claustrophobia, misophobia, syphilophobia, etc.)

Source: *A Standard Classified Nomenclature of Disease* (1933), p. 90.

DSM-I and DSM-II

This new system, however, met the needs of government but not necessarily those of patients and doctors. Psychiatric treatment at that time was still quite non-specific and too narrowly focused on the compilation of statistics. The volume was not especially helpful to psychiatrists from the military, from induction stations, and from the Veterans' Administration who were faced with cases that did not fit with the *SCM* system. For example, there were no terms for diagnosing reactions to the stress of combat.

The APA therefore struck a committee to work towards standardizing categories for all of medicine, and in 1952 the first *Diagnostic and Statistical Manual (DSM-I)* was published with a view to providing guidelines for the statistical recording and reporting of psychiatric conditions. Strangely, it contained no bibliographic references.

That psychoanalysis was still the dominant approach in psychiatry was evident in *DSM-I*, both in its organization and in the range of disorders included. For example, there were three major divisions of the functional (non-organic) disorders, into psychoses, psychoneuroses, and personality disorders. In *DSM-I*, the term 'disorder' was used 'generically' to delineate a group of related psychiatric syndromes, and each of these groups was further subdivided more specifically, into conditions known as 'reactions' (APA, 1952:9). Although agoraphobia was not named specifically, 'anxiety reaction' and 'phobic reaction' were (see below).

PSYCHONEUROTIC DISORDERS

– x DISORDERS OF PSYCHOGENIC ORIGIN OR WITHOUT CLEARLY DEFINED TANGIBLE CAUSE OR STRUCTURAL CHANGE

000-X00	Psychoneurotic reactions	*(318.5)**
000-x01	Anxiety reaction	*(310)*
000-x02	Dissociative reaction	*(311)*
000-x03	Conversion reaction	*(311)*
000-x04	Phobic reaction	*(312)*
000-x05	Obsessive compulsive reaction	*(313)*
000-x06	Depressive reaction	*(314)*
000-x0y	Psychoneurotic reaction, other	*(318.5)**

Source: *Diagnostic and Statistical Manual of Mental Disorders* (1952), p. 6.

The psychoneurotic disorders were defined by their chief characteristic, anxiety, which was 'directly felt and expressed, [and] automatically controlled by such defenses as depression, conversion, dissociation, displacement, phobia formation, or repetitive thoughts and acts' (APA, 1952:12). Anxiety was described as a 'danger signal,' 'produced by a threat from within the personality (e.g., by supercharged repressed emotions, including such aggressive impulses as hostility and resentment), with or without stimulation from such external situations as loss of love, loss of prestige, or threat of injury.' In the 'anxiety reaction,' which was distinguished from 'normal apprehensiveness or fear' (32), anxiety was diffuse and unrestricted to specific situations and objects. This reaction was contrasted with 'phobic reactions' or 'phobias,' in which the 'anxiety of these patients becomes detached from a specific idea, object, or situation in the daily life and is displaced to some symbolic idea or situation in the form of a specific neurotic fear.' Common examples of 'phobic reactions,' according to *DSM-I*, 'include fear of syphilis, dirt, closed places, high places, open places, animals, etc.' (33) (see below).

PSYCHONEUROTIC DISORDERS

The chief characteristic of these disorders is 'anxiety' which may be directly felt and expressed or which may be unconsciously and automatically controlled by the utilization of various psychological defense mechanisms (depression, conversion, displacement, etc.). In contrast to those with psychoses, patients with psychoneurotic disorders do not exhibit gross distortion or falsification of external reality (delusions, hallucinations, illusions) and they do not present gross disorganization of the personality. Longitudinal (lifelong) studies of individuals with such disorders usually present evidence of periodic or constant maladjustment of varying degree from early life. Special stress may bring about acute symptomatic expression of such disorders.

'Anxiety' in psychoneurotic disorders is a danger signal felt and perceived by the conscious portion of the personality. It is produced by a threat from within the personality (e.g., by supercharged repressed emotions, including such aggressive impulses as hostility and resentment), with or without stimulation from such external situations as loss of love, loss of prestige, or threat of injury. The various ways in which the patient attempts to handle this anxiety results in the various types of reactions listed below.

In recording such reactions the terms 'traumatic neurosis,' or 'traumatic reaction' will not be used; instead, the predominant type of reaction will be recorded, qualified by reference to other types of reactions as part of the symptomatology.

000-x01 Anxiety reaction

In this kind of reaction the anxiety is diffuse and not restricted to definite situations or objects, as in the case of phobic reactions. It is not controlled by any specific psychological defense mechanism as in other psychoneurotic reactions. This reaction is characterized by anxious expectation and frequently associated with somatic symptomatology. The condition is to be differentiated from normal apprehensiveness or fear. The term is synonymous with the former term 'anxiety state' ...

000-x04 Phobic reaction
The anxiety of these patients becomes detached from a specific idea, object, or situation in the daily life and is displaced to some symbolic idea or situation in the form of a specific neurotic fear. The commonly observed forms of phobic reaction include fear of syphilis, dirt, closed places, high places, open places, animals, etc. The patient attempts to control his anxiety by avoiding the phobic object or situation.

In recording this diagnosis the manifestations will be indicated. The term is synonymous with the former term 'phobia' and includes some of the cases formerly classified as 'anxiety hysteria.'

Source: *Diagnostic and Statistical Manual of Mental Disorders* (1952), pp. 32–3.

Enormously popular, *DSM-I* was reprinted twenty times following its release in 1952 and was distributed throughout the United States and to other countries. Yet in spite of its popularity the APA felt the need to integrate psychiatric nomenclature and classifications with the rest of medicine, that is, with the World Health Organization's International Classification of Diseases. Revisions commenced in 1965, and by December 1967, the APA Council had authorized publication of the new *DSM-II*, the system of which went into effect on 1 July 1968. As in *DSM-I*, there were no references or citations. But, as Herb Kutchins and Stuart Kirk remark in their important critique of the *DSM* system, *DSM-II* made 'no pretence of being [a] scientific' document; it was, rather, an administrative codebook that, like the first edition, sought to facilitate the recording of mental disorders and their conceptualization (Kutchins and Kirk, 1997:247).

Building on *DSM-I*, *DSM-II* contained many new categories and was organized in a new way. Unlike the first edition, it encouraged the recording of multiple diagnoses and associated physical conditions, and it changed some qualifying phrases and many definitions (APA, 1968:2–4). It redivided disease categories into ten major groups, rather than *DSM-I*'s three, but perhaps the most important change was that the 'phobic reactions' of *DSM-I* were now called 'phobic neuroses' in *DSM-II* (9). Though still consistent with the language of psychoanalysis, this particular shift was considered by the work committee to be, in their words, 'one of the most striking differences between DSM-I and DSM-II, and perhaps the one that will generate the strongest feelings.' They maintained that in the interest of assigning suitable labels to mental disorders, such a change was necessary (122–3).

Anxiety was considered the chief characteristic of neuroses and was still differentiated from phobias because anxieties were diffuse, abnormal apprehensions or fears, whereas phobias were 'characterized by intense fear of an object or situation which the patient consciously recognizes as no real danger to him.' Consistent with the tenets of psychoanalysis, phobias were 'generally attributed to fears displaced to the phobic object or situation from some other object of which the patient is unaware' (APA, 1968:40) (see below). But this allegiance to psychoanalysis, however subtle, would not continue. The publication of *DSM-III* would represent the first move in a steady marginalization of psychoanalysis by the APA.

THE DIAGNOSTIC NOMENCLATURE:

List of Mental Disorders and Their Code Numbers
...
IV. NEUROSES (300)

300   Neuroses
.0   Anxiety neurosis
.1   Hysterical neurosis
         .13* Hysterical neurosis, conversion type*
         .14* Hysterical neurosis, dissociative type*
.2   Phobic neurosis
.3   Obsessive compulsive neurosis
.4   Depressive neurosis
.5   Neurasthenic neurosis ((Neurasthenia))
.6   Depersonalization neurosis ((Depersonalization syndrome))
.7   Hypochondriacal neurosis
.8   Other neurosis
[.9   Unspecified neurosis]

Source: *Diagnostic and Statistical Manual of Mental Disorders* [*DSM-II*] (1968), p. 9.

IV. NEUROSES (300)

300 Neuroses

Anxiety is the chief characteristic of the neuroses. It may be felt and expressed directly, or it may be controlled unconsciously and automatically by conversion, displacement and various other psychological mechanisms. Generally, these mechanisms produce symptoms experienced as subjective distress from which the patient desires relief.

The neuroses, as contrasted to the psychoses, manifest neither gross distortion or misinterpretation of external reality, nor gross personality disorganization. A possible exception to this is hysterical neurosis, which some believe may occasionally be accompanied by hallucinations and other symptoms encountered in psychoses.

Traditionally, neurotic patients, however severely handicapped by their symptoms, are not classified as psychotic because they are aware that their mental functioning is disturbed.

300.0 Anxiety neurosis

This neurosis is characterized by anxious over-concern extending to panic and frequently associated with somatic symptoms. Unlike *Phobic neurosis* (q.v.), anxiety may occur under any circumstances and is not restricted to specific situations or objects. This disorder must be distinguished from normal apprehension or fear, which occurs in realistically dangerous situations.

300.1 Hysterical neurosis

This neurosis is characterized by an involuntary psychogenic loss or disorder of function. Symptoms characteristically begin and end suddenly in emotionally charged situations and are symbolic of the underlying conflicts. Often they can be modified by suggestion alone. [...]

300.2 Phobic neurosis

This condition is characterized by intense fear of an object or situation which the patient consciously recognizes as no real danger to him. His apprehension may be experienced as faint-ness, fatigue, palpitations, perspiration, nausea, tremor, and even panic. Phobias are generally attributed to fears displaced to the phobic object or situation from some other object of which the patient is unaware. A wide range of phobias has been described.

Source: *Diagnostic and Statistical Manual of Mental Disorders* [*DSM-II*] (1968), pp. 39 – 40.

DSM-III: The Paradigm Shifts

In fact, although *DSM-II*, published in 1968, largely still embodied a psychoanalytic framework, by the time it was released the psychoanalytic approach had begun to fall out of favour among APA members and among critics of psychiatry. Among these critics was the well-known psychiatrist and psychoanalyst Thomas Szasz (1974), who argued that psychiatric labels were arbitrary designations that served professional interests rather than patient needs. R.D. Laing (1969), also a psychiatrist and analyst, was particularly critical of traditional approaches to treating schizophrenia. Other detractors included the sociologist Erving Goffman (1961), who demonstrated in his study of asylums that deviant identities are socially constructed, and the philosopher and historian Michel Foucault (1978, 1987), who saw psychiatry, especially psychoanalysis, as enacting a set of power relations and criticized psychiatrists as being concerned only with normative social regulation (I take up this point again, in chapter 6). The United States government and the American private insurance industry saw psychiatry as too costly, and pharmaceutical companies wanted clearer diagnostic criteria in order to conduct more reliable clinical trials based on homogeneous patient samples.

Innocuously describing their motive as a 'growing recognition of the importance of diagnosis for both clinical practice and research' (APA, 1980:1), the APA saw a third edition of the *DSM* as a unique opportunity in which to respond to these pressures and criticisms. Interestingly, the APA's collective aspiration was consistent with that of early-twentieth-century psychiatrists, who aspired to elevate the status of their profession by 'establishing a psychiatry of the prosaic and routine' and providing people with insight into their normal everyday problems (Lunbeck, 1994:47). More important, however, is the fact that developing a revised third edition of the *DSM* was more than just a unique opportunity to respond to the APA's critics. It was, rather, a watershed moment in the history of psychiatry that had been approaching since the anti-psychiatric student revolutions of the 1960s. Accordingly, the emergence of *DSM-III* signalled an important (power) shift in the dominant voice of psychiatry from the supposedly less credible psychoanalysis back to biopsychiatry and well beyond it – to the 'politics of life itself' and a new ethics of normality (cf. Rose, 2001b).

To be sure, the Task Force charged with the work of revising *DSM-II* was driven by an invisible college of neo-Kraepelinian biological psychiatrists[2] who were not interested in simply updating psychiatric nosology but wanted a complete overhaul (Kutchins and Kirk, 1997: 42). The outcome of the process would be a set of reliable diagnostic concepts and the expansion of a differentiated mental health system in an increasingly medicalized American society (Rogler, 1997). As the Task Force chair, Robert Spitzer, argued in his introduction to the new manual, clinicians and investigators needed a 'common language with which to communicate about the disorders for which they have professional responsibility.' Proper treatment begins with an accurate diagnosis, he contended, and the 'efficacy of various treatment modalities can be compared only if patient groups are described using diagnostic terms that are clearly defined.' Promising to be an advance over *DSM-II*, the new and improved *DSM-III* – nearly 500 pages, as opposed to the 134 pages of *DSM-II* – offered several new features including expanded descriptions and additional diagnostic categories, some of which even had newly coined names (APA, 1980:1).

The need to standardize the process of diagnosis by clarifying diverse types of mental disorders was consistent with the Task Force's mandate to separate diagnostic labels from 'debatable aetiological theories,' that is, from psychoanalysis. This 'separation standard' meant the partitioning of symptoms into other disorders: affective, anxiety, somatoform, and dissociative. 'Neuroses' were relocated into the section on anxiety disorders, the main beneficiary of this redistribution. Diagnostic categories thereby expanded with the inclusion of new disorders and, as Rogler describes, the splitting of old ones into 'offspring disorders with taxonomic status equal to their parents'' (Rogler, 1997:11–14). Some categories were moved to other sections of the system, and others were collapsed and incorporated, or sometimes eliminated altogether. Like its precursors, *DSM-III* was meant to reflect the most current state of knowledge regarding mental disorders.[3]

Procedurally, the development of *DSM-III* was more or less the same as that of its predecessors, with versions drafted, circulated (among supporters, that is), and modified as necessary. There were, however, three changes to the process worth mentioning. First, a Committee on Women was struck and consulted to review *DSM-III* 'from their own perspective' (APA, 1980:4). Second, a multi-axial system was developed to ensure that information pertaining to treatment and its outcome was recorded on axes separating mental (Axes I and II) from physical disorders (Axis III) and reflecting other things such as severity of stressors (Axis IV) and level of adaptive functioning (Axis V) (8). Yet, as Rogler observes, while it was clear that a single class of information was no longer considered sufficient, it is not clear what the axis structure meant or how the relationship between axes was to be understood (Rogler, 1997:12; see also Cooksey and Brown, 1998).

Third, the Task Force conducted field trials; for previous editions of the *DSM*, new classifications had not undergone clinical trials before acquiring official status. The trials took place from 1977 to 1979, and consisted of the evaluation of 12,667 patients by approximately 550 practitioners in 212 different facilities, using drafts of *DSM-III*. To ensure the reliability of its categories, the Task Force asked pairs of clinicians to diagnose several hundred patients independently; and the results of this practice reflect, in the APA's words, 'far greater reliability than had previously been obtained with DSM-II' (APA, 1980:8).

Still, the reliability of the reliability studies was questionable. None of these trials are cited in the text, and as the psychologist Paula Caplan observed, 'one could get a large group of people to agree to call all horses "unicorns," so that their inter-rater reliability would be perfect, but that would not mean that any of them ever really saw unicorns' (Caplan, 1995:197–9). Kutchins and Kirk describe the field trials as 'uncontrolled, nonrandom surveys in which several hundred self-selected and unsupervised pairs of clinicians throughout the country attempted to diagnose nonrandomly selected patients and, after some sharing of information, made "independent" assessments of them' (Kirk and Kutchins in Caplan, 1995:201–2).

With this question concerning the reliability studies in mind, it is important to consider critically the reclassification of agoraphobia in *DSM-III*, beginning with the significant and controversial decision to eliminate the class of neuroses and the explicit rejection of psychoanalysis attendant in such a move. Psychoanalysts were not in favour of the *DSM-III* project and perceived it as 'the wholesale expurgation of psychodynamics from the psychiatric knowledge base.' As Dr Klaus P. Fink (whom we met in chapter 3) said in an interview with the historian Mitchell Wilson, 'I do not know ... who determined that this small group of people should try to reorganize psychiatric thinking in the United States but I am ... concerned that they have such an arrogant view of their mission and are not willing to incorporate some of the things which we have learned over the past 70 years' (Fink in Wilson, 1993:407). Not surprisingly, the decision to exclude the concept of neurosis from *DSM-III* was met with acrimonious resistance that threatened to embarrass the APA and prevent final approval of the new manual (Kutchins and Kirk, 1997:44–5). In order to get it approved, Chair Robert Spitzer, in a 'by-now familiar manner of compromising without giving up anything of real importance,' had to agree to include a statement of clarification of the concept in the manual's introduction (Wilson, 1993:407). As a result, 'Neurotic Disorders' were cross-listed in *DSM-III* to other chapters, on 'Affective,' 'Anxiety,' 'Somatoform,' 'Dissociative,' and 'Psychosexual Disorders' (APA, 1980:10).

So what becomes of agoraphobia in all this? It resides in the 'Anxiety Disorders' section, under the subcategory 'Phobic Disorders' (or phobic neuroses), but now with its very own designation. (Recall that in *DSM-II*, the subcategory 'Phobic Neurosis' was a single paragraph and did not mention agoraphobia specifically.) In *DSM-III*, anxiety is defined as either the predominant disturbance or the result of trying to overcome particular symptoms (such as a phobia). Phobic disorders are defined as a 'persistent and irrational fear of a specific object, activity, or situation that results in a compelling desire to avoid the dreaded object, activity, or situation (the phobic stimulus).' When irrational fear and concomitant avoidance behaviour infringe upon one's social role and functioning, however, then a diagnosis of phobic disorder is appropriate (APA, 1980:225) (see below).

Anxiety Disorders

In this group of disorders anxiety is either the predominant disturbance, as in Panic Disorder and Generalized Anxiety Disorder, or anxiety is experienced if the individual attempts to master the symptoms, as in confronting the dreaded object or situation in a Phobic Disorder or resisting the obsessions of compulsions in Obsessive Compulsive Disorder. Diagnosis of an Anxiety Disorder is not made if the anxiety is due to another disorder, such as Schizophrenia, an Affective Disorder, or an Organic Mental Disorder.

It has been estimated that from 2% to 4% of the general population has at some time had a disorder that this manual would classify as an Anxiety Disorder.

Panic Disorder, Phobic Disorders and Obsessive Compulsive Disorder are each apparently more common among family members of individuals with each of these disorders than in the general population.

PHOBIC DISORDERS (OR PHOBIC NEUROSES)
The essential feature is persistent and irrational fear of a specific object, activity, or situation that results in a compelling desire to avoid the dreaded object, activity or situation (the phobic stimulus). The fear is recognized by the individual as excessive or unreasonable in proportion to the actual dangerousness of the object, activity, or situation.

Irrational avoidance of objects, activities, or situations that has an insignificant effect on life adjustment is commonplace. For example, many individuals experience some irrational fear when unable to avoid contact with harmless insects or spiders, but this has no major effect on their lives. However, when the avoidance behavior or fear is a significant source of distress to the individual or interferes with social or role functioning, a diagnosis of a Phobic Disorder is warranted.

The Phobic Disorders are subdivided into three types: Agoraphobia, the most severe and pervasive form; Social Phobia; and Simple Phobia. Both Social and Simple Phobias generally involve a circumscribed stimulus, but Simple Phobia tends to have an earlier onset and better prognosis. When more than one type is present, multiple diagnoses should be made.

Although anxiety related to separation from parental figures is a form of phobic reaction, it is classified as Separation Anxiety Disorder, in the section Disorders Usually First Evident in Infancy, Childhood, or Adolescence (p. 50). Similarly, phobic avoidance limited to sexual activities is classified as a Psychosexual Disorder Not Elsewhere Classified (p. 282).

Although Simple Phobia is the most common type of Phobic Disorder in the general population, Agoraphobia is the most common among those seeking treatment.

300.21 Agoraphobia with Panic Attacks

300.22 Agoraphobia without Panic Attacks

The essential feature is a marked fear of being alone, or being in public places from which escape might be difficult or help not available in case of sudden incapacitation. Normal activities are increasingly constricted as the fears or avoidance behavior dominate the individual's life. The most common situations avoided involve being in crowds, such as on a busy street or in crowded stores, or being in tunnels, on bridges, on elevators, or on public transportation. Often these individuals insist that a family member or friend accompany them whenever they leave home.

The disturbance is not due to a major depressive episode, Obsessive Compulsive Disorder, Paranoid Personality Disorder, or Schizophrenia.

Often the initial phase of the disorder consists of recurrent panic attacks. (For a description of panic attacks, see p. 230.) The individual develops anticipatory fear of having such an attack and becomes reluctant or refuses to enter a variety of situations that are associated with these attacks. When there is a history of panic attacks (which may or may not be currently present) associated with avoidance behavior, the diagnosis of Agoraphobia with Panic Attacks should be made. Where there is no such history (or this information is lacking), the diagnosis of Agoraphobia without Panic Attacks should be made.

Associated features. Depression, anxiety, rituals, minor 'checking' compulsions, or rumination is frequently present.

Age at onset. Most frequently the onset is in the late teens or early 20s, but it can be much later.

Course. The severity of the disturbance waxes and wanes, and periods of complete remission are possible. The activities or situations that the individual dreads may change from day to day.

Impairment. During exacerbations of the illness the individual may be housebound. The avoidance of certain situations, such as being in elevators, may grossly interfere with social and occupational functioning.

Complications. Some individuals attempt to relieve their anxiety with alcohol, barbiturates, or antianxiety medications even to the extent of becoming physiologically dependent on them. Major Depression is another complication.

Predisposing factors. Separation Anxiety Disorder in childhood and sudden object loss apparently predispose to the development of Agoraphobia.

Prevalence. A study of the general population in a small city found that approximately 0.5% of the population had had Agoraphobia at some time.

Sex ratio. This disorder is more frequently diagnosed in women.

Differential diagnosis. In **Schizophrenia, Major Depression, Obsessive Compulsive Disorder** and **Paranoid Personality Disorder** there may be phobic avoidance of certain situations. The diagnosis of Agoraphobia is not made if a phobia is due to any of these disorders.

Diagnostic criteria for Agoraphobia

A. The individual has marked fear of and thus avoids being alone or in public places from which escape might be difficult or help not available in case of sudden incapacitation, e.g., crowds, tunnels, bridges, public transportation.

B. There is increasing constriction of normal activities until the fears or avoidance behavior dominate the individual's life.

C. Not due to a major depressive episode, Obsessive Compulsive Disorder, Paranoid Personality Disorder, or Schizophrenia.

Source: *Diagnostic and Statistical Manual of Mental Disorders* [*DSM-III*] (1980), pp. 225–7.

Regarding it as the commonest and most severe type of phobic disorder, *DSM-III* devotes one and a half pages specifically to 'Agoraphobia with' and 'Agoraphobia without Panic Attacks' (APA, 1980:225–6). Although agoraphobia without panic attacks is outlined in relatively comprehensive terms, what remains unexplicated is agoraphobia *with* panic attacks, which has a code number and heading but no accompanying text. The volume notes under 'Agoraphobia without Panic Attacks' that agoraphobia often begins with recurrent panic attacks, but then it directs readers to the subsection 'Anxiety States (or Anxiety Neuroses)' and the sub-subcategory 'Panic Disorder' a few pages later. There it states that when an individual becomes reluctant to be alone or in public places away from home owing to an anticipatory fear of helplessness or loss of control during a panic attack, then the diagnosis of agoraphobia with panic attacks is warranted (230). The sense here is that panic attacks may lead to agoraphobia and that agoraphobia is actually a *complication* of panic disorder, the primary condition (see below). This point is significant, because in the literature generated since the publication of *DSM-III*, the relationship between panic and agoraphobia remains unresolved in spite of the *DSM*'s classification of them in this way. Perhaps that is why a search for 'agoraphobia' in the electronic Medline catalogue turns up articles on both 'panic' and 'agoraphobia.'[4]

ANXIETY STATES (OR ANXIETY NEUROSES)
300.01 Panic Disorder
The essential features are recurrent panic (Anxiety) attacks that occur at times unpredictably, though certain situations, e.g., driving a car, may become associated with a panic attack. The same clinical picture occurring during marked physical exertion or a life-threatening situation is not termed a panic attack.

The panic attacks are manifested by the sudden onset of intense apprehension, fear, or terror, often associated with feelings of impending doom. The most common symptoms experienced during an attack are dyspnea; palpitations; chest pain or discomfort; choking or smothering sensations; dizziness, vertigo, or unsteady feelings; feelings of unreality (depersonalization or derealization); paresthesias; hot and cold flashes; sweating; faintness; trembling or shaking; and fear of dying, going crazy, or doing something uncontrolled during the attack. Attacks usually last minutes; more rarely, hours.

A common complication of this disorder is the development of an anticipatory fear of helplessness or loss of control during a panic attack, so that the individual becomes reluctant to be alone or in public places away from home. When many situations of the kind are avoided the diagnosis of Agoraphobia with Panic Attacks should be made (p. 226) rather than Panic Disorder.

Associated features. The individual often develops varying degrees of nervousness and apprehension between attacks. This nervousness and apprehension is characterized by the usual manifestations of apprehensive expectation, vigilance and scanning, motor tension, autonomic hyperactivity.

Age at onset. The disorder often begins in late adolescence or early adult life, but may occur initially in mid-adult life.

Course. The disorder may be limited to a single brief period lasting several weeks or months, recur several times, or become chronic.

Impairment. Except when the disorder is severe or complicated by Agoraphobia, it is rarely incapacitating.

Complications. The complication of Agoraphobia with Panic Attacks has been mentioned above. Other complications include abuse of alcohol and antianxiety medications, and Depressive Disorders.

Predisposing factors. Separation Anxiety Disorder in childhood and sudden object loss apparently predispose to the development of this disorder.

Prevalence. The disorder is apparently common.

Sex ratio. This condition is diagnosed much more commonly in women.

Differential diagnosis. Physical disorders such as **hypoglycemia**, **pheochromocytoma**, and **hyperthyroidism**, all of which can cause similar symptoms, must be ruled out.

In **Withdrawal** from some substances, such as **barbiturates**, and in some **Substance Intoxications**, such as due to **caffeine** or **amphetamines**, there may be panic attacks. Panic Disorder should not be diagnosed when the panic attacks are due to Substance-induced Organic Mental Disorder.

In **Schizophrenia, Major Depression**, or **Somatization Disorder** panic attacks may occur. However, the diagnosis of Panic Disorder is not made if the panic attacks are due to these other disorders.

Generalized Anxiety Disorder may be confused with the chronic anxiety that often develops between panic attacks in Panic Disorder. A history of recurrent panic attacks precludes Generalized Anxiety Disorder.

In **Simple** or **Social Phobia**, the individual may develop panic attacks if exposed to the phobic stimulus. However, in Panic Disorder, the individual is never certain which situations provoke panic attacks.

Diagnostic criteria for Panic Disorder

A. At least three panic attacks within a three-week period in circumstances other than during marked physical exertion or in a life-threatening situation. The attacks are not precipitated only by exposure to a circumscribed phobic stimulus.

B. Panic attacks are manifested by discrete periods of apprehension or fear, and at least four of the following symptoms appear during each attack:

    (1) dyspnea
    (2) palpitations
    (3) chest pain or discomfort
    (4) choking or smothering sensations
    (5) dizziness, vertigo, or unsteady feelings
    (6) feelings of unreality
    (7) paresthesias (tingling in hands or feet)
    (8) hot and cold flashes
    (9) sweating
    (10) faintness
    (11) trembling or shaking

(12) fear of dying, going crazy, or doing something uncontrolled during an attack

C. Not due to a physical disorder or another mental disorder,
such as Major Depression, Somatization Disorder, or Schizophrenia.

D. The disorder is not associated with Agoraphobia (p. 227).

Source: *Diagnostic and Statistical Manual of Mental Disorders* [*DSM-III*]
(1980), pp. 230–2.

In the category 'Agoraphobia without Panic Attacks,' where agoraphobia is evidently the primary (and only) condition, *DSM-III* states
that the essential feature of this disorder is a 'marked fear of being
alone, or being in public places from which escape might be difficult or
help not available in case of sudden incapacitation.' Noting that agoraphobia is more frequently diagnosed in women than in men, the volume describes avoidance behaviour of this type as getting in the way
of 'normal' activities, such as being in crowds, on busy streets, in
crowded stores, in tunnels, on bridges and elevators, or on public
transportation (APA, 1980:226–7). Apart from its indication that agoraphobia is more common among women, this official description is
ambiguous. The individual may or may not have a history of panic
attacks. Depression, anxiety rituals, compulsions, ruminations are frequently present, but agoraphobia without panic attacks is not due to
any of these. The individual's age at the onset of agoraphobia is the
late teens or early twenties, but it can begin much later. The activities
dreaded by the individual may change from day to day. The individual
may be housebound. The individual's avoidance of certain situations
may grossly interfere with his or her functioning.

In spite of its success and its considerable international influence,
given so much ambiguity it is difficult to be confident of *DSM-III*'s real
usefulness.

DSM-III-R, DSM-IV, and *DSM-IV-TR:* Revising the Revision

Soon after the release of *DSM-III*, when data emerged that did not cor-
respond with some of its diagnostic criteria, the APA decided that a

new edition of the manual was needed. Despite the 'extensive field testing' to which the volume laid claim, experience with the diagnostic criteria revealed, 'as expected, many instances in which criteria were not entirely clear, were inconsistent across categories, or were even contradictory.' The APA therefore embarked on the development of *DSM-III-R* ('Revised Edition'), framing it as another necessary step in the 'ongoing process of attempting to better understand mental disorders' (APA, 1987:xvii).

The process of revising *DSM-III* was much the same as for *DSM-II*. A Work Group was appointed, with members selected to include a 'broad' representation of clinical and research perspectives. Twenty-six advisory committees were formed, each with expertise in and responsibility for a particular area. Most proposals for revisions came from the members of these committees, although some came from outside (APA, 1987:xx). For the most part, clinical experience with *DSM-III* criteria dictated any fine-tuning that was required. Empirical data supporting the various proposals were given the most emphasis in decisions as to whether or not to make changes, but in the absence of data – in fact, 'for most proposals, data from empirical studies were lacking' – other things were considered, such as 'clinical experience, a judgement as to whether the proposal was likely to increase the reliability and validity of the diagnosis under consideration; or, in the case of a new diagnosis under consideration, the extent of the research support for the category as contrasted to its perceived potential for abuse' (xxi). National field trials were conducted for the development of diagnostic criteria (including for agoraphobia without history of panic disorder), and an ad hoc committee was appointed in 1985 to help the Work Group deal with controversies that arose in response to the proposed inclusion of three new psychiatric disorders, namely, paraphilic rapism, premenstrual dysphoric disorder, and masochistic personality disorder (Kutchins and Kirk, 1997:47).[5] Two drafts of *DSM-III-R* were circulated for critical review, and in May 1987, the revised manual, longer than *DSM-III* in having nearly 570 pages, was released with several new categories added and several others eliminated.

As for agoraphobia, its diagnostic parameters, once again, had 'evolved,' and several criteria for its classification were offered in a six-and-a-half-page section entitled 'Anxiety Disorders (or Anxiety and Phobic Neuroses),' which includes 'Panic Disorder with' and 'without Agoraphobia.' 'Panic Disorder' was now subdivided into Panic with Agoraphobia (300.21) (still with no accompanying explanation) and 'without Agoraphobia' (300.01). The previous category, 'Agoraphobia with Panic Attacks' (300.21), was eliminated, and 'Agoraphobia without Panic Attacks' was modified to become 'Agoraphobia without History of Panic Disorder' (300.22). Whereas in *DSM-III* agoraphobia had been the most common disorder among those seeking treatment (APA, 1987:226), in *DSM-III-R* the most common is said to be panic disorder. As well, an important new criterion of agoraphobia is included in *DSM-III-R*, namely, the experience or fear of embarrassment. Specifically, agoraphobia is described as 'the fear of being in places or situations from which escape might be difficult (or embarrassing), or in which help might not be available in the event of [the individual's] suddenly developing a symptom(s) that could be incapacitating or extremely embarrassing.' Also, it is noted, 'It is unclear whether Agoraphobia without History of Panic Disorder with limited symptom attacks represents a variant of Panic Disorder with Agoraphobia, and whether the same disorder without limited symptom attacks represents a disorder that is unrelated to Panic Disorder' (240). The description certainly is unclear, but what is especially unclear is how and when to decide which is the primary problem when the two appear together – the panic disorder or the agoraphobia (241).[6] Presumably a decision is to be made according to whether or not four of the criteria for panic are satisfied (see below).

Anxiety Disorders (or Anxiety and Phobic Neuroses)

The characteristic features of this group of disorders are symptoms of anxiety and avoidance behavior. In Panic Disorder and Generalized Anxiety Disorder, anxiety is usually the predominant symptom, and avoidance behavior is almost always present in Panic Disorder with Agoraphobia. In Phobic Disorders anxiety is experienced if the person confronts the dreaded object or situation. In Obsessive Compulsive Disorder anxiety is experienced if the person attempts to resist the obsessions of compulsions. Avoidance behavior is almost always present in Phobic Disorders, and frequently present in Obsessive Compulsive Disorder. The classification of Post-traumatic Stress disorder is controversial since the predominant symptom is the reexperiencing of a trauma, not anxiety or avoidance behavior. However, anxiety symptoms and avoidance behavior are extremely common, and symptoms of increased arousal are invariably present ...

Recent studies indicate that Anxiety Disorders are those most frequently found in the general population, Simple Phobia being the most common Anxiety Disorder in the general population, but Panic Disorder the most common among people seeking treatment. Panic Disorder, Phobic Disorders, and Obsessive Compulsive Disorder are all apparently more common among first-degree biologic relatives of people with each of these disorders than among the general population.

300.21 Panic Disorder with Agoraphobia
300.01 Panic Disorder without Agoraphobia
The essential features of these disorders are recurrent panic attacks, i.e., discrete periods of intense fear or discomfort, with at least four characteristic associated symptoms. The diagnoses are made only when it cannot be established that an organic factor initiated and maintained the disturbance.

The panic attacks usually last minutes or, more rarely, hours. The attacks, at least initially, are unexpected, i.e., they do not occur immediately before or on exposure to a situation that almost always causes anxiety (as in Simple Phobia). In addition, the attacks are not triggered by situations in which the person is the focus of others' attention (as in Social Phobia). The 'unexpected' aspect of the panic attacks is an essential feature of the disorder, although later in the course of the disturbance certain situations, e.g., driving a car or being in a crowded place, may become associated with having a panic attack. These situations increase the likelihood of an attack's occurring at some time while the person is in that situation, although not immediately upon entering the situation, as in Simple Phobia. In such a situation, the person fears having a panic attack, but is uncertain about when it may occur, or if it will occur at all.

Panic attacks typically begin with the sudden onset of intense apprehension, fear, or terror. Often there is a feeling of impending doom. Much more rarely, the person does not experience the attack as anxiety, but only as intense discomfort. During most panic attacks there are more than six associated symptoms. (Attacks involving four or more symptoms are arbitrarily defined as panic attacks; attacks involving fewer than four symptoms are limited symptom attacks. See Agoraphobia without History of Panic Disorder, p. 240.)

The symptoms experienced during an attack are: shortness of breath (dyspnea) or smothering sensations; dizziness, unsteady feelings, or faintness; choking; palpitations or accelerated heart rate; trembling or shaking; sweating; nausea or abdominal distress; depersonalization or derealization; numbness or tingling sensations (paresthesias; flushes (hot flashes) or chills; chest pain or discomfort; fear of dying; and fear of going crazy or doing something uncontrolled during the attack.

In the great majority of cases of Panic Disorder seen in clinical settings, the person has developed some symptoms of Agoraphobia. Agoraphobia is the fear of being in places or situations from which escape might be difficult (or embarrassing) or in which help might not be available in the event of a panic attack. As a result of this fear, there are either travel restrictions or need for a companion when away from home, or there is endurance of agoraphobic situations despite intense anxiety. Common agoraphobic situations include being outside the home alone, being in a crowd or standing in a line, being on a bridge, and travelling in a bus, train, or car. (Agoraphobia also includes those unusual cases in which persistent avoidance behavior originated during an active phase of Panic Disorder, but the person does not attribute subsequent avoidance behavior to fear of having a panic attack.)

Associated features. The person often develops varying degrees of nervousness and apprehension between attacks, usually focused on the fear of having another attack. A coexisting Depressive Disorder is often present.

Age at onset. The average age at onset is in the late 20s.

Course. Typically there are recurrent panic attacks several times a week or even daily. In very rare instances there is only a single attack, followed by a persistent fear of having another attack. The disorder may be limited to a single brief period lasting several weeks or months, may recur several times, or, more typically (particularly in Panic Disorder with Agoraphobia), may last for years, with varying periods of partial or full remission and exacerbation. During periods of partial remission, there may be recurrent limited symptom attacks (as defined above).

Impairment. Panic Disorder without Agoraphobia may be associated with no or only limited impairment in social and occupational functioning. Panic Disorder with Agoraphobia, by definition, is associated with varying degrees of constriction in lifestyle. When the Agoraphobia is severe, the person is nearly or completely housebound or unable to leave the house unaccompanied.

Complications. Complications include Psychoactive Substance Use Disorders, particularly alcohol and anxiolytics.

Predisposing factors. Separation Anxiety Disorder in childhood and sudden loss of social supports or disruption of important interpersonal relationships apparently predispose to the development of this disorder.

Prevalence. The disorder is common. In clinical settings Panic Disorder with Agoraphobia is much more common than Panic Disorder without Agoraphobia.

Sex ratio. In clinical samples, Panic Disorder without Agoraphobia is about equally common in males and in females; Panic Disorder with Agoraphobia is about twice as common in females as in males.

Differential diagnosis. The diagnosis is made only when it cannot be established that an organic factor initiated and maintained the disturbance. **Physical disorders** such as hypoglycemia, pheochromocytoma, and hyperthyroidism, all of which can cause similar symptoms, must be considered (see discussion of etiologic factors of Organic Anxiety Syndrome, p. 113).

In **withdrawal** from some substances, such as barbiturates, and in some **Psychoactive Substance-induced Intoxications,** such as those due to **caffeine** or **amphetamines,** there may be panic attacks. Panic Disorder should not be diagnosed when the panic attacks are due to ingestion of a psychoactive substance.

During a **Major Depressive Episode** there may be recurrent unexpected panic attacks, in which case diagnoses of both a Mood Disorder and Panic Disorder should be made. Similarly, if recurrent panic attacks occur during the course of **Somatization Disorder**, the additional diagnosis of Panic Disorder should be made.

Typically, people with Panic Disorder develop varying degrees of nervousness and apprehension between attacks. When this is focused on the fear of having another attack (as is usually the case), the additional diagnosis of **Generalized Anxiety Disorder** is not made. More rarely, however, the focus of concern may not be fear of having another panic attack, in which case the diagnosis of Generalized Anxiety Disorder should be considered.

In **Simple Phobia**, the person may develop panic attacks if exposed to the phobic stimulus. However, in such situations the panic attack occurs immediately before or upon exposure to the phobic situation and its intensity varies as the phobic stimulus approaches or withdraws. In Panic Disorder, by contrast, even when the attacks are associated with certain situations, such as being outside the home alone or standing in line, the person is never certain just when an attack will occur in that situation, or if it will occur at all. In **Social Phobia**, the person may develop panic attacks that are triggered only by being the focus of others' attention, whereas in Panic Disorder, the panic attacks are not, by definition, thus triggered. People with Panic Disorder may, however, have an unrelated Simple Phobia or Social Phobia.

Diagnostic criteria for Panic Disorder

A. At some time during the disturbance, one or more panic attacks (discrete periods of intense fear or discomfort) have occurred that were (1) unexpected, i.e., did not occur immediately before or on exposure to a situation that almost always caused anxiety, and (2) not triggered by situations in which the person was the focus of others' attention.

B. Either four attacks, as defined in criterion A, have occurred within a four-week period, or one or more attacks have been followed by a period of at least a month of persistent fear of having another attack.

C. At least four of the following symptoms developed during at least one of the attacks:

(1) shortness of breath (dyspnea) or smothering sensation
(2) dizziness, unsteady feelings, or faintness
(3) palpitations or accelerated heart rate (tachycardia)
(4) trembling or shaking
(5) sweating
(6) choking
(7) nausea or abdominal distress
(8) depersonalization or derealization
(9) numbness or tingling sensations (paresthesias)
(10) flushes (hot flashes) or chills
(11) chest pain or discomfort
(12) fear of dying
(13) fear of going crazy or of doing something uncontrolled

Note: Attacks involving four or more symptoms are panic attacks; attacks involving few than four symptoms are limited symptom attacks (see Agoraphobia without History of Panic disorder, p. 241).

D. During at least some of the attacks, at least four of the C symptoms developed suddenly and increased in intensity within ten minutes of the beginning of the first C symptom noticed in the attack.

E. It cannot be established that an organic factor initiated and maintained the disturbance, e.g., Amphetamine or Caffeine Intoxication, hyperthyroidism.

Note: Mitral valve prolapse may be an associated condition, but does not preclude a diagnosis of Panic Disorder.

Types of Panic Disorder

Diagnostic criteria for 300.21 Panic Disorder with Agoraphobia

A. Meets the criteria for Panic Disorder

B. Agoraphobia: Fear of being in places or situations from which escape might be difficult (or embarrassing) or in which help might not be available in the event of a panic attack. (Include cases in which persistent avoidance behavior originated during an active phase of Panic Disorder, even if the person does not attribute the avoidance behavior to fear of having a panic attack.) As a result of this fear, the person either restricts travel or needs a companion when away from home, or else endures agoraphobic situations despite intense anxiety. Common agoraphobic situations include being outside the home alone, being in a crowd or standing in a line, being on a bridge, and travelling in a bus, train, or car.

Specify current severity of agoraphobic avoidance:

Mild: Some avoidance (or endurance with distress), but relatively normal lifestyle, e.g., travels unaccompanied when necessary, such as to work or to shop; otherwise avoids travelling alone.

Moderate: Avoidance results in constricted lifestyle, e.g., the person is able to leave the house alone, but not to go more than a few miles unaccompanied.

Severe: Avoidance results in being nearly or completely housebound or unable to leave the house unaccompanied.

In Partial Remission: No current agoraphobic avoidance, but some agoraphobic avoidance during the past six months.

In Full Remission: No current agoraphobic avoidance and none during the past six months.

Specify current severity of panic attacks:

Mild: During the past month attacks have been intermediate between 'mild' and 'severe.'

Severe: During the past month, there have been at least eight panic attacks.

In Partial Remission: The condition has been intermediate between 'In Full Remission' and 'Mild.'

In Full Remission: During the past six months, there have been no panic or limited symptom attacks.

Diagnostic criteria for 300.01 Panic Disorder without Agoraphobia

A. Meets the criteria for Panic Disorder.

B. Absence of Agoraphobia, as defined above.

Specify current severity of panic attacks, as defined above.

300.22 Agoraphobia without History of Panic Disorder
The essential feature of this disorder is Agoraphobia without a history of Panic Disorder. Agoraphobia is the fear of being in places or situations from which escape might be difficult (or embarrassing), or in which help might not be available in the event of suddenly developing a symptom(s) that could be incapacitating or extremely embarrassing. As a result of this fear, the person either restricts travel or needs a companion when away from home, or else endures agoraphobic situations despite intense anxiety. Common agoraphobic situations include being outside the home alone, being in a crowd or standing in a line, being on a bridge, and traveling in a bus, train, or car.

Usually the person is afraid of having a *limited symptom attack*, that is, developing a single or small number of symptoms, such as becoming dizzy or falling, depersonalization or derealization, loss of bladder or bowel control, vomiting, or having cardiac distress. In some of these cases, such symptoms have occurred in the past, and the person may be preoccupied with fears of their recurrence. In other cases, the person has never experienced the symptom(s), but nevertheless fears that the symptom 'could' develop and incapacitate him or her or be extremely embarrassing. In a small number of cases the person fears feeling incapacitated in some way, but is unable to specify what symptom he or she fears.

It is unclear whether Agoraphobia without History of Panic disorder with limited symptom attacks represents a variant of Panic Disorder with Agoraphobia, and whether the same disorder without limited symptom attacks represents a disorder that is unrelated to Panic Disorder.

Associated features. Personality disturbance, particularly features of Avoidant Personality Disorder, may be present.

Age at onset. Age at onset is variable, but the disorder most commonly begins in the 20s or 30s.

Course. Typically, the disorder persists for years.

Impairment. In clinical samples the impairment is usually severe.

Complications. Some people subsequently develop Panic Disorder.

Predisposing factors. No information.

Prevalence. In clinical samples the disorder is rare. It may, however, be more common in the general population.

Sex ratio. The disorder is diagnosed far more commonly in females than in males.

Differential diagnosis. In a **psychotic disorder with persecutory features**, the person may avoid situations that he or she believes make him or her vulnerable to being attacked. In **severe Major Depressive Episode**, the person may avoid situations that he or she experiences as overwhelming. In neither of these cases, however, does the person fear suddenly developing a symptom that would be extremely embarrassing or incapacitating.

In **Panic Disorder with Agoraphobia**, the panic attacks may be in full remission while the agoraphobia persists, but a history of Panic Disorder would preclude a current diagnosis of Agoraphobia without History of Panic Disorder. (Note: Panic Disorder does not preclude a preexisting diagnosis of Agoraphobia without History of Panic Disorder.) In extremely severe cases of **Social Phobia**, the person may avoid the same kinds of situations that are avoided in Agoraphobia without History of Panic Disorder. The motivation, however, is to avoid doing something or acting in a way that would be embarrassing or humiliating rather than to avoid the sudden development of a symptom.

Diagnostic criteria for 300.22 Agoraphobia without History of Panic Disorder

A. Agoraphobia: Fear of being in places or situations from which escape might be difficult (or embarrassing) or in which help might not be available in the event of suddenly developing a symptom(s) that could be incapacitating or extremely embarrassing. Examples include: dizziness or falling, depersonalization or derealization, loss of bladder or bowel control, vomiting, or cardiac distress. As a result of this fear, the person either restricts travel or needs a companion when away from home, or else endures agoraphobic situations despite intense anxiety. Common agoraphobic situations include being outside the home alone, being in a crowd or standing in a line, being on a bridge, and traveling in a bus, train, or car.

B. Has never met the criteria for Panic Disorder.

Specify with or without limited symptom attacks (see p. 240).

Source: *Diagnostic and Statistical Manual of Mental Disorders* [*DSM-III-R*] (1987), pp. 235–41.

Although *DSM-III-R* was touted as representing a great improvement over all previous *DSMs*, the first meeting to discuss *DSM-IV* was held only months after the release of *DSM-III-R*. Again, a Task Force was established, this time headed by the psychiatrist Allen Frances, and out of this body were established thirteen Work Groups, each responsible for a section of the new manual.[7]

In the meantime, the World Health Organization's *International*

Classification of Diseases (*ICD-10*) had been published. Those who worked on both projects tried as much as possible to coordinate their efforts (APA, 1994:xx–xxi). Medicine was by now fully evidence-based in its orientation, and psychiatry was no exception. The *DSM-IV* Task Force accordingly established a formal evidentiary process for its Work Groups to follow. This was a three-stage process consisting of an expansive review of existing literature, re-analysis of existing data sets, and twelve issue-specific field trials (xviii). Unlike with early editions of the *DSM*, where follow-up was impossible owing to the absence of citations, a five-volume *DSM-IV Sourcebook* was also created, containing condensed versions of the literature reviews, reports of the data re-analyses, reports of the field trials, and a final summary of the rationale for each Work Group's decisions (xx). And, to avoid controversy and conflict, Frances announced the fundamental rule that no changes to the *DSM* would be accepted without an explicit rationale and sound empirical support (xx).[8] At first glance this rule appears to represent a step in the right direction, given the lack of bibliographic accountability of previous *DSM*s. But as Kutchins and Kirk point out, the implication of Frances's policy was that, in the absence of evidence, the questionable categories of *DSM-III* and *DSM-III-R* were actually institutionalized by default (Kutchins and Kirk, 1997:48).

DSM-IV was published in 1994 at a staggering length of 900 pages. The manual's near doubling in size resulted from the inclusion not only of new disorders and more information about them, but also of such things as an annotated listing of the changes in *DSM-IV* and an outline of indigenous (culture-bound) syndromes. While *DSM-III-R* had displayed some cultural sensitivity in the section entitled 'Cautions in the Use of DSM-III-R,' it had not elaborated the issue to the extent that *DSM-IV* did. Despite this increase in cultural sensitivity, however, it is evident that *DSM-IV* still failed to consider a number of important issues, such as gender difference in the diagnosis of depression, phobias, and personality disorders, and the potential skewing of data resulting from the disproportionate representation of middle-class whites in the clinical populations upon which some of the field trials were based.

As for the classification of agoraphobia, the major section, entitled 'Anxiety Disorders,' begins with a brief summary of all the conditions included within it. It is noteworthy that the psychoanalytic term 'neurosis,' still relatively frequent in *DSM-III-R*, has been completely banished from this new edition. It is significant, in fact, that in *DSM-IV* the contribution of genetics to the development of panic disorder is discussed – a discussion that reinforces the APA's attempt to disengage from psychoanalytic theories and its full (re)turn to positivist bio-psychiatry.

Agoraphobia by itself is 'not a codable disorder'; it occurs in the context of 'panic disorder with agoraphobia' and 'agoraphobia without history of panic disorder.' Nevertheless, *DSM-IV* contains one and a half pages on agoraphobia, including – unlike *DSM-III-R* – a discussion of its 'features' and a summary of the criteria for the disorder, as well as an outline of its relationship to panic disorder. The description of agoraphobia is essentially the same, but now notes that 'individuals' avoidance of situations may impair their ability to travel to work or carry out homemaking responsibilities (e.g., grocery shopping, taking children to the doctor)' (APA, 1994:396). In contrast, *DSM-III* had noted only an 'increasing constriction of normal activities' (APA, 1980:227), and in *DSM-III-R* 'Panic Disorder with Agoraphobia,' by definition, is even more vaguely associated with 'varying degrees of constriction in lifestyle.' In that edition, the severity of agoraphobic avoidance ranged from 'mild,' in which case the individual was able to lead a 'relatively normal lifestyle' and to travel alone as necessary – to get to work and to shop – to 'severe,' in which case the individual was 'nearly or completely housebound or unable to leave the house accompanied' (APA, 1987:239).

The indefinite boundary between agoraphobia and simple and social phobias is also acknowledged in *DSM-IV*: 'The differential diagnosis ... can be difficult because all of these conditions are characterized by avoidance of specific situations.' This difficulty is, however, more or less dismissed with the unqualified assertion that 'anxiety or phobic avoidance is not better accounted for by another mental disorder' (APA, 1994:396–7). Several pages later readers are given some guidance as to how to distinguish among phobias, but even then it is noted that 'some presentations fall between ... prototypes and require clinical judgement in the selection of the most appropriate diagnosis' (401).

From there the manual moves into a description of panic disorder, and includes an expanded section containing the titles 'Associated Features and Disorders' (including descriptive features and mental disorders, laboratory findings, and physical examination findings and general medical conditions), 'Specific Culture and Gender Features,' and – gesturing in the direction of genetics – 'Familial Pattern.' Diagnosis with or without agoraphobia is to be made accordingly, but concerns about a future panic attack or its implications often lead the individual to develop avoidance behaviour that then qualifies him or her for a diagnosis of panic disorder with agoraphobia. That said, the manual does recognize that 'some cultural or ethnic groups restrict the participation of women in public life, and [that] this must be distinguished from Agoraphobia' (APA, 1994:399). Panic disorder without agoraphobia is said to occur twice as often in women as in men, and panic disorder with agoraphobia is diagnosed three times as often. The onset of panic disorder is said to be typically between late adolescence and the mid-thirties, but can occur earlier or later.[9] Agoraphobia, if it develops, usually occurs within a year of recurrent panic attacks, but the relationship between agoraphobia and panic disorder is described as highly variable: 'In some cases, a decrease or remission of Panic Attacks may be followed closely by a corresponding decrease in agoraphobic avoidance and anxiety. In others, Agoraphobia may become chronic regardless of the presence or absence of Panic Attacks' (397–9).

Following an extensive discussion of differential diagnosis (especially interesting are the guidelines for choosing among panic disorder, social phobia, and specific phobia), the diagnostic criteria for panic disorder without agoraphobia and those for panic disorder with agoraphobia are conveniently listed in user-friendly bulleted lists. Then comes agoraphobia without history of panic disorder.

It remains unexplained why there is no category entitled 'Agoraphobia with History of Panic Disorder,' that is, why panic disorder is primary when the two disorders occur together, although this edition of the *DSM*, finally, acknowledges that in the end, 'relatively little is known about the course of Agoraphobia Without History of Panic Disorder' (APA, 1994:404). Recall that in *DSM-III*, code number 300.21 *was* 'Agoraphobia with Panic Attacks' (APA, 1980:226). That code became 'Panic Disorder with Agoraphobia' in *DSM-III-R* and *DSM-IV*, where the two disorders are distinguished on the basis of a *fear* of the 'occurrence of incapacitating or extremely embarrassing panic-like symptoms or limited-symptom attacks rather than full Panic Attacks.' Individuals with this fear, it is noted, 'have Agoraphobia (see p. 396) (Criterion A). The "panic-like symptoms" include any of the 13 symptoms listed for Panic Attack (see p. 394) or other symptoms that may be incapacitating or embarrassing' (403) (see below).

Anxiety Disorders

The following disorders are contained in this section: Panic Disorder Without Agoraphobia, Panic Disorder With Agoraphobia, Agoraphobia Without History of Panic Disorder, ... Because Panic Attacks and Agoraphobia occur in the context of several ... disorders, criteria sets for a Panic Attack and for Agoraphobia are listed separately at the beginning of this section.

A **Panic Attack** is a discrete period in which there is the sudden onset of intense apprehension, fearfulness, or terror, often associated with feelings of impending doom. During these attacks, symptoms such as shortness of breath, palpitations, chest pain or discomfort, choking or smothering sensations, and fear of 'going crazy' or losing control are present.

Agoraphobia is anxiety about, or avoidance of, places or situations from which escape might be difficult (or embarrassing) or in which help may not be available in the event of having a Panic Attack or panic-like symptoms.

Panic Disorder Without Agoraphobia is characterized by recurrent unexpected Panic Attacks about which there is persistent concern. **Panic Disorder With Agoraphobia** is characterized by both recurrent unexpected Panic Attacks and Agoraphobia.

Agoraphobia Without History of Panic Disorder is characterized by the presence of Agoraphobia and panic-like symptoms without a history of unexpected Panic Attacks.

...

Panic Attack

• **Criteria for Panic Attack**

Note: A Panic Attack is not a codable disorder. Code the specific diagnosis in which the Panic Attack occurs (e.g., 300.21 Panic Disorder with Agoraphobia [p. 402]).

A discrete period of intense fear of discomfort, in which four (or more) of the following symptoms developed abruptly and reached a peak within 10 minutes:

(1) palpitations, pounding heart, or accelerated heart rate
(2) sweating
(3) trembling or shaking
(4) sensations of shortness of breath or smothering
(5) feeling of choking
(6) chest pain or discomfort
(7) nausea or abdominal distress
(8) feeling dizzy, unsteady, lightheaded, or faint
(9) derealization (feelings of unreality) or depersonalization (being detached from oneself)
(10) fear of losing control or going crazy
(11) fear of dying
(12) paresthesias (numbness or tingling sensations)
(13) chills or hot flushes

Agoraphobia

Features

... The essential feature of Agoraphobia is anxiety about being in places or situations from which escape might be difficult (or embarrassing) or in which help may not be available in the event of having a Panic Attack (see p. 394) or panic-like symptoms ... The anxiety typically leads to a pervasive avoidance of a variety of situations that may include being alone outside the home or being home alone; being in a crowd of people; traveling in an automobile, bus, or airplane; or being on a bridge or in an elevator. Some individuals are able to expose themselves to the feared situations but endure these experiences with considerable dread. Often an individual is better able to confront a feared situation when accompanied by a companion (Criterion B). Individuals' avoidance of situations may impair their ability to travel to work or to carry out homemaking responsibilities (e.g., grocery shopping, taking children to the doctor).

A. Criteria for Agoraphobia

Note: Agoraphobia is not a codable disorder. Code the specific disorder in which the Agoraphobia occurs (e.g., 300.21 Panic Disorder With Agoraphobia [p. 402] or 300.22 Agoraphobia Without History of Panic Disorder [p. 404]).

A. Anxiety about being in places or situations from which escape might be difficult (or embarrassing) or in which help may not be available in the event of having an unexpected or situationally predisposed Panic Attack or panic-like symptoms. Agoraphobic fears typically involve characteristic clusters of situations that include being outside the home alone; being in a crowd or standing in a line; being on a bridge; and travelling in a bus, train, or automobile.

   Note: Consider the diagnosis of Specific Phobia if the avoidance is limited to one or only a few specific situations, or Social Phobia if the avoidance is limited to social situations.

B. The situations are avoided (e.g., travel is restricted) or else are endured with marked distress or with anxiety about having a Panic Attack or panic-like symptoms, or require the presence of a companion.

C. The anxiety or phobic avoidance is not better accounted for by another mental disorder...

Panic Disorder

• **Diagnostic criteria for 300.01 Panic Disorder Without Agoraphobia**

A. Both (1) and (2).
(1) recurrent unexpected Panic Attacks (see p. 395)
(2) at least one of the attacks has been followed by 1 month (or more) of one (or more) of the following:

   a. persistent concern about having additional attacks
   b. worry about the implications of the attack or its consequences (e.g., losing control, having a heart attack, 'going crazy')

c. a significant change in behavior related to the attacks

B. Absence of Agoraphobia (see p. 396).

C. The Panic Attacks are not due to the direct physiological effects of a substance (e.g., a drug of abuse, a medication) or a general medical condition (e.g., hyperthyroidism).

D. The panic Attacks are not better accounted for by another mental disorder, such as Social Phobia (e.g., occurring on exposure to feared social situations), Specific Phobia (e.g., on exposure to a specific phobic situations), Obsessive-Compulsive Disorder (e.g., on exposure to dirt in someone with an obsession about contamination), Posttraumatic Stress Disorder (e.g., in response to stimuli associated with a severe stressor), or Separation Anxiety Disorder (e.g., in response to being away from home or close relatives).

• **Diagnostic criteria for 300.21 Panic Disorder With Agoraphobia**

A. Both (1) and (2).
(1) recurrent unexpected Panic Attacks (see p. 395)
(2) at least one of the attacks has been followed by 1 month (or more) of one (or more) of the following:

a. persistent concern about having additional attacks
b. worry about the implications of the attack or its consequences (e.g., losing control, having a heart attack, 'going crazy')
c. a significant change in behavior related to the attacks

B. The presence of Agoraphobia (see p. 396).

C. The Panic Attacks are not due to the direct physiological effects of a substance (e.g., a drug of abuse, a medication) or a general medical condition (e.g., hyperthyroidism).

D. The Panic Attacks are not better accounted for by another mental disorder, such as Social Phobia (e.g., occurring on exposure to feared social situations, Specific Phobia (e.g., on exposure to a specific phobic situations), Obsessive-Compulsive Disorder (e.g., on exposure to dirt in someone with an obsession about contamination), Posttraumatic Stress Disorder (e.g., in response to stimuli associated with a severe stressor), or Separation Anxiety Disorder (e.g., in response to being away from home or close relatives).

• **Diagnostic criteria for 300.22 Agoraphobia Without History of Panic Disorder**

A. The presence of Agoraphobia (see p. 396) related to fear of developing panic-like symptoms (e.g., dizziness or diarrhea).

B. Criteria have never been met for Panic Disorder (see p. 402).

C. The disturbance is not due to the direct physiological effects of a substance (e.g., a drug of abuse, a medication) or a general medical condition.

D. If an associated general medical condition is present, the fear described in Criterion A is clearly in excess of that usually associated with the condition.

Source: *Diagnostic and Statistical Manual of Mental Disorders* [*DSM-IV*] (1994), pp. 393–405.

The most recent version of the *DSM* is *DSM-IV-TR* ('Text Revision'), published in 2000 and roughly the same length as *DSM-IV*. With a *DSM-V* not expected for another six years (at that point), the APA decided that that was too long a time to wait for an updating of the information in the text that would keep it consistent with current research. The goals of this text revision included correcting any errors in *DSM-IV*, ensuring that all information was up to date, incorporating information acquired since the literature reviews of *DSM-IV* were completed in 1992, enhancing the educational value of *DSM-IV*, and updating the *ICD-9-CM* codes changed since the *DSM-IV* Coding Update (APA, 2000:xxix). Following from the protocol established for *DSM-IV*, all changes had to be supported empirically, but that meant that, once again, problematic criteria could pass through the revision process unmodified owing to an absence of contradictory data. Nevertheless, revisions were limited to the text sections only, and no proposals for new disorders, subtypes, or changes in the appendix categories were considered. In fact *DSM-IV-TR* does not present itself as a new edition of the *DSM*, even though technically it is a different manual. In other words, the volume invariably refers to itself as *DSM-IV* rather than *DSM-IV-TR* (making it difficult to know where *DSM-IV* stops and *DSM-IV-TR* begins).

The process of revising the text of *DSM-IV* began in 1997 and followed roughly the same procedures as for previous revisions, with the establishment of a Task Force and specialized Work Groups to deal with each section. Comprehensive literature reviews of research published since 1992 were carried out. Each Work Group drafted proposed changes where necessary, and accompanied the proposals with written justifications for the changes, along with relevant references (which, as before, were not included in the volume, but were made available for purchase as a separate volume known as the *Sourcebook*). Following review at various levels, final drafts were produced and eventually approved by the APA's Committee on Psychiatric Diagnosis and Assessment (APA, 2000:xxx). Most of the changes, deriving from evidence based on literature reviews, were in the sections 'Associated Features and Disorders,' 'Culture,' 'Age,' 'Gender,' 'Prevalence,' 'Course,' and 'Familial Patterns.' In some cases, the 'Differential Diagnosis' section was also expanded.

Although the section on anxiety disorders and agoraphobia is generally the same in this edition, there are some changes. The text delineating types of panic attacks and their association with specific anxiety disorders has been updated. Information about triggers to panic attacks has been expanded, as has been the list of associated medical conditions and the accounts of prevalence, familial patterns, and differential diagnoses. Agoraphobia on its own is still 'not a codable disorder,' and must be coded in relation to the specific disorder in which it occurs (APA, 2000:433). The category 'Agoraphobia without History of Panic Disorder' retains essentially the same features as 'Panic Disorder with Agoraphobia,' except that the focus of the individual's fear is now on the possibility of developing embarrassing symptoms while outside and not being able to get help (441). (For a diagnosis of agoraphobia without history of panic disorder, the *full* criteria for panic disorder must never have been met, so the number of panic-like symptoms remains less than four.)

Leaking Boundaries

What all these changes to the *DSM* suggest is that in spite of the effort that has gone into classifying agoraphobia, the boundaries between the relevant categories are 'leaky.' This suggestion is confirmed by the psychiatric literature generated, particularly since the publication of *DSM-III*, when the APA began to devote itself to a neo-Kraepelinian 'science' of mental disease classification. Accordingly, a great deal of energy has been spent over the last two to three decades debating where exactly agoraphobia fits. For example, the relationship between agoraphobia and other phobias, especially simple and social phobias, was a steady subject of interest in the 1980s and 1990s, and there was evidence on both sides that they may or may not be wholly discrete disorders (see Boyd et al., 1990; Roth and Argyle, 1988).

There was similarly no consensus on whether or not basic personality traits and disorders play a role in the development of agoraphobia. Studies conducted in the late 1980s found a 'preponderance of dependent, avoidant, and histrionic diagnoses and traits,' and that 'patients who exhibited a greater number of [these] personality traits were also significantly more symptomatic, more neurotic, and ... less extraverted' than others (Mavissakalian and Hamann, 1988:542). Another study contradicted these findings; agoraphobia 'was not associated with higher rates of axis II [personality] disorders in PAD [panic disorder agoraphobia] patients,' the suggestion being that the role of personality disorders as 'preexisting or even predisposing factors to anxiety states ... should be viewed cautiously.' Some personality traits, according to this study, 'can be related to behavioral and life-style changes induced by the clinical symptoms during the course of illnesses' (Sciuto et al., 1991:450). A later study based on a sample of patients with panic disorder with agoraphobia in remission, however, determined that 'avoidant behavioral and attitudinal patterns may be enduring personality characteristics of panic disorder with agoraphobia patients' (Mavissakalian and Hamann, 1992:305). Even in periods of stable remission, patients displayed 'a greater tendency than normals to see themselves as rather unassertive, indecisive, self-critical, and emotional individuals, who are easily frustrated and often feel rejected when criticized' (308).

Another source of debate has been the relationship between panic disorder and agoraphobia. This debate hinged, and still hinges, on two central problems. The first stems from the *DSM* criteria that subsume certain diagnoses under others, the modification(s) that occurred with the release of *DSM-III-R*, and the concomitant difficulty in delineating among panic, panic with agoraphobia, and agoraphobia without panic. It is worth quoting one article at length:

> Essentially, panic had been viewed in DSM-III as a frequently comorbid symptom of agoraphobia, whereas, in DSM-III-R, agoraphobia is seen as a severe complication of panic ... Furthermore, DSM-III criteria for agoraphobia required an 'increasing constriction of the normal activities until the fear of avoidance behavior dominates the individual's life'... However, in DSM-III-R criteria for PDA [panic disorder and agoraphobia] and AWOPD [agoraphobia without panic disorder], this threshold impairment criterion is eliminated, so that very mild agoraphobic avoidance ... would cause a subject to be considered as having PDA, resulting perhaps in a dilution of a PDA sample with subjects phenomenologically more similar to a PD sample ... Thus it is difficult to compare the results of studies conducted with DSM-III and DSM-III-R criteria. (Goisman et al., 1994:72–3)

A significant proportion of researchers and clinicians take the position that agoraphobia is actually a conditioned response to panic attacks, that agoraphobia *without* panic is really very rare. This view would account for the clear tendency for doctors to use the terms 'panic disorder' and 'agoraphobia' interchangeably throughout the literature. Such a view may be particular to American clinicians and researchers; in the United Kingdom there is more support for the idea that agoraphobia does occur without panic. In fact, while there is some evidence that agoraphobia is more commonly associated with panic attacks (Pollard and Henderson, 1987), there is also evidence that a substantial number of agoraphobics do not meet the *DSM-III* criteria for panic. Research shows considerable overlap between agoraphobia and panic disorder, but it also shows that it is possible for agoraphobia and panic to occur in pure forms, and that agoraphobia is a heterogeneous disorder that develops along several different pathways other than panic

(Weissman et al., 1986:789). Even a clinical report written very recently – that is, after the publication of *DSM-III-R* and *DSM-IV* – illustrates how this might occur. In four 'presentations of agoraphobia without panic,' one person was fearful of developing a migraine headache away from home. Another was worried that he would have spontaneous and uncontrollable bowel movements in situations where he did not have ready access to a restroom. The third avoided flying, most public situations, hospitals, and being away from home at night for fear that she might vomit. And the fourth patient had frequent episodes of tachycardia (rapid heart beat) and thumping in his chest (but yet had never manifested the four symptoms required to qualify officially for a *DSM-III-R* panic attack) (Pollard et al., 1996). In other words, agoraphobia can 'develop in response to fears of a variety of symptom attacks other than panic' (61–2).

This clinical assertion was corroborated by an epidemiological survey of 3,021 respondents classified as having agoraphobia with panic. The investigators found that there were 'marked differences in symptomatology, course, and associated impairments between panic disorder and agoraphobia,' calling into question the view of agoraphobia as a 'secondary complication of spontaneous panic attacks or paniclike experiences' (Wittchen et al., 1998:1017). Another recent study from Germany similarly found that many panic patients do not develop avoidance behaviour. The investigators interpret this to mean that 'evidently there must be other factors than just the existence of panic attacks in general, which either predispose, or, on the other hand, protect individuals from developing avoidance behavior' (Langs et al., 2000:44). They conclude that the development of agoraphobic avoidance in panic patients is not coincidental, nor a straightforward process (47–8). This divide points to the possibility that epidemiological studies may actually have overestimated the prevalence of agoraphobia without panic disorder. It also indicates a lack of diagnostic clarity between agoraphobia and simple phobia, especially if we consider the possibility that agoraphobia may not be a fear of leaving the house per se, but rather a fear of specific stimuli located outside the house (see Hallam, 1978).

The second problem contributing to the lack of consensus about the relationship between panic and agoraphobia derives from the methodological discrepancy inherent in clinical versus random community (epidemiological) sampling. Most of what is known about agoraphobia comes from research done on clinical populations, but, as we saw in chapter 4, clinical populations constitute a very select group, 'subject to a raft of knowable and unknowable epidemiologic biases, which makes scientific inference difficult' (Sackett in Edlund, 1990:15). Clinical studies may yield fewer agoraphobics without panic than do epidemiological studies. For example, a clinical study of 562 subjects using rigorous agoraphobia criteria[10] found that whereas there were some agoraphobics who did not experience panic (n=30), there were far more who did (n=363) (Goisman et al., 1994). But, as Weissman observes, in clinical practice clinicians usually see only agoraphobics who have had panic symptoms, since an individual who suffers only from agoraphobic social withdrawal may never go to the doctor (Weissman et al., 1986:787). Only 23 per cent of agoraphobics actually seek treatment (Boyd et al., 1990:317), and the agoraphobics who do seek treatment – the subjects of clinical studies – are arguably not only affluent whites, as we saw in chapter 4, but also the individuals with the most severe symptoms and in the most need of help. This factor may explain why so many practitioners subscribe to the idea that agoraphobia is simply a secondary complication of the primary panic disorder – the patients they actually see come for help with their panic because panic is more intrusive, more obviously disruptive of their lives. Agoraphobia without panic, on the other hand, is possibly much easier to live with, once one makes the necessary accommodations. It could equally be the case, however, that patients with the mildest symptoms are the ones most able to seek psychiatric assistance, which would leave the most severe agoraphobics unaccounted for. Either way, psychiatrists cannot treat people who do not seek treatment, nor can reports based on the patients who do manage to make their way to treatment be taken as absolutely representative of agoraphobia as it is found in the general population.[11]

These two problems interrelate to the extent that the incongruity between clinical and epidemiological findings exacerbates the tenuous nature of the *DSM* criteria. Epidemiological surveys may offer a more representative picture of disease at the community level, but clinical studies may tell a better story about what goes on in practitioners' offices, and we cannot ignore the fact that clinical commentary is the predominant source of information about agoraphobia. Moreover, the *DSM* criteria are both supported and disputed by a great deal of conflicting research. It may be better to think of agoraphobia and panic as two discrete syndromes that commonly co-occur. Perhaps the names should be changed to avoid implying a primary-secondary relationship and 'an etiological relationship that has not yet been established, as the current system, overtly or implicitly, seems to do [imply]' (Goisman et al., 1994:77). Alternatively, the disorders could be viewed on a continuum (Goisman et al., 1995:1438). As it stands, the classification of agoraphobia has persisted as a site of conflict for the last two decades, a conflict rooted squarely within the *DSM* framework(s):

> We have had three different sets of official criteria for agoraphobia without a history of panic disorder in 15 years (DSM-III, DSM-III-R, and DSM-IV), clear variance in the application of the criteria even within one version of DSM ... significant discrepancies between clinical and community samples within one set of criteria (DSM-IV ...), and at least two equally plausible but contradictory theoretical explanations of these findings. (1439)

Although the exponential increase in publishing on agoraphobia in recent decades may reflect a greater wealth of knowledge about this illness, it also reveals a surprising lack of consensus on its classification. No two patients are alike, the category shifts relentlessly, and the question of where agoraphobia fits in relation to panic (and other mental disorders) remains unresolved.

Systematic efforts respecting the *DSM* ultimately failed to settle conclusively and reliably the various issues of classification and operationalization (researchers' use of different interview schedules based on different *DSM*s is a case in point). The change in diagnostic criteria from one *DSM* to the next and the frequent tendency to use them interchangeably results in a kind of *dis-order* with implications for the methods of research and treatment of agoraphobia. With the relationship between agoraphobia and panic disorder perpetually unclear and indefinite, the two terms are conflated constantly – between reports, by Medline, and even within individual articles, which often do not distinguish between agoraphobics who panic and those who do not. Compounding this inconsistency is the fact that current research frequently cites old *DSM* criteria. It seems to be common practice for researchers to use whichever edition they happen to have on hand, thereby defeating the central purpose of the *DSM*, which was, purportedly, to have a unifying effect on psychiatry and psychiatric research. That the APA is constantly in the process of releasing new (but not necessarily improved) editions of the *DSM* makes it reasonable to expect that the next edition may contain within it yet another set of revised criteria. With different studies utilizing different editions of the *DSM*, and each edition of the *DSM* calling into question the status of research based on its own previous criteria,[12] we are faced with a rather chaotic state of affairs. Even if we give the APA's efforts the benefit of the doubt and credit each new edition of the *DSM* as representing 'scientific progress' and the accumulating research as contributing to the fine-tuning of what is known about agoraphobia, the categories stipulated therein still raise important questions. What about the patients who do not quite fit the *DSM* schema(s)? Is there room in the *DSM* for heterogeneity among patients? Over twenty years have passed since Dr R.S. Hallam complained of 'diagnostic vagueness,' and agoraphobia *still* has no 'underlying unity and coherence' (Hallam, 1978:317).

Psychoanalysis and a Call to Science

The marginalization of psychoanalysis and biopsychosocial explanation of mental disease is also important here because it reveals a very particular interpretation of social order or, rather, disorder. The current literature, in its biological neo-positivism, suggests that social disorder – represented by diseases like agoraphobia – results from the rejection of 'normal' society, a rejection implicit in the very symptoms of agoraphobia.

Consequently, the discourse of this disorder has depicted society in regulative terms such that the literature and diagnostic criteria do more than simply constitute accounts of a disease, its symptoms, causation, and treatment; rather, they encompass certain normative guidelines for 'governing the living,' that is, 'techniques and procedures for directing human behavior' (Foucault, 1994c:81). In other words, as Foucault has shown, psychiatry has served as a technology of bio-power and subjectification that acts upon the conduct of individuals. (It should be noted here that although psychoanalysis was rejected by mainstream biopsychiatry, for Foucault it was just as culpable in its effects as a normalizing episteme; see chapter 6).

Still, irrespective of Foucault's anti-psychiatric critique (of psychoanalysis and mainstream psychiatry alike), the broader, that is, dominant, discourse of agoraphobia also tells a story about what kind of psychiatric explanation shall count, at least for the APA – an issue recently taken up by the American psychiatrist Allan Compton. A vocal proponent of making psychoanalysis more scientific if it is to survive its veritable exile from mainstream psychiatry, Compton published several articles in which he argued for an overhaul of *DSM-IV*'s nosology to reincorporate the *DSM*'s earlier psychoanalytic influence. The development of sound treatment outcome studies – something psychoanalysts historically have resisted – is, in Compton's estimation, the most effective means to such an end. Writing on phobias and anxiety in particular, he observes that in 'recent years almost innumerable papers on phobic conditions have appeared in the psychiatric literature, while none have come from psychoanalysis' (Compton, 1992a: 206). As he puts it, this is 'certainly not a sign of avid psychoanalytic interest in this most common clinical condition' (Compton, 1992b:230). Although there is extensive interest in pharmaceuticals and cognitive-behaviour therapies, psychoanalysts have failed to contribute to the discussions on treatment, and psychoanalysis has possibly even 'lost its clinical moorings' (Compton, 1992a:207). If psychoanalysis is to regain its credibility, Compton argues, treatment results need to be presented in a scientific manner. He acknowledges that case studies, the traditional psychoanalytic forum for reporting on results, have a certain value, but psychoanalysts need to delineate clear boundaries around the conditions being treated in descriptive, not theoretical, terms (223–4).

In other words, Compton is arguing that if psychoanalysts are to reclaim their rightful place in the world of mainstream psychiatry, they need to play more by the APA's rules. He sees the *DSM* as a 'route to legitimacy' and a 'guideline to what is "real" in the realm of psychopathology,' and something that analysts have 'backed away from' (Compton, 1998:692). Without a clearer system of classification in psychoanalysis, 'results cannot be aggregated in a meaningful fashion [and the] validation of psychoanalytic hypotheses, or choices among competing hypotheses, depends largely upon the comparison of therapeutic results' (Compton, 1992a:224). To this end, he asserts that the terminology needs to change, at least with regard to agoraphobia. Since agoraphobia tends to include fears of a number of things (such as elevators, travel, closed spaces, and so forth), it would be more appropriate that its nomenclature reflect this plurality (Compton, 1992c:414). In the final instalment of his four-part series Compton builds on this point by saying that the criteria for what does and does not count as a phobia are 'to most analysts ... arbitrary, artificial and unduly restrictive in clinical practice [but] necessary for research' (Compton, 1992d:435). He contends that psychoanalysts are in a position to improve upon this state of affairs, but they have as yet failed to develop a coherent theory of phobias out of a refusal to use demographic data and statistical methods. Of course, implicit in this statement is the assumption that other psychiatric disciplines have done better by using demographic data and statistical methods. Yet, as I have tried to show, there is still no coherent theory. To be sure, practitioners today cannot even agree on whether panic and agoraphobia are separate or synonymous disorders. For example, in a panel discussion chaired by Compton in 1995, participants simultaneously referred to the disease as 'agoraphobia and panic states,' 'agoraphobia/panic,' 'panic disorder and agoraphobia,' 'panic disorder without agoraphobia,' 'anxiety disorders,' 'neurosis,' 'panic,' and, simply, 'agoraphobia' (Compton et al., 1995:212).

In a more recent article, Compton takes up his own challenge and begins the task of constructing the research he called for in the earlier series. He offers a rationale and a design for a preliminary research project intended to challenge the 'hegemonic knowledge claims of the DSM system' by offering a 'reliable, psychoanalytically influenced nosology' (Compton, 1998:700) as a first step towards enabling reliable outcome studies of psychoanalytic treatment for agoraphobia (715). Once the validity and reliability of its criteria are tested and refined by the inclusion of psychodynamic concepts, he argues, the ground will be prepared for the outcome studies so desperately needed by the profession. He also laments that psychoanalysis is under considerable duress (691). Given the tendency of psychoanalysis to disparage diagnosis, treatment, and science, it comes as no surprise that the discipline is 'criticized as unscientific and ... of little treatment value by those who are not psychoanalysts' (692). The failure to produce convincing generalizations based on traditional rational and empirical methods has not helped to shore up the status of this approach. As Compton writes, 'those steps which in other sciences are reasonably designated as "advances in knowledge" have not been taken in psychoanalysis. We have not met our obligation to be part of science as a cumulative endeavor ... evaluating the feasibility of generalization as mere "number crunching"' (693). If psychoanalysis is to participate in the advance of knowledge, Compton insists, then analysts need to take the same steps as in any other clinical science: the 'careful design of studies; parsimonious hypotheses; replicable data; empirical methodology in data analysis, not just in data collection, assemblage of outcome results; and comparative evaluation of treatment efficacy' (694).

Big Pharma

It remains to be seen whether or not Compton's remedy for psychoanalysts' veritable exile from mainstream psychiatry will be taken up. In the meantime, pharmaceuticals have been significantly more influential among contemporary psychiatrists, making it difficult to imagine Compton's 'call to science' being embraced by psychoanalysts. They do not seem as willing as the behaviourists, for example, to conform to the normative empirical standards of mainstream, neo-positivist biopsychiatry.

The widespread prescription and use of pharmaceuticals is also significant when considered in relation to the number of diagnoses of agoraphobia that are made. As we saw in chapter 1, prevalence figures as high as 5 per cent of the American population have been cited (Rosenbaum et al., 1995:A4), roughly 12.5 million people (the strong majority of whom are women) – all potential consumers of benzodiazepines and antidepressants.

To be sure, the sale of these classes of drugs has been a substantial source of revenue for drug companies; it is not insignificant that in the mid-1980s, panic disorder was commonly referred to as 'Upjohn illness' (Healy, 1990:159). The Pharmacia & Upjohn company, for example, one of the 'big boys' (Wyke, 1987:4)[13] of drug manufacturing and a major producer of alprazolam (a benzodiazepine frequently prescribed for the management of panic), earned $321 million USD from sales of alprazolam in 1998, up from $279 million USD in 1997 and 1996 (Pharmacia & Upjohn, 1998:35).[14] This drug was one of the 'top 10 brand name pharmaceutical products,' as measured by $327 million in global sales in 2000 (Salomon Smith Barney, 2002). (After 2002, Xanax sales dropped owing to its release from patent protection, in September that year;[15] see *Med Ad News*, 2002; Pfizer, 2003:5).

In Canada, the Patented Medicine Prices Review Board reports that patented drugs used to treat conditions of the nervous system, the category under which antidepressants and benzodiazepines would be classified, accounted for $655.9 million in 1998 and 15.1 per cent of all pharmaceutical sales in Canada that year. Moreover, these figures represent a growth of 39.6 per cent, or $186 million dollars, from the year before. By 2002, sales in this category had more than doubled those in 1998, exceeding $1.4 billion and ranking second only to sales of cardiovascular drugs in driving the overall and dramatic growth of drug sales in Canada in 2002 (Canada, Patented Medicine Prices Review Board, 2002). In total, the Canadian pharmaceutical industry earned $4.3 billion in 1998 (Canada, Patented Medicine Prices Review Board, 1998), and by 2002, total drug sales had reached $8.8 billion dollars.[16] Sales figures for imipramine, an antidepressant also widely prescribed to agoraphobics, were not publicly available, but the market reporter Lisa Jarvis predicted in 2000 that global antidepressant sales would increase from their then value of $11.1 billion USD to $13 billion USD by 2005 (Jarvis, 2000).[17] It turns out that her prediction was much too modest: IMS Health, a Canadian company that tracks prescription drug trends, recently reported that in 2003, global sales of antidepressants were already at $19.5 billion (Reuters, 2004).

It is probably self-evident that the marketing of pharmaceuticals has been crucial to these enormous profits. Promotional activities can encompass everything from choosing what to name a drug, to providing incentives for physicians such as trips to conferences, fridges for their offices, textbooks for medical students, cash bonuses and other gifts, to keeping clinics in good supply of free drug samples, to sponsoring patient groups (see Johnson, 2000), and even to the underreporting or selective reporting of unfavourable clinical drug trial results, and the over-reporting of favourable studies (Healy, 2001:324). Pharmaceutical companies are highly adept at gathering and distributing evidence that serves their business interests and to this end may convene 'consensus conferences' and publish the proceedings. They have also been known to sponsor symposia at professional meetings, and/or fund the publication of special supplements to professional journals (Healy, 2000:20). Another technique increasingly being used by the pharmaceutical industry is the commissioning of 'celebrity researchers' to ghostwrite scientific papers. Healy writes:

> Companies now sell diseases rather than just drugs. To do this, where they used celebrity endorsements before, they turn to celebrity academics now. Where papers were placed in the lay media by PR companies before, academic papers are now increasingly written by medical writing agencies and placed in the leading journals in the field. Where company products were previously judged on the basis of independent research, and research publications were distributed by companies if they coincided with company interests, companies now design and conduct their own studies to produce indications that suit their commercial interests. Clini-

cians meanwhile continue to believe that they are not unduly influenced by pharmaceutical companies. (Healy, 2004b:240–1; see also Healy, 2004a; Johnson, 2003)

Thus the most successfully marketed products 'make the invisible visible' through niche marketing (Healy, 1990:153). That is, they master 'the art of branding,' in which the drug for a given condition and its associated symptoms is defined as capable of 'fulfilling unmet needs' (Parry, 2003).[18] Through influential direct-to-consumer advertising (Thomaselli, 2003) and by 'being intentionally general,' ads for things like antidepressants and minor tranquillizers, particularly after the terrorist attacks of 11 September 2001 in New York, seduce us emotionally, obscuring details about who might actually need the drug (Parpis, 2001:11). Collectively, these incentives and marketing initiatives contribute to 'a market-development package, which, almost unnoticed by psychiatrists, has developed to the point where it has the power to rewrite psychiatric textbooks' (Healy, 2002:6).

With upwards of $1 billion being spent annually on marketing alone, all this is financed, of course, by a given pharmaceutical company's profits from drugs already successfully marketed and sold. Marketing considerations 'have a significant effect in determining how pharmaceutical research and development funds are allocated,' so demand – not disease – dictates (Myers, 1992:229). In fact, psychiatric concepts have become, as Healy also argues, 'products in a market-place in a way that leaves the rise and fall of psychiatric theories subject to the vagaries of industrial regulation and patenting' (Healy, 2002:6).

As already suggested, marketing plays a role not only in decisions as to how research and development funds are spent, but also in decisions as to which indications or claims for a new drug will be researched and subsequently advertised. Marketing research can be used *prior* to drug development as a means of 'designing clinical trials that address market needs' and 'providing guidance to new business development/product management to ensure that the product is positioned to showcase the clinical properties that R&D has created based on prior assessments of market need' (Bartone, 1992:296). But, as Healy (2002) demonstrates, what it means to 'address market needs' is a matter of interpretation. And, when faced with increasing competition, pharmaceutical companies can simply choose to market old drugs for new indications (Jarvis, 2000). Research and development 'may also be

influenced by marketing's need for clinical evidence to promote a specific competitive advantage for a product,' so the needs of shareholders
and medical needs therefore often conflict (Myers, 1992:222). In some
cases, researchers themselves may benefit, when they own the very
company that stands to gain from the research – a state of affairs
that, although it has caused some concern, is perhaps inevitable in a
'resource-based economy slowly going down the tubes' (Livingstone
in McIlroy, 2001:A6).

One implication of all this is that in the last few decades the academic and corporate pharmaceutical worlds have become disturbingly
close bedfellows, a relationship – if not a conflict of interests – that in
pharmaceutical trials is all too often concealed (see Healy, 2004a). For
example, in Canada, between 16 per cent and 30 per cent of all research
at big medical schools (McGill, Queen's, Toronto, and British Columbia) is funded by pharmaceutical and biotech companies, a state of
affairs raising questions as to the possibility that 'links with drug companies change the way scientists work' (McIlroy, 2001:A1 and A5).
Another implication is that R&D funds may be used to develop profitable pharmaceuticals that satisfy consumer needs but actually contribute little or nothing to health care. The possibility is that the extensive
research that has been generated over the last two decades has not
been medically, so much as *market*, driven.

The (Not So) New Biological Positivism

A major element of this research is, of course, its empiricism, though
the evidence-based psychiatry that has emerged since the publication
of *DSM-III* was not an innovation of late-twentieth-century medicine.
The Parisian researcher P.C.A. Louis, considered to be the founder of
'numerical medicine,' analysed two thousand cases of tuberculosis in
1825, long before the concept of probability and the field of statistics
had been fully developed (Duffin, 1999:77). But in the context of psychiatry's (re)turn to positivist biopsychiatry, the contemporary discourse of agoraphobia has become noticeably exclusionary. As we
have seen, it is exclusionary in that psychoanalysis and psychosocial
explanation have been marginalized, but also because, as many feminist scholars have convincingly argued, positivist epistemology has
never been particularly good at capturing real, lived experience. This
failure should not be understated when considering a disease that is
diagnosed so disproportionately in women.

The discourse of agoraphobia is also exclusionary in that medical ideas about agoraphobia, in so far as they are based on patients' functionality, reflect a biopolitical conception of society that overlaps considerably with a functionalist view of social order. To be sure, as much as the *DSM* was intended to guide psychiatrists in the practice of diagnosis (however successful it has or has not been in this endeavour), historically it has served – like functionalism – as a kind of moral and ideological prescription for how people *should* live if society is to operate smoothly. Consider, for example, this famous passage by Talcott Parsons, written fifty years ago:

> The marriage bond is, in our society, the main structural keystone of the kinship system ... Very definite expectations in the definition of role, combined with a complex system of interrelated sanctions, both positive and negative, go far to guarantee stability and maintenance of standards of performance ...
>
> To be the main 'breadwinner' of his family is a primary role of the normal adult male in our society. The corollary of this role is his far smaller participation than that of his wife in the internal affairs of the household. Consequently, 'housekeeping' and the care of children is still the primary functional content of the adult feminine role in the 'utilitarian' division of labor. (Parsons, 1954:187–91)

We might compare this with the criteria in the *DSM*: 'Individuals' avoidance of situations may impair their ability to travel to work or carry out homemaking responsibilities (e.g., grocery shopping, taking children to the doctor)' (APA, 1994:396). Amazingly, this 'homemaking' criterion was a new addition to the *DSM* in 1994. Given this criterion and the fact that by the time it was added most agoraphobics, clearly, were women, it must be said that agoraphobia has the potential to cause a real disruption to the normal gendered order of things.[19] Moreover, to return to Iris Fodor's argument, psychiatry's message to contemporary women is double-edged, in telling women that the stereotypic feminine role is increasingly unacceptable, yet family responsibilities must be a priority. Once again, in Fodor's words, women 'are expected to be "out there" in the world and still put their families first' (Fodor, 1992:201).

Apart from the obviously gendered, if contradictory, definition of disease deployed by *DSM-IV*, through which it draws from and reinforces a Parsonian conception of society, the notion that health can be measured by the ability to work is significant in that it articulates economic productivity and pathology together. Granted, homemaking has had a long-standing history of not being valued as much as paid work per se, but the point here is that in the *DSM*, the agoraphobic person (most often a woman) is defined (at least in part) through her or his decreased productivity and consumption. As noted in this book's introduction, agoraphobia has both social and economic costs. The disorder is bad for the economy, and although not working (for pay) may still pass as consistent with ideal feminine behaviour, the resistance to shopping could be a sign of mental pathology. This view has been demonstrated time and again in the behaviourist literature, in that shopping alone has frequently been set as a desirable goal in behavioural treatment. When doctors sanction shopping as a goal by incorporating it into treatment programs (that nurses, more often than not, subsequently carry out), they are transmitting – reifying and legitimating – an ideological cultural imperative to their patients. This imperative reflects dominant ideals of femininity and consumption and (as in the case of 'Mr Prince') masculinity and work as they *should* be occurring *normally*.

Signifying a collective denial of the cultural basis of science, and consistent with Parsons's assertion that 'our occupational system' requires 'rationality ... universalistic norms, and ... functional specificity' (Parsons, 1954:191), the *DSM* has invariably conceived of society as systematic, classifiable, and orderly. (Of course, operating from this principle guarantees legitimacy to its claims to medical truth.) By deeming pathological those people who do not conform to the limits it prescribes as 'normal' (working, homemaking), the *DSM* and the literature it has generated have constructed as transgressive any living outside the assumed boundaries of modern society. Conservative functionalist (economic) assumptions are encoded in the categories of the *DSM* and the medical literature it has generated, thereby shaping the lens through which individual psychiatrists gaze at their patients.

But make no mistake: I am not suggesting that this is a one-way transmission of these values. Medical notions both draw from and reinforce the social fabric and, in so doing, reflect an ethical agenda alongside society's social/moral prescriptions. Each standard and category in the *DSM* 'valorizes some point of view and silences another,' seamlessly obscuring the politics and contestations surrounding its assembly (witness the conflicts over homosexuality, PMS, and so forth). Yet we rarely see such 'artifacts [as] embodying moral ... choices that in turn craft people's identities, aspirations, and dignity' (Bowker and Star, 1999:4–5). It is in this respect that the *DSM*, an information artefact implying asociality yet fraught with normative dimensions, converges with the social world (82). Moreover, failing to acknowledge the slippery slope of 'objectivity,' the *DSM* seeks to eliminate social accounts of mental disease in its exclusion of psychoanalytic concepts, such as 'neurosis' and 'reaction.' Yet ironically, as Metzl has demonstrated in his incisive study of post-1950s American print representations of psychotropic medications, biopsychiatry and the discourse of psychopharmacology have ended up producing the same discursive effect as psychoanalysis in restoring the very gender roles and hierarchy for which psychoanalysis has been so severely criticized (Metzl, 2003).

To be sure, the kind of social order that the *DSM* espouses informs the vast empiricist literature that has been generated since the 1980s. The once ubiquitous case report, though useful for conveying newsy accounts of illness, is nowadays regarded with scientific scepticism as to its generalizability. Such reports tended to be single-authored publications, written in the first person and in a popular and accessible (read, unscientific) style. For example, one 'clinical parable' begins:

> A harvest moon hovered fleetingly behind banks of wispy clouds as Mary wended her way cheerfully from the local dance hall. Her mind was racing with recollections of the past few hours – minor flirtation and the prospect of still more pleasant liaisons ... Her stiletto heels rattled along the lonely country lane. Suddenly ... she missed her footing and slid into the roadside ditch ... All at once Mary found herself sinking into a slimy morass ... she was quite convinced that there would be no escape from total submersion and suffocation in a God-forsaken bog ... Ruefully she clawed her way back to the road and surveyed the damage; nothing worse than a pair of laddered tights and a soggy skirt. Or so it seemed. But the greater harm was still to show. (Martin, 1979:2170)

Another begins in the voice of an agoraphobic patient:

> I gripped the pram as tightly as I could, thankful that I had it to hold on to. My breathing was becoming laboured, surely my heart was going to burst, right here on the street in front of everybody. I must try to hang on, we're almost at the school, I mustn't run, it would only draw attention to myself, frighten the kids. Suddenly my scalp had pins and needles all

over it, tears welled in my eyes. I began to get a funny sensation in my ears, a sensation of enormous pressure. I told myself I was having a brain haemorrhage. (Hodgkinson, 1981b:37)

As prose of a sort, case reports are more likely to have imaginative titles such as 'Agoraphobia: Far from the Madding Crowd' (Hodgkinson, 1981b); 'Agoraphobia: Another Brick in the Wall' (Wondrak, 1980); 'Behind Closed Doors' (Lim, 1982); 'Imprisoned by Fear' (Lim, 1985); 'Learning to Enjoy the Great Outdoors' (Hodgkinson, 1981a); and 'Dependency in Agoraphobia: A Woman in Need' (King, 1981). Rather than being formulaic expressions of empiricist studies, the titles are inspired by what it *means* and how it *feels* to suffer from this 'baffling syndrome' (Martin, 1979:2170). To this end, they tend to offer extensive detail about the interventions made. They not only outline the steps in treatment and patients' progress from visit to visit and week to week, but also illustrate quite vividly the settings in which these encounters between patient and therapist take place:

> Mr Prince lived in a prestigious part of Hackney. In sharp contrast to the rest of the borough, the area was exceptionally clean, with well cared for houses and gardens.
>
> The door was opened to my knock by a short slim man who stood behind the door. He appeared subdued as I introduced myself. I was reluctant to go in because a huge fierce-looking black dog stood in the corridor barking ferociously.
>
> 'Are you sure it is all right? Does your dog bite?' I asked. 'Come in, it's all right. He won't bite you,' said Mr Prince. I cautiously edged myself into the house. (Lim, 1985:18)

But as a 'variety of the personal essay, the case report struggles with the problems of subjectivity and contingency, and these problems have earned it the suspicion of clinical scientists' (Hunter, 1991:94). Although there are some case reports among the current scholarship, writers using behavioural methods have for the most part published controlled and uncontrolled, often multi-authored, studies.[20] Moreover, the language of the 'scientific method' – lacking in affect and emotion – obscures any sense of individuality or agency on the part of the agoraphobics participating in the research.

Whereas in the late nineteenth and early twentieth centuries physicians (and planners and theorists) assumed that, at bottom, social disorder and agoraphobia came from the changes brought by modern society, I argue that lately the assumption has been – as reflected in the psychiatric literature – that social disorder comes from the refusal of rationalism and the scientific method,[21] and that scientific reason is the ultimate route to good health. In this view, a rejection of society is implied by the very symptoms of agoraphobia, and the colonization of its presumed irrationality by the 'agoraphobia industry' provides an avenue to reclaiming the suffering individuals to the modern (patriarchal capitalist) world, thereby restoring social order through reason and science.[22] At once celebrating and repudiating as pathological the still so-called private sphere, the *scientification* of agoraphobia denies the social in social life. As the imperative of standardized evidence collection has become the central feature of contemporary psychiatry, the laboratory – not the street – has become the 'real' context for agoraphobia, thereby obscuring the social and effectively severing the patient from ownership of her or his own condition (see Bowker, 1998:275). The tension between biomedicine as defender of the human body against disease and biomedicine as an entity that generates its knowledge and procedures by objectifying the human body as 'passive biomass' (Waldby, 2000:7) is exemplified by the tendency in this literature to refer to patients as 'Ss' – thereby reifying them as impersonal, medicalized research *subjects* to be experimented upon (cf. Hunter, 1991:134). Amounting to a hyper-rational science of social order, the collectively constructed theory of society implicit in recent psychiatric literature assumes an 'objective' understanding of bodies and disease and claims to be unproblematically extracted from *social* life. We might attribute this claim to what Waldby has termed the 'biomedical imagination,' or 'biomedicine's speculative and explanatory universe, the kind of propositional world that it makes for itself' (Waldby, 1996:5).

The science of agoraphobia has thus emerged as a discursive formation (Foucault, 2002) that presumes to exclude the social, and is legitimated by research and reporting in which the social is nowhere to be found – indeed, such abstraction from the social is integral for conveying a scientific message (cf. Knorr-Cetina, 1981, especially chap. 2; Latour and Woolgar, 1979, especially chap. 2). In contrast, its profound sociality is essentially what has been perceived by mainstream psychiatrists to be wrong with psychoanalysis – it is intensely personal, disdainful of the *DSM* classification system, and therefore deeply unscientific. Written in a passive and disinterested voice, as if to suggest that the appearance of scientific detachment somehow guarantees

the unquestionable objectivity of the research, the neo-positivist literature constitutes a discourse that seems 'to rise above uncertainty,
power struggles, and the impermanence of the compromises' (Bowker,
1998:259).[23] With each edition of the *DSM* it has been increasingly difficult to find signs of the 'social' within the discourse of agoraphobia (if
by 'social' we mean the opposite of 'scientific,' or 'values' versus
'facts'). Unlike the early literature, this writing is directly informed by
a *DSM* that 'enforces a certain understanding of context, place, and
time ... [and] makes a certain set of discoveries (which validate its own
framework) much more likely than an alternative set outside of the
framework.' To clarify, the issue is not that the definitions contained in
the *DSM* are good or bad, but that they represent dangerous and 'arbitrary ways of cutting up [a] world' that is 'always slightly out of reach'
(Bowker, 1998:273; see also Bowker and Star, 1999:5).

Yet there is a certain 'complicity between biomedical knowledge and
non-scientific systems of thought.' As Waldby observes, 'biomedical
knowledge cannot ... be quarantined from general ideas operative in
the culture, even when it understands its concepts to be carefully and
directly deduced from the factual evidence of the body.' Biomedicine
'constantly absorbs, translates and recirculates "non-scientific" ideas ...
about social order, about culture ... in its technical discourses.' In effect,
then, biomedical discourse can be seen as a discourse of culture to a
certain extent, in that it is implicitly bound up with broader cultural
narratives and power relations inherent in the distinctions it makes
between the normal and the pathological (Waldby, 1996:5–6). Accordingly, the divisions in the *DSM* are heavy with social, ethical, and political meaning and 'do not describe the world as it is in any simple sense
[but rather] model it' (Bowker, 1998:286–91).

To the extent that classifications of all kinds are ubiquitous and
invisible in society, and given that 'we stand for the most part in formal
ignorance of the social and moral order created by these invisible
potent entities' (Bowker and Star, 1999:3), it is arguable that this search
for knowledge about agoraphobia is not undirected. Evelyn Fox Keller
asks 'how the very framing of the questions' that scientists ask might
'already commit us to the possibility' of certain social initiatives. She
focuses in particular on eugenics (Keller, 1992:77), but her argument
can be applied equally here. She writes,

> Our confidence in the purity of scientific knowledge ... works ... to fore-
> close the questions we would otherwise ask about the aims of science,

about the ways in which both the form and content of scientific knowledge have been shaped by the motivations driving it (either from below,
in the consciousness or unconscious of individual scientists, or from
above, in the programs of the sponsoring agencies). (83)

Keller's remark is particularly incisive when read in the context of a
1988 article by Robert Spitzer and Janet Williams, long-time chair and
member, respectively, of the APA Work Group formed to revise *DSM-
III*. Briefly, the article argued for a new structured diagnostic interview
schedule (the 'SCID') that could be used to make *DSM-III-R* anxiety
disorders diagnoses in adults. The authors write:

> We believe that the inclusion of revised diagnostic criteria and the fact
> that it is modelled on the clinical diagnostic interview will make this
> instrument a valuable tool for diagnosing patients with Anxiety Disor-
> ders for psychopharmacologic research. This instrument is already being
> used for patient selection in a multinational study of the efficacy of alpra-
> zolam in the treatment of Panic Disorder and Agoraphobia, sponsored by
> the Upjohn Company. (Spitzer and Williams, 1988:56)

In this case, Upjohn's research (that is, marketing) agenda literally *preceded* – perhaps even created the need for – a new interview schedule
that could better differentiate among anxiety disorders and that would
allow investigators to maximize the homogeneity of their patient samples. Most important, though, is the fundamental assumption embedded in the act of revising the interview schedule, namely, that people
can be sorted out, that they *can* be ordered – and more accurately at
that.

It is on this basis that an agoraphobic 'bandwagon' (Fujimura, 1992)
has developed. This notion of bandwagons is certainly one we could
use to describe the activities of mainstream psychiatry and other social
groups having a vested interest in subscribing to the *DSM* framework
since the release of its third edition in 1980. We have seen, for example,
that while cognitive-behavioural psychologists leave plenty of room in
their ideas for social therapies and explanations, they also appear to
recognize that in order to stay in the research game, they must adopt
psychiatry's 'conventionalized ways' (178). Psychoanalysts also offer a
clear example of what happens when practitioners or researchers do
not conform: professional excommunication.

The *DSM* and the literature it has generated have been very success-

ful in 'enrolling many members of multiple social worlds in constructing a new and at least temporarily stable definition' of agoraphobia (cf.
Fujimura, 1992:176–7). Participants in many different social worlds
work with agoraphobia, and all assume a certain conception of social
order. And, through their work, they see to it that social order will happen. The very goal of all the various forms of treatment – restoring a
patient to a 'normal' state – flags this assumption as a central organizing principle of psychiatry. Accordingly, the science of psychiatry as we
know it – motivated by this desire for social order(ing) – can work only
with the standardized *DSM* classification system in place, bolstered
and reinforced as it is by research designed very much in its own image.
Moreover, the reification of agoraphobia as a monolithic entity is necessary if different social worlds are to be able to talk about the disorder
among themselves. We may recall that the Work Groups responsible for
the *DSM*, even in its earliest incarnations, stated openly that standard-
ization across military and mainstream psychiatry was their central
objective in creating (and subsequently revising) the manual.

Yet the sensibility of order that we have been discussing turns on
another assumption, that is, besides the assumption that people and
diseases can be classified and ordered. What I am referring to now is
the fundamental – and problematic – assumption that diseases (and
their causation) can be apprehended with certainty. Working from the
premise that a disease *can* be defined in effect amounts to having a
taken-for-granted disease concept as a kind of black box. Having disease concepts as black boxes ensures the efficacy of medicine as a form
of organized knowledge about the world and enables it to proceed as a
form of collective action. Taken-for-granted disease concepts can even
be seen as the basis of social order in medicine; at the very heart of all
medical transactions, then, disease concepts are of central importance
in the doctor-patient relationship. It is imperative that everyone concerned, especially the doctors, know what they are dealing with. But
the fact is, as several attempts to define disease demonstrate, they do
not.

Talcott Parsons, for example, approached the concept of disease
from the perspective of social action and, of course, social roles. He
emphasized illness rather than disease, defining it as an impairment of
the individual's 'teleonomic' capacities, that is, her or his capacity to
maintain equilibrium of the organic and action-level subsystems and
'to undertake successful goal-oriented courses of functioning, especially behavior' (Parsons, 1978:591). Both the *DSM* and all the litera-

ture it has generated are in accord with this view; as *DSM-III* stated, for example, one sign of agoraphobia was the 'increasing constriction of normal activities' (APA, 1980:227).

Illness for Parsons was dysfunction, and something that gave rise to what he called the 'sick role.' This included both the status and the treatment of individuals whose normally expected levels of health were impaired (Parsons, 1978:591). Parsons's definition is notable for its having gone beyond the internal anatomical-physiological components to present sickness as a socially sanctioned form of deviance, subject to medicine as an agent of social control (596). Parsons illuminates the sociality of illness, but not only are his ideas prescriptive (and ideological), they are circular as well. He fails to explain the interdependence of the various parts of the body/society but only asserts it; what is health is simply not disease, and what is disease is simply not health. This raises the question of when exactly someone is 'sick.' Parsons also equates the individual body's subsystems with those of the larger society, but it is difficult to discern with certainty what each needs in order to be considered 'healthy.' Moreover, if the system (corporeal or social) is self-correcting (as the concepts of teleonomy and equilibrium suggest), then is somebody ever *really* sick in this model? The chicken pox, for example, may not in fact qualify as disease according to Parsons's logic. Although the chicken pox does set the individual back in all the ways we think of as 'being sick,' it also represents the body's internal mechanisms for improving health – by virtue of *having* the chicken pox, the body immunizes itself. This suggests that the individual is actually even healthier with the disease than without it. Finally, Parsons takes for granted the stability of social norms from which diseases deviate. However, as we shall see in the next chapter, the norms of disease are not so stable, for, as Hunter writes, 'each patient is potentially abnormal, an anomalous instance of disease. "Normal" science in medicine is like "normal rhythm" in Shakespeare's blank verse: the meter, we know, is iambic pentameter, but we are often hard pressed to find a classic invariant line' (Hunter, 1991:18).

Alongside Parsons's functionalist (and sociological) conception of disease, historians have observed that within medicine the concept of disease has been understood mainly in terms of two theories, the ontological and the physiological. Briefly, the ontological theory views disease as an external invader. Disease originates outside the body as a specific, objective entity (germ theory and tuberculosis come to mind here). The physiological theory of disease attributes causation to the disturbance of functions already operating within the individual, such as genetic or auto-immune diseases. As categories imposed by historians and philosophers, the ontological and physiological designations have helped twentieth-century writers about medicine to organize conceptually debates that have persisted since their introduction in ancient Roman and Greek medicine (see Hudson, 1987; King, 1982; Risse, 1978).

These theories of disease also illuminate the ways in which medical knowledges are constructed simply by virtue of the fact that they often appear simultaneously in one disease picture. Trying to demarcate the two theories of causation, therefore, may be a red herring, in that diseases usually do not fit within any one category. As Lester King has argued, disease causation must be understood not as a singular phenomenon, but as the outcome of interactions among several causal factors (King, 1982:203). I would add to this notion, by maintaining that diseases are better understood as 'effects' enabled by social and physical conditions of possibility. Still, King's point is instructive, in that it is difficult if not impossible to pin a disease down to any one cause.

A theory of causation aside, the concept of disease also largely depends on what is considered 'normal' culturally. For example, epidemiological research that looks at the 'why' and the 'when' of diseases depends on the range of normal within the given population. In other words, if in a particular group *everyone* is afraid to go outside, such a fear may not be considered a problem per se. As Rose states, 'What is common is all right, we presume' (Rose, 1985:32). Certainly the fear many women have of going out (alone at night) would not be considered pathological, that is, agoraphobic; rather it is considered prudent (cf. Gardner, 1994). Diagnosis is not value-free, nor is it immune to cultural constraint. What passes for 'normal' has political implications, and it matters very much who is doing the looking (see Engelhardt, 1976, 1978; Margolis, 1976, 1986).

In light of these issues, I contend that disease concepts are historically and culturally contextual shifting bits of knowledge, better understood as social processes – as scientific and popular representations of illness, of causation theories, and of cultural imperatives. As Rosenberg argues, a disease can be said not to exist until it is agreed that it does by naming it and responding to symptoms of it that are identified, categorized, and linked (hence my use of the term 'disease' to describe agoraphobia in this text; see Rosenberg, 1992:xiii). We have also seen that disease classifications are not naturally given, and that the collation of symptoms into discrete categories and lists of criteria comes with a risk of overemphasizing some symptoms at the expense of others (Engel, 1960:463). What is seen as worthy of mention at one time and place may not be so in another, however, so the same phenomenon may be considered pathological in a first instance and normal in a second, as was the case with homosexuality (eventually eliminated from *DSM-III-R*) (Ziporyn, 1992:51).

The especially intriguing thing about disease concepts and their indefiniteness is that we (doctors especially) proceed as though we really know what is meant by the concept of disease, when what we are really doing is operating on the basis of *ideas* of disease and causation. Harold Garfinkel's ethnomethodology illuminates this type of conventionalized behaviour. He wrote in 1967, 'For the purposes of *conducting their everyday affairs* persons refuse to permit each to understand "what they are really talking about" in this way.' The 'anticipation that persons *will* understand' is a sanctioned property of discourse (Garfinkel, 1967:41). The concept of disease similarly presumes a '"seen but un-noticed" background of common understandings' (44).

Arguably, then, every single entry in the *DSM* is merely a *hypothesis* about how the individual is expected to – should – act when she or he is mentally ill. By deeming pathological those people who do not conform to prescribed standards of 'normal' behaviour (i.e., working and homemaking), the *DSM* and the literature generated on the basis of its criteria offer an essentialist conception of gender, if not of human nature. Moreover, since absolute precision regarding the concept of disease is not possible, it seems especially significant that mental/emotional symptoms have proved particularly difficult to name. 'Panic' and 'agoraphobia' are conflated regularly, and words like 'disease,' 'syndrome,' 'disorder,' 'illness,' and 'symptom' are used interchangeably even though they all technically refer to different aspects of ill health, and despite the fact that causation cannot technically be known.[24] If the symptoms of agoraphobia have not really changed over the years, but yet we do not know what the concept of disease really means – or whether the panic component of agoraphobia is primary or secondary – then from where does the idea of agoraphobia get its stability?

To borrow from Bruno Latour, as long as all the elements of a (disease) black box 'act as one,' the only thing that seems to matter is its 'input and output' (Latour, 1987:3, 131). Failing to provide us with a definitive framework by which to define disease both generally and particularly, theories of disease are at best tools that force us to make sense of the ways that these ideas known as diseases – these knowledges – are socially constructed. Yet the black box–ness of disease and its causation is also suggestive of the possibility that medical actors unwittingly – through their professed objectivity – subvert the boundary between 'fiction' and 'non-fiction' (cf. Barrett, 1999:16–7). If we accept this point, then it becomes possible to destabilize the assumptions informing the way medical texts are perceived.

6 Conclusion:
Doing Agoraphobia(s) – The Social
Relations of Psychiatric Knowledge

So far I have examined agoraphobia as it has been mobilized in psychiatric texts, but I have not yet fully explored the theoretical implications of this mobilization. Specifically, the psychiatric reports under discussion here have historically constituted a central venue in which doctors can dialogue with one another about (this) disease and thereby collectively construct various psychiatric realities. To be sure, psychiatrists put much stock in medical reports, as they are crucial for their work. But in addition to being professionally important, these texts are 'vivid documents of social history' (Hansen, 1992:106). They are indispensable historical artefacts that provide access to doctors' voices and especially their perceptions of patients in broad historical terms. In other words, this book has emphasized – albeit implicitly – that doctors 'write disease,' and the role of medical reports in the enactment of agoraphobia.

With such an emphasis in mind, I focus in this closing chapter on embodiment as a means of further demonstrating the sociality of agoraphobia. I argue that the mutual engagement between the writing and publishing of psychiatric texts and the reiteration of normative cultural categories implicit within them has been a significant vehicle for the materialization of agoraphobic bodies. In analysing disease categories, not only in terms of their social construction but also in terms of their materialization, this final chapter illuminates the sociocultural process of embodiment as one that unfolds in and through (disease) categories. We have seen that psychiatric classification is a critical point of inter-

Sections of this chapter are taken from Reuter (2002).

section between the psychiatric and the cultural; by examining the exclusionary discourse of the disease, this book illuminates how relations of power construct the 'Other' and inform a range of cultural classifications that are embedded within psychiatric categories, namely, gender, 'race,' and class. That psychiatric classifications contain this sociocultural narrative within them poses a challenge to the assumed singularity of disease concepts. It also forces us to reconsider our assumptions about embodiment. I begin with Foucault.

In *The Birth of the Clinic* (1973), Foucault posits an epistemic shift in medical practice, contending that with the emergence of modern medicine, the diseased body was radically and conceptually transformed into a discursive site.[1] With the development of the 'clinic,' diseases changed from being conceptualized as *dwellers in* to *conditions of* the human body (from Mol and Law, 1999). The body was – is – both the object of medical knowledge, the 'clinic,' and the medical gaze and its tools; and it was – is – also the living body, embodied humanness, the 'fleshy condition for, or, better, the fleshy situatedness of, our modes of living' (Mol and Law, 1999). This epistemic shift made possible a rational, positive science of 'man' whereby the individual could be both 'subject and object of his [*sic*] own knowledge,' constituting himself 'in his own eyes as an object of science.' As Foucault writes, 'the gaze is no longer reductive, it is, rather, that which establishes the individual in his irreducible quality. And thus it becomes possible to organize a rational language around it.' He goes on: 'The *object* of discourse may equally well be a *subject*, without the figures of objectivity being in any way altered. It is this *formal* reorganization, *in depth*, rather than the abandonment of theories and old systems, that made *clinical experience* possible.' At last, he observes, 'one could ... hold a scientifically structured discourse about an individual' (Foucault, 1973:xiv). To the extent that it was concerned with 'man's being as object of positive knowledge' – that is, with 'the philosophical status of man' (197–8) – medicine thus came to have an importance that was not only methodological but also ontological.

This dualistic subject-object ontology is manifested in clinical writing about agoraphobia, and it is reflected in physicians' tendency to direct their attention not to the (whole) patient but to the signs that differentiate one disease from another, a tendency illustrative of what Foucault describes as 'a new "carving up" of things' (Foucault, 1973:xviii). Doctors do not ask, 'What is the matter with you?' – a question characteristic of eighteenth-century doctor-patient encounters (xviii); they have replaced it with 'that other question: "Where does it hurt?"' (xviii). Recall Carl Westphal's patient 'Mr C.,' for example, a 32-year-old commercial traveller who complained of a 'feeling of fear' that would overtake him whenever he attempted to walk through open spaces: 'After questioning,' Mr C. indicated 'that the feeling is located more in the head than in the area of the heart, although the heart palpitates' (Westphal 1988 [1871]:60). A second patient, 'Mr N.,' was a 24-year-old merchant who could not cross open spaces or go for long walks or rides in taxis, buses, carriages, or the train. Nor could he spend time in theatres, concert halls, or larger rooms where crowds assembled. In all these situations, 'the response [was] an immediate breakout of intense anxiety, which is introduced by an ascending feeling of warmth from the abdomen to the head along with strong palpitations of the heart' (66). We may remember that with these and his other patients, Westphal paid protracted attention to anatomical details, including in his investigation a thorough eye examination and, in one case, extensive measurement of the patient's physical features.

Following Foucault, we may recognize in these examples of Westphal's practice 'the operation of the clinic and the principle of its entire discourse' (Foucault, 1973:xviii) whereby, through practices of objectification, patients – human beings – are transformed into subjects of medicine – that is, into patients. These transformative practices include the 'modes of inquiry which try to give themselves the status of sciences'; the 'dividing practices' that differentiate between, for example, the mad and the sane, the sick and the healthy, or, as we might say, the vertiginous epileptoid and the neuropathic; and, finally, humans' turning themselves into subjects, through recognition of themselves as subjects of, for example, sexuality (Foucault, 1982:208; also 1978), surveillance (Foucault, 1979), or, as I am arguing, disease. Foucault demonstrates that historically patients have been both subjects of disease theories and objects of the clinical gaze deployed according to a standard of 'normal' functioning – according to the binary of health and morbidity in the normal and the pathological (Foucault, 1973:35; see also Canguilhem, 1991). His characterization of modern medical work and the clinical gaze serves as a very useful starting point for thinking about disease and representations of agoraphobia in particular. But although the concept of the gaze is useful for understanding how modern medicine functions, it is also limited, because it posits bodies as docile and monolithic subject-objects of psychiatry, thereby failing to account for the diversity of agoraphobic bodies that emerge in apparent defiance of the diagnostic norms meant to constrain them.

On the one hand, the plurality of agoraphobic bodies has been mobilized by the differing characterizations offered in each representation of agoraphobia (as well as by the symptoms described and experienced, the effects of agoraphobia on daily living, gendered differences, and varied clinical approaches). On the other hand, this plurality of bodies also has melded together to form a singular discourse of agoraphobia generated by the physicians who write and publish about it. Two related theoretical responses are possible here.

First, the body is never simply a body, but an enacted body whose meaning – in this case, agoraphobia – is always shifting. Second, a theory of the body as meaningfully enacted destabilizes not only the *DSM*-professed uniformity of agoraphobia, but also the presumed distinction between the discursive and the material. This destabilization involves a challenge to the divide between 'words and things' that has, especially within recent feminist scholarship, caused so much 'perplexity and irritation' for the privileging of materialist explanations for women's oppression at the expense of meaning (Barrett, 1999:18–19). This point is especially key in the light of previous sociological interpretations of agoraphobia that focus only on women's subordinate status relative to men, to the exclusion of other social factors that historically have contributed to the gendering (and racializing and classing) of this disease.

Materialist feminists have been resistant to this turn to culture and discourse, seeing it as 'an ideologically suspect attempt to deny material reality' (Barrett, 1999:25). But, to borrow from Hortense Spillers's work (on slavery), 'we might concede, at the very least, that sticks and bricks *might* break our bones, but words will most certainly *kill* us' (Spillers, 1987:68). To distinguish between the material and the discursive is to assume, wrongly, that the discursive has no materiality. As we have seen in this study, the discursive – the discourse of agoraphobia – has had the very important material effect of narrating social order. The tension implicit in the separation of the material from the discursive is evident in doctors' use of disease theories in their accounts, and in the cultural assumptions upon which their theories about the disease are based.

The important point for now is that the examination of symptoms, the theorization of causation, the attempts at treatment, and, most fundamentally, the construction of the individuals concerned as something to repair and to write about rendered these agoraphobic bodies Foucaultian subject-objects of a psychiatric gaze. A strictly Foucaultian (archaeological) analysis, however, limits us to an understanding of bodies as docile and monolithic. I contend that the practices and discourses of agoraphobia – the material and the discursive – together produced variable embodied agoraphobic subjectivities.

Annemarie Mol and John Law's study of 'hypoglycaemic enactment' is instructive here. Mol and Law replace the dualistic question of what it means to *have* or *be* a body with the question of what it means to *do* a body, and they propose a theory of the body as *enacted* by the various practices associated with it. The notion that diseased bodies – in their case, hypoglycaemic, and in my case, agoraphobic – are enacted may be illuminated, for example, by details in the psychiatric literature. This jump from diseased minds to diseased bodies may strike readers as problematic, but I would argue that agoraphobia represents the conceptual inadequacy of this particular dualism par excellence. As Shilling astutely observes, the mind is inextricable from the body 'as a result of the mind's location *within* the body' (Shilling, 1993:13).

In the psychiatric literature on agoraphobia, we see patients who do things like panic, avoid crowds, stay at home, lie about their problem, walk with a companion, take remedies, attend clinics, and so forth. Although we as readers of this psychiatric literature have no 'real' access to what the patients did (being left to read their actions through the lens of doctors' writings), it stands to reason that, as with Mol and Law's hypoglycaemic patients, the actions the patients engaged in *enacted* their agoraphobic embodiment. In other words, the body is 'enacted' through patients' practices – what we might describe as 'doing agoraphobia.'

The ways in which patients deport themselves and move through open spaces, however indirectly we may apprehend these as readers of psychiatric literature, represent only part of a range of actions through which agoraphobia 'gets done.' By examining, measuring, testing, and listening to their patients talk about their experiences, doctors also enact agoraphobia. But they also do so through *writing* the disease in the form of articles and reports, so I expand upon Mol and Law's concept of enactment to include, then, the writing and publishing that psychiatrists do. As Berg and Bowker observe in their study of medical records and bodies, 'knowing *in the practice of medicine* is ... dependent on writing,' and, like medical records, medical literature '*mediates* the relations that it organizes [and] the bodies that are configured through it' (Berg and Bowker, 1997:514). I contend that the case literature helps 'perform the medical body,' that in other words there is a convergence here: representations inscribe themselves in the bodies they represent, such that the patient's body becomes its representation (519).

Note that this convergence does not happen uniformly. As we have seen, agoraphobia has been many things – vertigo, epilepsy, neuropathy, a symptom, a disease, a disease of men, a disease of women, the result of debauchery, punishment for masturbation, a neurotic defence, and more. Yet agoraphobia's variable ontologies have been mobilized as aspects of some monolithic entity and projected as a virtual object ('Agoraphobia') behind the variety of agoraphobias that were performed (cf. Mol, 1998:161). In reality, every examination, conversation, designation – every publication – constituted a different 'enactment' of this kind of body. What Mol writes in an analysis of atherosclerosis can be applied to agoraphobia: 'The material manipulated, the concerns addressed, the reality performed, all vary from one place to another. The ontology incorporated ... in the diagnosis, treatment, and prevention of [agoraphobia] is multiple' (1998:161–2). So not only have doctors and patients enacted agoraphobia together, they have enacted many agoraphobias through a range of practices. Not least of these have been the telling and writing of the disease. But here I must also draw the reader's attention to the constitutive epistemology of these practices, for the enactment of agoraphobia cannot be understood outside of culture. Judith Butler's study (1993) of the sexing of bodies illustrates this point.

Butler contends that gender is a performance in that it is a repetition of conventions and norms, and power relations 'cited' and concealed. The reiteration of norms is a process that is dependent for meaning upon the creation, exclusion, and maintenance of an abjected Other – bodies that fall outside the shifting boundaries of normality and are, by implication, defined as abnormal, or as bodies that do not matter. As part of a productive process that unfolds within a regulative structure, social norms make the material constitution and cultural intelligibility of *certain* bodies – those that do matter – possible. In other words, bodies that do not matter provide a constitutive outside for those that do. Abnormal bodies – in Butler's case, homosexual, and in my case, diseased (agoraphobic) – constitute the materialization of norms that, in their reiteration, create and re-create an ongoing structure of exclusion and its relations of power. An individual's identity and experiences are produced, mediated, and constrained by this process.

The point is that bodies may be something that we *do* or enact, but the *doing* is rendered intelligible and relevant (only) through normative knowledge categories, in this context the category (and subcategories) of disease. When doctors have made certain claims about agoraphobics and, for example, their excessive behaviours, they have invoked assumptions and categories of morality couched in the language of disease causation. Accordingly, there is a sense in which theories and categories have mediated the practices involved in enacting agoraphobia – a sense in which they have constituted the normative conceptual structure through which agoraphobic bodies have been enacted. Bodies can thus be said, as Butler puts it, to 'only appear, only endure, only live within the productive constraints of certain ... regulatory schemas' (Butler, 1993:xi). In other words, a body is never just a body, but a body with normative meaning – the outcome of power relations. Multiple agoraphobias may be enacted through various practices, but these practices are meaningful only through the grid of culture. They are made intelligible and relevant only through normative categories, in this case the concepts and language of mental disease, which includes ideas about gender, 'race,' and class as well as questions of epistemology (i.e., questions as to which approach to understanding agoraphobia shall count as knowledge).

Ian Hacking's discussion of multiple personality disorder further illustrates the link among bodies, reiteration, and theories of disease. He writes: 'Psychiatry did not discover that early and repeated child abuse causes multiple personality. It forged that connection, in the way that a blacksmith turns formless molten metal into tempered steel.' He continues: 'I am pursuing a ... profound concern, namely, the way in which the very idea of the cause was forged. Once we have that idea, we have a very powerful tool for making up people, or indeed, for making up ourselves' (Hacking, 1995:94–5). With these remarks, Hacking underscores the ontological *and* epistemological process by which particular material subjectivities – in this case, agoraphobic bodies – were made intelligible through normative structures called up in the representation of this disease. As Hacking also writes, 'a seemingly innocent theory on causation ... becomes formative and regulatory' (95).

Doctors and patients together enacted agoraphobic bodies, and these enactments derived their meaning from cultural disease ideas and categories. Enactments are thus both material and discursive to the extent that they are inextricable from meaning structures. Given our earlier discussion of the variability of agoraphobic bodies, it is also worth noting, however, that the process of reiteration Butler describes is neither closed nor stable. The lines of inclusion and exclusion upon which normative classifications depend are always shifting because people interpret and reiterate the norms in particular contexts. Norms are not solid or unwavering, so agoraphobia has not successfully mobilized as a single or complete identity. In other words, each reiteration of agoraphobic norms (the impetus to theorize and classify the disease indicates that these exist) reflects a different disease. Here we might revisit (and adapt) Mol: Agoraphobia is *'performed* in a variety of ways, or better ... the name ['agoraphobia'] is used for different objects – which also have names of their own' (Mol, 1998:161). While enactments necessarily reiterate cultural meaning structures, which, when 'cited,' affirm relations of power, *'different* [medical reports and] *different* practices of reading and writing are intertwined with the production of *different* patient's [*sic*] bodies, different bodies politic, and different bodies of knowledge' (Berg and Bowker, 1997:514).

The concept of reiteration illuminates an understanding of agoraphobic bodies as (multiply) enacted reiterations in three respects. First, as we have seen, the materiality of agoraphobic bodies is constituted in and through disease categories that are normative and regulative. This constitution has implications in and for the bodies so produced because bodies are intelligible only within these meaning structures. Certainly, agoraphobic bodies could not be understood as such outside the essential conceptual framework of medicine premised on the bifurcation of normal and pathological. But the concept of reiteration demonstrates that it is in and through this conceptual framework that agoraphobic bodies historically have materialized. In this respect, discourses such as that of psychiatry – through the positioning of pathology as the constitutive outsider to health – have shaped the social world through the normative frameworks that they create and deploy by virtue of the authority accorded to (medical) science.

Second, reiterations of agoraphobia are necessarily open-ended, as is confirmed by the varied images of this disease apparent in the literature. Each reiteration of agoraphobia has been different and particular – in terms of sociohistorical context, the patient presenting, the doctor diagnosing, the method of apprehension and treatment, the theory of causation invoked, the *DSM* in use, and so forth. The numerous agoraphobic patients who have presented themselves to physicians have combined to generate a single discourse of agoraphobia, but this study reveals that a plurality of different ideas about agoraphobia has helped to enact a plurality of agoraphobic bodies. That several theories of causation and methods of classification of the disease were in circulation over time and often at the same time – that the discourse of agoraphobia was fragmented in this respect – destabilizes the notion of *an* agoraphobic body, as well as the notion that agoraphobia is a unified category. The attendant sense of friction and plurality calls into question contemporary lay and medical notions of what agoraphobia is and has implications for how other pathologies are understood. The social process of classification, as it both relates to and produces ontologically variable phenomena, is disrupted, and the problem of order that is imposed by the categorization of 'symptoms that matter' is exasperated.[2] Psychiatric and cultural categories are called up in particular bodies in ways that actually reveal both the power of the categories and their vulnerability, as each embodied agoraphobic person takes them up – reiterates them – differently.

Third, the concept of reiteration also helps situate the practices implied by the notion of 'enactment' within their linguistic, symbolic, and normative contexts. Practical actions – enactments – can be understood only in terms of the normative categories of knowledge that are called up in their execution. We could also say that agoraphobic bodies have been the outcome of *knowledgable* practices in that they have represented the enactment of knowledge categories. In attempting to impose stability on their patients' bodies, medical theories have guaranteed these symptomatic beings a recognizable and enduring social existence (cf. Butler, 1997:20), even while exacerbating their instability through the open-endedness of norms. Discursive categories have been necessary for their meaningful material existence, and at the centre of the process has been the social differentiation of these bodies through abjection, the constitutive distinction made between the normal and the pathological.

In sum, agoraphobic bodies derive their intelligibility through the regulative and normative meaning structures of psychiatric discourse. Enactments and reiterations are equally pluralistic, but also indistinguishable to the extent that enactments of agoraphobia can make no sense outside a normative conceptual order that designates which aspects of agoraphobia shall be 'given to be seen' (Rajchman, 1991). Mol and Law's theory of the body as enacted gives an account of the practical and active component of embodiment, enabling us to theorize practices associated with agoraphobia, not the least of which has been the publication of clinical literature, as central to its enactment. As I have tried to demonstrate, however, actions are necessarily attached to meaning structures, and it is in this respect that agoraphobias are at once reiterated and enacted. In other words, the body is not merely where a disease happens but also the material-discursive instantiation of disease and cultural categories. The theories of disease and the ideas about culture and the social that are invoked in writings about agoraphobia amount to the deployment of discursive structures of abjection that regulate the material intelligibility of this disease. Pushing this point further, the enactment of bodies through particular practices also involves the enactment of certain exclusions of bodies, and of diseases not enacted.

As we have seen, Foucault's ideas illuminate the extent to which patients have been the subject-objects of modern disease discourse, of the Clinic and its gaze. But Foucault's concept of the subject-object may not permit us to transcend the dilemma of conceiving the body in either material or discursive terms. He demonstrates that phenomena are the effects of power/knowledge systems and boundary drawing projects that make some identities or attributes intelligible to the exclusion of others, but the identities or attributes that are measured as part of such boundary projects do not represent inherent properties of subjects or objects. Subjectivity and objectivity are constituted through and within particular practices – they do not pre-exist (see Barad, 1998:106). I contend that it is necessary to extend Foucault's concept of the subject-object by considering the role of the material-discursive in agoraphobia. Diseased bodies are 'intra-acted' in and by published psychiatric literature (along with other things).

Yet, almost in spite of this critical reformulation, the 'old,' dualistic genre of medical knowing is still evident in the literature upon which this study is based. Practitioners scrutinize diseases in a very particular way that is the driving force, the essential ideology, of medical practice. This way of knowing the body marks a crucial difference between the 'person presenting symptoms' of agoraphobia and 'the agoraphobe,' or the sense in which pathology *essentially* defines an individual's very identity. 'The agoraphobe' is a subject-object in relation to the discipline of psychiatry and its gaze. A material-discursive account of agoraphobia enhances our understanding of the multiplicity and materialization of agoraphobic bodies, but it is important to preserve Foucault's insight into psychiatry as a set of power relations, relations that are central in the history of psychiatry in general and agoraphobia in particular.

A major emphasis in this study has been the marginalization of psychoanalysis by mainstream, neo-positivist biopsychiatry. The point of this aspect of my study has not been to rally in support of a psychoanalytic understanding of agoraphobia per se, as though it were somehow outside the exclusionary relations of psychiatric knowledge by virtue of having itself been excluded from them. Although psychoanalysis offered a refreshing departure from strictly biological explanations of mental illness, the basic premises and concepts of psychoanalysis have come under intense and important criticism. To clarify, as compared with positivist and neo-positivist psychiatry, psychoanalysis was for all intents and purposes *social* – but only in a very qualified sense, to the extent that Freud's ideas were specific to his milieu. It can be no coincidence, for example, that in seeking to offer an account of how values are reproduced and internalized, the mind as he described it, divided as it was into private and public, mirrored the bourgeois ideological doctrine of separate spheres. Subsequent psychoanalytic literature did the same by adopting Freud's framework (irrespective of modifications and developments in theory). Feminists have also taken particular issue with his asocial account of subjectivity, as though subjectivity simply develops out of inherent and invariable desires. They have contested the universalistic claims of psychoanalysis, arguing for further pluralism in at least two respects.

First, to the extent that dominant values are encoded in its framework, psychoanalysis presumes a homogeneous society. There is a tendency towards normative heterosexuality as well as an exclusive emphasis on the unfolding of the family drama as the key moment in the origin and development of the psyche. The Oedipus complex, that crucial trans-historical foundation of Freudian theory, presumes the family, or rather a certain kind of family, to be fundamental to the development of subjectivity. Yet non-familial events could equally be cast in that developmental role. As Michèle Barrett writes, it is not that 'psychoanalysis overtly preaches "familialism" as a good thing (although it may do on occasion) but that its entire frame of reference is locked into the assumption that all interpretation proceeds from the centrality of "original" family experiences.' She continues, 'Its operation is [thus] deeply "familialist" in the sense that it cannot imagine anything else' (Barrett, 1991:117). Through its insistence that the self can be understood solely in terms of the psyche, it offers only a partial concept of the social: psychoanalysis forecloses on the relevance of social processes that are not explicitly familialist even as it offers an account of their internalization.

Second, this foreclosure informs feminist critiques that target the failure of psychoanalysis – recall its association of civilization (read, middle-class whiteness) with neuroses – to explain how we become 'raced' and classed. Elizabeth Abel writes that the 'traditional indifference of psychoanalysis to racial, class, and cultural differences, and the tendency of psychoanalysis to insulate subjectivity from social practices and discourses all run contrary to a feminism increasingly attuned to the power of social exigencies and differences in the constitution of subjectivity.' If psychoanalysis is to be useful for contemporary feminism, she argues, it 'needs some infusion of the social – whether the "social" is construed as the technologies that regulate desire or ... as the roles of race and class in a diversified construction of subjectivity' (Abel, 1990:184).

Abel's remark is ironic, given that it was the perceived *over-sociality* of psychoanalysis that gave rise to its eventual exclusion from mainstream psychiatry following the publication of *DSM-III*. Still, she has a point: informed by a bourgeois sensibility, psychoanalysis reflects class ideals (crystallized by the requirement that patients pay a fee for this service as a condition of treatment). But I would not characterize its silence on 'race' and class, as Abel puts it, as (merely) a sign of 'indifference.' The impact of 'indifference,' as I tried to show in chapter 4, is that a silent or absent discourse still speaks volumes.

Similarly, given the powerful associations between 'race' and disease that were common when Freud was writing (and, disturbingly, still are common today), it is arguable that as both a medical scientist and a Jew he constructed psychoanalysis as racially neutral in order to eclipse the racial 'truth' of medicine and psychiatry. Emil Kraepelin for example, the leading nineteenth-century German psychiatrist whose ideas inspired the biopsychiatric (re)turn following *DSM-III*, spoke of the 'frequency of psychopathic predisposition in Jews ... their harping criticism, their rhetorical and theatrical abilities' (Kraepelin, 1992 [1919]:264). These characteristics spoke to a need to 'domesticate' the Jews, and, epitomizing the modern medical subject, even 'Jewish physicians themselves accepted the premise of their own potential mental collapse because of the stress of the "modern life" into which they entered simply by becoming part of the medical establishment' (Gilman, 1993:93). Since most early analysts were Jews, 'the lure of psychoanalysis for them may well have been its claims for a universalization of human experience and an active exclusion of the importance of race from its theoretical framework' (6) – and, I add, from its conception of social order.

But in spite of its subversive potential within the realm of medicine, as a central force in the larger transformation of the West into a 'therapeutic culture' (Barrett, 1991:115), psychoanalysis has been criticized as a normalizing episteme. Foucault, of course, is the best-known exponent of this particular line of thinking, and has characterized psychoanalysis as a regime of truth through which individuals become subjects of (its) knowledge and through which social cohesion could be maintained. He has argued against psychiatry as a non-autonomous human science and technology of power, and in particular against psychoanalysis as a discourse (and practice) of normalization. As he wrote in the first volume of *The History of Sexuality*, 'one denounces Freud's conformism, the normalizing functions of psychoanalysis ... and all the effects of integration ensured by the "science" of sex and the barely equivocal practices of sexology' (Foucault, 1978:5). Even though psychoanalysis challenged dominant biogenic notions of mental illness – 'it assumes an adversary position with respect to the theory of degenerescence' or the 'perversion-heredity-degenerescence system' (119) – Foucault contended that the personality should be understood as a style of behaviour and not as an objective theory of a totality of functional components (Dreyfus, 1987:312). As he wrote in *The Order of Things*, 'nothing is more alien to psychoanalysis than anything resembling a general theory of man' (Foucault, 1970:376).

In later work, Foucault focused on the social effects of the human sciences, locating the conditions of possibility for pathology within the social world (and even sociology). He wrote, 'The analyses of our psychologists and sociologists, which turn the patient into a deviant and which seek the origin of the morbid in the abnormal are ... above all a projection of cultural themes' (Foucault, 1987:63). Psychoanalysis, therefore, was not liberating but rather represented the zenith of a 'normalizing confessional technology' developed by early Christians (Dreyfus, 1987:318). Foucault was interested in 'truth-effects' and argued that the individual with desires – the focus of psychoanalytic theory – was produced first by Catholic confessional practices that imposed 'meticulous rules of self-examination' and 'attributed more and more importance in penance ... to all the insinuations of the flesh: thoughts, desires, voluptuous imaginings, delectations, combined movements of the body and the soul; henceforth all this had to enter, in detail, into the process of confession and guidance.' He went on to say, 'According to the new pastoral, sex must not be named imprudently, but its aspects, its correlations, and its effects must be pursued down to their slenderest ramifications ... everything had to be told' (Foucault, 1978:19). Desire was an 'evil that afflicted the whole man,' and one had always to be suspicious, and always to work to understand the true motivations behind it. Quoting from an actual confession manual, Foucault demonstrated its remarkable resonance with Freud's psychoanalytic method:

> Examine diligently, therefore, all the faculties of your soul: memory, understanding, and will. Examine with precision all your senses as well ... Examine, moreover, all your thoughts, every word you speak, and all your actions. Examine even unto your dreams, to know if, once awakened, you did not give them your consent. And finally, do not think that in so sensitive and perilous a matter as this, there is anything trivial or insignificant. (20)

Like confessional practices, psychoanalysis was a technique for the deployment of sexuality, having 'the task of alleviating the effects of repression (for those who were in a position to resort to psychoanalysis) that this prohibition [on incest] was capable of causing' and allowing 'individuals to express their incestuous desire in discourse' (129).

The danger in this, however, was that psychoanalysts were thus the arbiters of lifestyle, and the self-inspection of psychoanalysis/confession had become a way of life, a technology of the self (Foucault, 1988) seeping out past the limits of a period of therapy and the examination of a specific problem, and manifesting as norms based on an alleged science of human nature, the 'philosophical status of man' (Foucault, 1973:198), and consistent with the individualism of Western liberal democracies, where psychological expertise and psychotherapeutics in general have emerged to play a crucial role in the government of subjectivity (see Rose, 1989). Biopower and normative social control, effected through the production of psychoanalytic truth, permeated every aspect of people's lives, turning everyone into self-normalizing and self-regulating subjects who strive to ensure that all their actions and thoughts conform to what science had shown to be normal, healthy, and productive (Dreyfus, 1987:319).[3] As Dreyfus writes, 'the ultimate form of alienation in our society is not repression but the constitution of the isolated individual subject to which all psychiatries contribute.' Dreyfus continues,

> Just as an individual ... comes to have a one-dimensional, normalizing understanding of reality, which every anomaly must finally be made to yield to its truth and confirm his systematic interpretation, so our culture, in its pursuit of objective truth and the total ordering of all beings for the sake of efficiency, health, and productivity, focused in the paradigms of the panopticon and the confessional couch, has reached a stage in which human beings can only show up as sexual individuals, each striving to be a normal subject so as to maximize his [sic] human potential. (330)

Moreover, the threat of sexuality, produced as dangerous by psychoanalysis, was accessible only in the context of 'the calm violence' (Foucault, 1970:377) of the analyst-patient relationship, that is, with the guidance of an authority, the analyst, whose expert knowledge provided the necessary remedy for the psychical threat looming within. In other words, empirical knowledge of the individual was made possible by 'the regulated organization of persons under the gaze of authority' (Rose, 1994:61).

Of all the psychiatries, Foucault was most critical of psychoanalysis, arguing that it was, from its origins in the nineteenth century, a 'reconstitution of medical power as truth-producer, in a space arranged so that the production would always remain perfectly adapted to that power' (Foucault, 1994e:47). Yet it was much more explicitly social than recent positivist interpretations. Indeed, the recent (re)turn to positivist biopsychiatry epitomizes the authoritative gaze Foucault describes; the privilege and power of the *DSM*, as a technology implicated in the government of human subjects (Rose, 1989:ix) through the regulation and organization of the 'normal' and the 'mentally ill' is a testament to this. I am not quite ready, therefore, to let go of Foucault's subject-object, for without it there would be no pathological Other(ing) by/for the Clinic – psychoanalytic or otherwise – to take as problematic. As Foucault himself has stated, 'power relations constituted the a priori of psychiatric practice. They condition the operation of the mental institution; they distributed relationships between individuals within it; they governed the forms of medical intervention' (Foucault, 1994e:48).

Accordingly, I maintain that agoraphobic bodies occupy a theoretically vital position in relation to the Clinic. The process of their truth-production as subject-objects of a certain (diagnosable) type has been an implicit concern of this book, alongside my endeavour to provide a material-discursive account of agoraphobia. As a disease concept that contains within it a normative theory of social order, agoraphobia has shown itself to have a highly variable and shifting ontology. The conception of society it invokes, what I have termed the 'psychiatric narrative,' encompasses a set of regulative cultural assumptions and practices, revealing that the process of narrating social order entails the crucial inextricability of psychiatric-scientific discourse and dominant sociocultural imperatives of power and exclusion.

Notes

1. Introduction: A Sociology of Psychiatry

1 This is a scene from the movie *Copycat*, in which Sigourney Weaver plays an agoraphobic forensic psychiatrist.
2 This is an un-refereed website.
3 The online version of the article included a link to a quiz entitled 'Are You a Phobia Expert?' The preamble read: 'Phobia, schmobia. Why can't people just get over themselves?' And later: 'Everybody knows about claustrophobia (confined spaces), acrophobia (heights) and agoraphobia (public spaces), but there's a lot more out there to worry about. Here are 10 other everyday phobias you might not even realize you have – until now' (Gregg, 2001).
4 See Berrios and Link (1995) for a good, if short, account of the history of anxiety disorders. It is written primarily from the perspective of French and German physicians but is relatively consistent with the English-language account offered here.
5 See Micale (1995 especially pp. 66–88) and Tomes (1994) for expanded versions of this brief historiography of hysteria.
6 See Rose (1998) for his especially lucid analysis of the psychological sciences as a technology of power within liberal democracies. As he explains (following Foucault), such societies do not exercise power through the domination and coercion of their citizens; rather, they achieve government through educating citizens to be 'free' to act in accordance with certain norms and to regulate themselves: 'The apparently "public" issue of rationalities of government is fundamentally linked to the apparently "private" question of how we should behave, how we should regulate our own conduct, how we should judge our behavior and that of others' (Rose, 1998:76–7).

7 In its early days the discourse of agoraphobia unfolded in the United States, the United Kingdom, and certain other countries such as France and Germany. It is still a culture-bound disorder not highly prevalent outside North America and Western Europe. That being said, according to *DSM-IV-TR*, epidemiological studies have found panic disorder throughout the world. Accordingly, there has been some recent recognition by the American Psychiatric Association that cultural considerations need to be taken into account when applying the manual's criteria to different ethnic and cultural groups. In *DSM-IV-TR*, for example, information related to cultural considerations is included with the categories in order to 'increase sensitivity to variations in how mental disorders may be expressed in different cultures and ... reduce the possible effect of unintended bias stemming from the clinician's own cultural background' (APA, 2000:xxxiv). The manual's authors note that in 'some cultures, Panic Attacks may involve intense fear of witchcraft or magic,' and that 'some cultural or ethnic groups restrict the participation of women in public life, and this must be distinguished from Agoraphobia' (436). Still, the discourse of this disease is normatively and persistently American. This character is due in large part to the *DSM* and the central role this document and its values have played (especially since 1980) in shaping contemporary psychiatry both in the United States and elsewhere. To ensure that they receive funding and that their ideas (and publications) are taken seriously, American and non-American psychiatrists alike have had to adopt the categories of the *DSM*, or risk professional marginalization.

8 Since collecting my data, Medline has expanded its scope to include literature from 1950.

2. Urban Modernity and Social Change: Diagnosing Alienation

1   Cf. Hansen (1992), who makes this argument about the 'discovery' of homosexuality in America.

2   Hansen notes that late-nineteenth-century American physicians recognized that 'cities might [also] harbor numerous [sexual] inverts' (Hansen, 1992:116).

3   Freud pursued these ideas in *Civilization and Its Discontents* as well, arguing that the demands of instinct and the moral restrictions of civilization were in constant conflict (because there was a 'tendency on the part of civilization to restrict sexual life') (Freud, 1982 [1929]:41). Freud did not attribute modern psychical problems solely to the pressures of modern urban living. He cited several expert opinions on the topic and asserted that while they

were not wrong, they failed to consider the 'undue suppression of the sexual life in civilized peoples (or classes) as a result of the "civilized" sexual morality which prevails among them' (1950b [1908]:80). As we shall see later, subsequent psychoanalytic understandings of agoraphobia expressed a similar concern through their preoccupation with urban streets as threatening and seductive.

4 Modern urban phobias were among their concerns (see Vidler, 1993, 2000). Agoraphobia in particular was taken as proof of the dangers of urbanism, and as one planner, Camillo Sitte (1843–1903), wrote, 'recently a unique nervous disorder has been diagnosed – "agoraphobia" ... a very new and modern ailment. Numerous people are said to suffer from it, always experiencing a certain anxiety or discomfort, whenever they have to walk across a vast empty place.' He continued, 'One naturally feels very cozy in small, old plazas,' but in 'our modern gigantic plazas, with their yawning emptiness and oppressive ennui, the inhabitants of snug old towns suffer attacks of this fashionable agoraphobia' (Sitte, 1965 [1889]:45). Credit for the discovery of this passage in Sitte's text goes to Vidler; see in particular his *Warped Space* (Vidler, 2000) for a much richer account of the relationship between modern urban space and phobic anxiety than I have been able to offer here.

5 Cf. Lefebvre, who refers to them as 'doctors of space' (Lefebvre, 1991:99).

3. Explaining Agoraphobia: Three Frameworks

1 Rosenberg observes a persistent dichotomy within psychiatric practice between that which takes place in institutions (hospitals, asylums) and that which takes place in private practices with still-functioning but symptom-bearing patients (Rosenberg, 1992:251).

2 Westphal also described a fourth case, of a man with hypochondria who suffered bouts of agoraphobia.

3 He tried cultivating their will power, having them walk daily through the areas they feared, giving them wine, beer, and various remedies, and even applying electrical shocks to the upper spine, neck, and jaw.

4 I thank an anonymous reviewer for the insight that 'psychiatrists understand that poverty is a root cause of many if not most psychiatric disorders, but they do not give their patients money (perhaps they should!).'

5 Antidepressants fall into four major sub-categories, namely, tricyclics, monoamine oxidase inhibitors (MAOIs), heterocyclics, and selective serotonin reuptake inhibitors (SSRIs) (Canadian Pharmaceutical Association, 1996:4). Tricylcic antidepressants include clomipramine (also used to treat

obsessive-compulsiveness), desipramine, doxepin, lofrepramine, nortrip-
tyline, trimipramine. SSRIs that appear in this literature are mostly fluoxetine and fluvoxamine. References to MAOIs are largely to phenelzine.

6 This debate has widened along with the growth of the antidepressants market and an accompanying increase in diagnoses of depression. See Healy
(1997, 2000).

7 Valued for its effect of fear reduction and its ability to block panic before it
happens (Laybourne and Redding, 1985; Mavissakalian, 1993; Schwartz and
Val, 1984), imipramine has long been preferred by physicians, despite evidence that the MAOI phenelzine is equally or more effective (Harnett, 1990;
Lydiard and Ballenger, 1987; Mountjoy et al., 1977; Ravaris, 1981; Rohs and
Noyes, 1978; Sheehan et al., 1980). Presumably the preference for imipramine over phenelzine relates to the dietary restrictions associated with
MAOIs; nor does imipramine have the unwanted side effect of weight gain,
for which phenelzine is known (see Pohl et al., 1982; Solyom et al., 1991).

8 Anxiolytics can also be subdivided into two main categories, namely, high
potency benzodiazepines (such as Xanax) and azaspirodecanediones (such
as buspirone) (Canadian Pharmaceutical Association, 1996:7). The benzodiazepines – also known as 'housewives' pills' (Harding, 1986:52) – have been
the more popular of the two.

9 I develop this point in chapter 5.

10 An anecdote by Theodor Reik is worth quoting at length: 'Freud did not
often speak about himself and his intimate life. My impression is that he
became more confidential after his seventieth birthday; at least he then told
me some things about himself which I could never have guessed. One
memory is the most important. I accidentally met him one evening in the
Kaertnerstrasse in Vienna and accompanied him home. We talked mostly
about analytic cases during the walk. When we crossed a street that had
heavy traffic, Freud hesitated as if he did not want to cross. I attributed the
hesitancy to the caution of the old man, but to my astonishment he took my
arm and said, "You see, there is a survival of my old agoraphobia, which
troubled me much in my younger years." We crossed the street and picked
up our conversation after his remark, which had been casually made. His
confession of a lingering fear of crossing open places ... made ... a strong
impression upon me ... The free admission that his neurosis had left this
scar on his emotional life would have added to my admiration of his great
personality' (Reik, 1948:15).

11 This anecdote is actually taken from an essay on the psychopathology of
hysteria. It describes such a common symptom of agoraphobia – the inability to go into shops alone – that it warrants inclusion here.

12 Although Tucker (not an analyst) blames mothers for their daughters' mental demise, fathers were not entirely free of culpability. He wrote that the 'personality and influence of the father also contribute to the problem, particularly if he is overprotective or overpunitive, and there may be a problem in the patient's relationship to both parents. However, the father is more frequently a passive individual who plays a relatively minor role of influence on the patient' (Tucker, 1956:829).

13 Separation anxiety and over-parenting are not fundamentally psychoanalytic concepts per se, so it is important to note that practitioners of other persuasions also examine the question of parental over- and under-protectiveness. See, for example, Arrindell and Emmelkamp (1986); Parker (1979); Solyom et al. (1976); also Faravelli et al. (1991); Shear (1996); Silove (1986); Wiborg and Dahl (1997).

14 Another incident also played an important role in Peter's turnaround, namely, his overhearing Fink on the phone reprimanding someone in German. Peter was reminded of his 'very energetic' father, who 'handled the occupation forces in a clever way protecting his family and the village from excessive demands and arbitrariness' (Fink, 1989:484).

15 His *Fears and Phobias*, published in 1969, is still widely cited today.

16 Recently an attempt was made by Yaniv to disprove the view that the high cost of psychotherapy helps to ensure its success. The thinking behind such a view is that because clients pay a fee they may try harder to get well in order to justify the expense. Yaniv (who, it should be noted, is affiliated with the Israeli National Insurance Institute) contends that there is 'little scientific evidence supporting the effectiveness of psychotherapy in these conditions' (Yaniv, 1998:238). Advocating publicly funded treatment (for mild disorders) in community clinics or through corporate-financed mental health programs, he maintains that 'while psychotherapy reduces the risk of suffering an attack on the way to/from work, the cost of therapy might reduce the tendency to take risks, thus acting to undermine treatment.' In other words, the high cost of psychotherapy may actually encourage work avoidance in less severe cases, thereby aggravating the phobic disorder and adversely affecting the economy (240). As an insurer, Yaniv's interest in reducing costs borne by third-party payers is self-evident. But he is not alone in his denigration of psychoanalysis for its lack of scientific status. With the groundwork for its decline laid by the release of *DSM-III*, psychoanalysis has long been an easy target for scientific rationalists, and in this respect it is no surprise that its published contribution to the discourse of agoraphobia significantly diminished after 1980, even though the number of both psychoanalysts and psychoanalytic patients has increased. See Mitchell and Black (1995:xviii).

17 See Cobb (1983) for a review of exposure *in vivo*, and Ferentz (1990) for a general overview of therapies including exposure.
18 Therapists debate various issues pertaining to cognitive and behaviour therapies, such as the merits of cognitive therapies versus exposure methods, but frequently the therapies are used together. See Bouchard et al. (1996); Burke et al. (1997); Emmelkamp et al. (1978); Hout et al. (1994); Last et al. (1984); Norton et al. (1983).

4. The Prerogative of Being 'Normal': Gender, 'Race,' and Class

1 Who, by accommodating their fear, were in effect behaving like women, thereby feminizing agoraphobia in yet another respect.
2 'Passing' in this sense has added significance in the contemporary context. A relatively recent study of agoraphobia and sex-role stereotyping revealed that agoraphobic women were more stereotypically feminine and less masculine. The authors, Chambless and Mason, argued that fearful behaviour was more acceptable for women because 'women are taught and allowed to be fearful and to perceive themselves as incompetent and helpless without male assistance.' They found that not only were women more likely to become agoraphobic, but even among a mixed sample, women were more avoidant, especially when 'functioning without the protective shield of men.' As Chambless and Mason put it, 'a society that does not teach women to be instrumental, competent and assertive rather than just nurturant and expressive, is one that breeds phobic women' (Chambless and Mason, 1986:234).
3 The indefinite boundaries between masculinity and femininity, war neurosis and agoraphobia are suggested even more evocatively by the words of a military psychiatrist who wrote in 1981 that 'agoraphobia does not respect ... military rank' (Hudson, 1981:511–12). Although neither of the two patients he describes in his report had actually served in any war (one was a newly inducted officer and the other an electronics technician), the writer makes a point of saying that agoraphobia 'has an important bearing on military psychiatry because it is a common disorder' and occurs in 'physicians, college professors and officers, as well as enlisted men' (511–12). In other words, it could easily be missed in military *men* who *have* experienced combat, a possibility suggesting that war neurosis and agoraphobia actually may have overlapped.
4 In a clear case of life imitating art, these words resonate with an article that recently appeared in the *Globe and Mail* detailing the discovery by some members of Canada's military that it is in fact all right and even desirable

for male soldiers to cry. The writer describes how 'a major with decades of experience in the ... toughest, most battle-hardened regiments, found himself in a circle with 30 of his military comrades, crying, confessing and searching for his inner soldier.' The sensitivity training seminar in which this outpouring took place opened 'emotional channels that had been blocked by years in the military, where the expression of feelings has long been discouraged.' Advocates of institutionalized sensitivity training were 'laughed out of a lot of offices,' because, in the words of the major described above, 'You were taught to hide your feelings. To show your feelings was to show weakness ... Boys don't cry. They fight.' This point was underscored by the comments of Sergeant Patricia Callahan at the end of the article: 'I never saw this before ... Men are in there crying. I think it's long overdue.' See Cheney (2001:A3).

5 It is worth noting that here doctors made a point of describing the physical features of their female patients, but did not do so when describing their male patients. For example, Dr Potter's (1882) patient was a brunette, Dr Van Horn's (1886) was 'of a large, robust frame,' and Dr Records's (1896) was of medium size with fair complexion and blue eyes.

6 An anecdote may serve to clarify. A colleague once began to tell me a story about a young man in her class, a 'big black guy.' As it turned out, his *blackness* had absolutely nothing to do with the story she then proceeded to tell about him. In an ethnomethodological sense, her racialization of this man exemplifies just how common it is to hear people mention 'race' when they are describing people who are not white, yet it is 'normal' to talk about white people as *just* people, and it is 'normal' to *assume* and *imagine* the people who are *just* people as being white.

7 The irony, though, is that racialized bodies historically have been considered different enough to be racialized and too different to be normal, yet 'same enough' (like lab mice) to be reliably experimented upon, with the results safely applicable to whites.

8 1.28 for African Americans as against 1.00 for whites, with $P < 0.01$; 1.00 for the highest quartile of SES (socioeconomic status) as against 1.80 for the lowest quartile, with $P < 0.001$. See Boyd et al. (1990:318).

9 The Tuskegee study is not the only example of the abuse of African Americans for the purposes of medical experimentation. See also Lederer (1995:115–16) for a description of the antebellum gynaecologist J. Marion Sims's experiment with three Alabama slaves whom he purchased expressly for the purpose of practising a technique for repairing postpartum vaginal tears. Lederer also describes the work of another physician on remedies for heatstroke, which he tested on a slave made to sit naked on

a stool inside a heated pit. The cultural effects of these damaging research practices were compounded by the prospect of urban 'night-doctors' taking African Americans away dead or alive for use in medical research (Gamble, 1997b:1774). Gloria Fry observes that coinciding with the great migration of African Americans to industrial urban centres between 1880 and the end of the First World War, the entrenched notion that city people were in danger of being kidnapped and murdered was possibly the most effective rumour deliberately circulated by Southern labour-conscious whites seeking to prevent blacks from migrating to the North (Fry, 1975:171–3; see also p. 210). As one statement in an 1896 issue of the *Journal of American Folklore* read, 'On dark nights negroes in cities consider it dangerous to walk alone on the streets because the "night-doctor" is abroad. He does not hesitate to choke colored people to death in order to obtain their bodies for dissection. The genesis of this belief from the well-known practice of grave-robbing for medical colleges, several of which are located in Southern cities, is sufficiently evident' (in Fry, 1975:173). Though no evidence has been found that these 'night riders' actually existed, through the substantial folklore about it the situation was defined as real and was therefore real in its consequences (cf. Thomas and Thomas, 1928 [1919]). So a move from this specific fear among African Americans to *agoraphobic* fear did not require the exercise of much imagination; here is a passage from a *Boston Herald* article, also described by Gloria Fry: 'The colored women are so worked up over this phantom that they will not venture out at night, or in the daytime in any sequestered place' (in Fry, 1975:201).

10 Whites had the lowest admission rates, especially for persons aged 25 to 44 (United States Department of Health and Human Services, 1987:74).

11 In 1998, African Americans paid a total of 89.8 million visits to physicians in their offices, whereas whites saw physicians in their offices 702.2 million times. This translates into 259 visits per 100 African Americans, and 317 visits per 100 whites.

12 I owe this insight to Jackie Duffin.

5. The *DSM* and the Decline of the Social

1 See Moncrieff and Crawford (2001) for their analysis of continuity and change within British psychiatry in the twentieth century. On the basis of a historical examination of the contents of the *British Journal of Psychiatry*, they argue that there is little support for the widely held notion that major shifts have occurred in the explanatory paradigms used by psychiatry, though they acknowledge that such a claim may not be supported by the

examination of only one journal. I contend that the analysis of psychiatric history must be anchored in the history of specific diseases, because as this book's examination of the psychiatric literature on agoraphobia reveals, the major psychiatric disciplines involved (physical medicine, psychoanalysis, and behaviourism) have coexisted throughout the history of this disease, with each dominating at different points in time. This development *is* suggestive of different paradigms, albeit indiscrete ones.

2 A contemporary of Freud's, Emil Kraepelin (1856–1926) was a German psychiatrist famous for his attempt to classify definite disease entities, especially manic-depressive psychosis and schizophrenia, and for his belief that empirical research was necessary if one wanted to demonstrate that serious mental disorders were organic and biochemical in origin. See Kraepelin (1962 [1918]).

3 Elizabeth Lunbeck writes of early-twentieth-century American psychiatrists: 'They were constantly chronicling their discipline's progress; they were united in their conviction that its Dark Ages were just behind them' (Lunbeck, 1994:6). A reading of the prefaces to *DSM-III* and later editions prompts the conclusion that not much has changed in this regard.

4 Clark rightly observes that anxiety (in this case *agoraphobic* anxiety) and panic 'represent two very different kinds of experience' yet are closely associated in modern clinical accounts. Panic tends to subside, whereas anxiety tends to be more 'insidious, long-lasting and far-reaching in its effects' (Clark, 1995:565). In this text I deliberately consider panic and agoraphobia together for the simple reason that the doctors and researchers do not distinguish between them very well, particularly in the most recent (post–*DSM-III*) discourse.

5 As well, gay activists had staged protests against the inclusion of homosexuality as a mental disorder at annual APA conventions, and finally the APA had no choice but to capitulate. See Caplan (1995) for an account of the controversies that surrounded these categories.

6 Tucked into the description of 'Agoraphobia without History of Panic Disorder' is the statement that in 'Panic Disorder with Agoraphobia, the panic attacks may be in full remission while the agoraphobia persists, but a history of Panic Disorder would preclude a current diagnosis of Agoraphobia without History of Panic Disorder. (Note: Panic Disorder does not preclude a pre-existing diagnosis of Agoraphobia without History of Panic Disorder.)'

7 It is interesting to note that Allen Frances had previously practised psychoanalysis. See, for example, Frances and Dunn (1975).

8 This marked an improvement over previous *DSM*s, but still no biblio-

graphic citations were included. To access these, one had to purchase the *Sourcebook*.

9 Note that in this manual the onset is described as later than it was in the earlier manuals, coinciding with the fact that by this time women were marrying increasingly later in life. Given that most agoraphobic women are married, there is a correlation suggested here between marriage and this mental illness.

10 That is, agoraphobia without panic disorder was diagnosed only when no panic criteria were met.

11 A 1987 study comparing the baseline characteristics and treatment outcomes of two panic disorder/agoraphobia populations who differed in their method of referral (indirectly solicited versus self-referred) found that indirectly solicited patients were more chronically and severely symptomatic, and more likely to accept treatment and remain in treatment than self-referred patients (Aronson, 1987). This finding suggests that treatment outcome studies may be affected by sample selection biases not dissimilar to those that preclude absolute comparisons between community and clinical findings.

12 It is common practice for studies to invoke old *DSM* criteria even when new ones are available at the time the research takes place. In some instances this may be owing to the lag-time between submission and publication of journal articles, or the possibility that the research began prior to the release of the newest *DSM*, but the practice still raises the issue of the validity of research results once new criteria have been adopted.

13 A description given prior to the 1995 merger between Upjohn and Pharmacia, when Upjohn was just Upjohn.

14 As noted in chapter 3, benzodiazepines continue to be prescribed for panic despite the fact that SSRIs are recommended as the preferred treatment approach.

15 This put Pfizer – the number one advertiser in medical/surgical journals in 2003 (May, 2004) – in direct competition with manufacturers of the generic version of this drug, the sales of which, by the end of 2002, totalled $635 million (*Drug Topics*, 2003). In 2002, sales of Xanax reached only $314 million (*PR Newswire*, 2003), and by 2003, following the 2002 merger of Pharmacia & Upjohn with the Monsanto agricultural biotechnology company (to become 'Pharmacia') and the subsequent acquisition of 'Pharmacia' in April 2003 by the Pfizer company (which purchased it for $56 billion dollars and so became the largest drug company in the world), sales of alprazolam diminished further, to $238 million dollars (Pfizer, 2003:7). This drop in sales sparked a massive advertising campaign that put Xanax on

the 'top 25' list of advertised pharmaceutical brands in 2003 (May, 2004:48). Pfizer recorded a growth in total pharmaceutical revenue in the United States of 12 and 32 per cent in 2002 and 2003 respectively, and internationally of 12 and 55 per cent in 2002 and 2003.

16 These figures include generic and patented drugs for both human and veterinary use.

17 Much of these profits have been earned in the United States, where, as Foote and Etheredge (2000) observe, antidepressant sales have grown from $2 billion USD in 1993 to over $7 billion USD in 1998. This growth may reflect improvements in existing technology, namely, the development of SSRIs, and/or simply the fruits of effective marketing. But it may also reflect a cultural tendency to over-medicalize and over-medicate ordinary exigencies of living. Cf. Metzl and Angel (2004).

18 Xanax is considered a 'legendary example' of this marketing strategy. See Parry (2003).

19 And, like Parsons's famous and deeply problematic AGIL model of the social system (i.e., Adaptation, Goal Attainment, Integration, and Latency; see Parsons [1951]), the DSM also provides 'boxes' in which all individuals are supposed to fit one way or another. Interestingly, however, the DSM contains no code for 'normal,' unlike Parsons, who outlines normal behaviour very clearly, at least in terms of gender roles.

20 Yet even some of the case literature reads like scientific reports. See, for example, Biran (1987); Kolko (1984); Jackson and Elton (1985).

21 In her essay 'The Rationality of Mania' (2000), Emily Martin locates the notions that 'rational thought would produce order, knowledge, and scientific truth' and that 'rational arrangements of time, space and bodies would yield efficient and productive societies' in the early part of the twentieth century. Judging from the amount and kind of research done in recent decades, I contend that these assumptions are certainly characteristic of recent neo-positivist biopsychiatry.

22 Cf. Martin (2000).

23 Bowker is concerned with the International Classification of Disease, a statistical manual very similar in its form and purpose to the DSM but pertaining to diseases in general. The reader may recall that DSM-III was intended to go beyond the ICD (9th edition), which did not address mental illnesses adequately.

24 Some diseases have no symptoms; some symptoms can themselves have symptoms (witness agoraphobia, which has been at different times a symptom of neurosis or anxiety disorder with its own symptoms). Sometimes symptoms are mistaken for diseases, as are syndromes, a term often used to

describe 'nameless diseases' (see Ziporyn, 1992:99–128). Diseases and disorders are often confused, though psychiatrists still distinguish between them, working from the premise that 'diseases represent a disturbed anatomical structure, while disorders represent a disturbed physiological function' (214 n16).

6. Conclusion: Doing Agoraphobia(s) – The Social Relations of Psychiatric Knowledge

1 The chronological inaccuracies and generalizations of Foucault's medical historical work have been the subject of much criticism and debate. Still, the point he makes is useful to consider because the 'gaze' he describes is a common point of departure for many critiques of medicine.
2 I owe this insight to Bart Simon.
3 Dreyfus notes that Foucault addressed only the Lacanian revision of Freud and speculates that object-relations theory, which emphasizes pre-Oedipal factors, shows the limitations of a purely Oedipal account and therefore approached Foucault's understanding of the self somewhat more favourably. Still, both the Lacanian and the object-relationist theories make causal claims that justify the normal/pathological structure, of which Foucault was deeply critical. See Dreyfus (1987:332 n5).

References

ABC News. 1999. 'Treatment for Panic Attacks.' *20/20*. Broadcast 24 February.

Abel, E. 1990. 'Race, Class, and Psychoanalysis? Opening Questions.' Pp. 184–204 in *Conflicts in Feminism*, ed. M. Hirsch and E.F. Keller. New York: Routledge.

Abraham, K. 1973 [1913]. 'A Constitutional Basis of Locomotor Anxiety.' Trans. D. Bryan and A. Strachey. Pp. 235–43 in *Selected Papers of Karl Abraham*, ed. E. Jones. London: Hogarth Press and the Institute of Psycho-Analysis.

Adler, J. 1997. 'The Dueling Diagnoses of Darwin (Discussion).' *Journal of the American Medical Association* 277:1275.

Agar, S.W. 1886. 'Some Social Questions in Connection with Nervous Disease.' *Birmingham Medical Review* 20:1–21.

Ahmad, T., J. Wardle, and P. Hayward. 1992. 'Physical Symptoms and Illness Attributions in Agoraphobia and Panic.' *Behavior Research and Therapy* 30:493–500.

Alexander, F. 1930. *The Psychoanalysis of the Total Personality: The Application of Freud's Theory of the Ego to the Neuroses*. New York and Washington, DC: Nervous and Mental Disease Publishing Co.

Allen, K.W. 1981. 'Nursing Care Study: Behavioural Treatment of an Agoraphobic.' *Nursing Times* 77(7):268–72.

American Medical Association. 1933. *A Standard Classified Nomenclature of Disease*. New York: Commonwealth Fund.

American Medico-Psychological Association [AMPA]. 1918. *Statistical Manual for the Use of Institutions for the Insane*. New York: n.p.

– 1920. *Statistical Manual for the Use of Institutions for Mental Diseases*. 2nd ed. Utica, NY: State Hospitals Press.

American Psychiatric Association [APA]. 1934. *Statistical Manual for the Use of Hospitals for Mental Diseases*. 6th ed. Utica, NY: Utica State Hospitals Press.

- 1952. *Diagnostic and Statistical Manual of Mental Disorders.* Washington, DC: American Psychiatric Association.
- 1968. *Diagnostic and Statistical Manual of Mental Disorders [DSM-II].* Washington, DC: American Psychiatric Association.
- 1980. *Diagnostic and Statistical Manual of Mental Disorders [DSM-III].* Washington, DC: American Psychiatric Association.
- 1987. *Diagnostic and Statistical Manual of Mental Disorders [DSM-III-R].* Washington, DC: American Psychiatric Association.
- 1994. *Diagnostic and Statistical Manual of Mental Disorders [DSM-IV].* Washington, DC: American Psychiatric Association.
- 2000. *Diagnostic and Statistical Manual of Mental Disorders [DSM-IV-TR].* Washington, DC: American Psychiatric Association.

Andrews, G., S. Freed, and M. Teesson. 1994. 'Proximity and Anticipation of a Negative Outcome in Phobias.' *Behavior Research and Therapy* 32(6):643–5.

Aronson, T.A. 1987. 'A Follow-up of Two Panic Disorder–Agoraphobic Study Populations: The Role of Recruitment Biases.' *Journal of Nervous and Mental Disease* 175(10):595–8.

Arrindell, W.A., and P.M. Emmelkamp. 1986. 'Marital Adjustment, Intimacy and Needs in Female Agoraphobics and Their Partners: A Controlled Study.' *British Journal of Psychiatry* 149:592–602.

Atwood, C.E. 1903. 'Do Our Present Ways of Living Tend to the Increase of Certain Forms of Nervous and Mental Disorder?' *New York Medical Journal* 77:1070–3.

August, A. 1994. 'How Separate a Sphere? Poor Women and Paid Work in Late-Victorian London.' *Journal of Family History* 19(3):285–309.

Bakker, A., A.J. van Balkom, P. Spinhoven, B.M. Blaauw, and R. van Dyck. 1998. 'Follow-up on the Treatment of Panic Disorder with or without Agoraphobia: A Quantitative Review.' *Journal of Nervous and Mental Disease* 186(7):414–19.

Ball, C.R. 1916. 'Discussion re: Patrick, 1916.' *Journal of the American Medical Association* 67:185.

Ballenger, J.C. 1987. 'Unrecognized Prevalence of Panic Disorder in Primary Care, Internal Medicine, and Cardiology.' *American Journal of Cardiology* 60:39J–47J.

Bandelow, B., J. Zohar, E. Hollander, S. Kasper, and H.J. Moller. 2002. 'World Federation of Societies of Biological Psychiatry (WFSBP) Guidelines for the Pharmacological Treatment of Anxiety, Obsessive-Compulsive, and Post-traumatic Stress Disorders.' *World Journal of Biological Psychiatry* 3(4):171–99.

Barad, K. 1999. 'Getting Real: Technoscientific Practices and the Materialization of Reality.' *Differences* 10(2):87–128.

Barker, P. 1991. *Regeneration*. London: Viking.

Barloon, T.J., and R. Noyes. 1997a. 'Charles Darwin and Panic Disorder.' *Journal of the American Medical Association* 277(2):138–41.

– 1997b. 'In Reply.' *Journal of the American Medical Association* 277:1276–7.

Barrett, M. 1991. *The Politics of Truth: From Marx to Foucault*. Oxford: Polity Press.

– 1999. *Imagination in Theory: Culture, Writing, Words, and Things*. New York: New York University Press.

Bartone, N. 1992. 'The Role of Marketing Research during Drug Development.' *Journal of Drug Issues* 22(2):295–303.

Beard, G.M. 1881. *American Nervousness, Its Causes and Consequences, A Supplement to Nervous Exhaustion (Neurasthenia)*. New York: Putnam.

Benedikt, M. 1870. 'Über Platzschwindel.' *Allgemeine Wiener Medizinische Zeitung* 15:488 90.

Benjamin, W. 1973. *Charles Baudelaire: A Lyric Poet in the Era of High Capitalism*. London: NLB.

Benjamin, W., and P. Demetz. 1978. *Reflections: Essays, Aphorisms, Autobiographical Writings*. New York: Harcourt Brace Jovanovich.

Berg, M., and G.C. Bowker. 1997. 'The Multiple Bodies of the Medical Record – Toward a Sociology of an Artefact.' *Sociological Quarterly* 38:513–37.

Bergler, E. 1935. 'Psychoanalysis of a Case of Agoraphobia.' *Psychoanalytic Review* 22:392–408.

Bernheimer, C., and C. Kahane, eds. 1985. *In Dora's Case: Freud – Hysteria – Feminism*. New York: Columbia University Press.

Berrios, G.E., and C. Link. 1995. 'Anxiety Disorders: Clinical Section.' Pp. 545–62 in *A History of Clinical Psychiatry: The Origin and History of Psychiatric Disorders*, ed. G.E. Berrios and R. Porter. New York: New York University Press.

Bignold, B.C. 1960. 'Agoraphobia: A Review of Ten Cases.' *Medical Journal of Australia* 2:332–3.

Biran, M.W. 1987. 'Two-stage Therapy for Agoraphobia.' *American Journal of Psychotherapy* 41(1):127–36.

Birk, L. 1978. 'Behavior Therapy and Behavioral Psychotherapy.' Pp. 433–58 in *The Harvard Guide to Modern Psychiatry*, ed. A.M. Nicholi, Jr. Cambridge, MA, and London: Belknap Press of Harvard University Press.

Blanco, I.M. 1989. 'Comments on "From Symmetry to Asymmetry" by Klaus Fink.' *International Journal of Psycho-Analysis* 70(pt 3):491–8.

Blodgett, A.N. 1887. 'A Case of Agoraphobia.' *Boston Medical and Surgical Journal* 117:407–10.

Booth, D.S. 1916. 'Discussion re: Patrick, 1916.' *Journal of the American Medical Association* 67:185.

Bordo, S. 1993. *Unbearable Weight: Feminism, Western Culture, and the Body.* Berkeley: University of California Press.

Botts, S.R. 1997. 'Managing Generalized Anxiety Disorder.' *Drug Topics*: S9–S12. Available online at ProQuest.

Bouchard, S., J. Gauthier, B. Laberge, D. French, M.H. Pelletier, and C. Godbout. 1996. 'Exposure versus Cognitive Restructuring in the Treatment of Panic Disorder with Agoraphobia.' *Behavior Research and Therapy* 34(3):213–24.

Bowker, G.C. 1998. 'The Kindness of Strangers: Kinds and Politics and Classification Systems.' *Library Trends* 47(2):255–93.

Bowker, G.C., and S.L. Star. 1999. *Sorting Things Out: Classification and Its Consequences.* Cambridge, MA: MIT Press.

Boyd, J.H., D.S. Rae, J.W. Thompson, B.J. Burns, K. Bourdon, B.Z. Locke, and D.A. Regier. 1990. 'Phobia: Prevalence and Risk Factors.' *Social Psychiatry and Psychiatric Epidemiology* 25(6):314–23.

Bradley, M.E. 1975. 'Nursing Care Study: Treatment of a Phobic Condition.' *Nursing Times* 71(25):964–7.

Briggs, L. 2000. 'The Race of Hysteria: "Overcivilization" and the "Savage" Woman in Late Nineteenth-Century Obstetrics and Gynecology.' *American Quarterly* 52(2):246–73.

Brooker, C. 1980. 'Nursing Care Study: The Behavioural Management of a Complex Case.' *Nursing Times* 76(9):367–9.

Brown, A.T. 1986. 'Coping with Agoraphobia: A Study of Strategies and Help-Seeking Behaviour.' Ph.D. thesis, Department of Sociology and Social Administration, University of Southampton.

Bruce, S.E., R.G. Vaslie, R.M. Goisman, C. Salzman, M. Spencer, J.T. Machan, and M.B. Keller. 2003. 'Are Benzodiazepines Still the Medication of Choice for Patients with Panic Disorder with or without Agoraphobia?' *American Journal of Psychiatry* 160(8):1432–8.

Burgin, V. 1993. 'The City in Pieces.' *New Formations* 20:33–45.

Burke, M., L.M. Drummond, and D.W. Johnston. 1997. 'Treatment Choice for Agoraphobic Women: Exposure or Cognitive-Behaviour Therapy?' *British Journal of Clinical Psychology* 36(pt 3):409–20.

Butler, J. 1993. *Bodies That Matter: On the Discursive Limits of 'Sex.'* New York: Routledge.

– 1997. *The Psychic Life of Power: Theories in Subjection.* Stanford: Stanford University Press.

Campbell, R.J. 1996. *Psychiatric Dictionary.* New York: Oxford University Press.

Canada, Patented Medicine Prices Review Board. 1998. 'Eleventh Annual

Report Year Ending December 31, 1998.' Ottawa: Patented Medicine Prices Review Board.

– 2002. 'Annual Report 2002.' Available online at http://www.pmprbcepmb. gc.ca/english/View.asp?x=223&mp=68. Accessed 15 June 2004.

Canadian Pharmaceutical Association. 1996. *Compendium of Pharmaceuticals and Specialties (Canada)*. Vol. 31. Ottawa: Canadian Pharmaceutical Association.

Canguilhem, G. 1989. *The Normal and the Pathological*. New York: Zone Books.

Caplan, P.J. 1995. *They Say You're Crazy: How The World's Most Powerful Psychiatrists Decide Who's Normal*. Reading, MA: Addison-Wesley.

Chambless, D.L., A.T. Beck, E.J. Gracely, and J.R. Grisham. 2000. 'Relationship of Cognitions to Fear of Somatic Symptoms: A Test of the Cognitive Theory of Panic.' *Depression and Anxiety* 11(1):1–9.

Chambless, D.L., and J. Mason. 1986. 'Sex, Sex-Role Stereotyping, and Agoraphobia.' *Behavior Research and Therapy* 24(2):231–5.

Cheney, P. 2001. 'Why Our Soldiers Are Fighting Tears.' *Globe and Mail*, 27 March, p. A3.

Chesler, P. 1972. *Women and Madness*. Garden City, NY: Doubleday.

Cixous, H., and C. Clément. 1986 [1975]. *The Newly Born Woman*. Trans. B. Wing. Minneapolis: University of Minnesota Press.

Clark, M. 1995. 'Anxiety Disorders: Social Section.' Pp. 563–72 in *A History of Clinical Psychiatry: The Origin and History of Psychiatric Disorders*, ed. G.E. Berrios and R. Porter. New York: New York University Press.

Clark, U.F. 1963. 'The Treatment of Hysterical Spasm and Agoraphobia by Behaviour Therapy.' *Behaviour Research and Therapy* 1(2–4):245–50.

Cloitre, M., K.A. Yonkers, T. Pearlstein, M. Altemus, K.W Davidson, T.A. Pigott, M.K. Shear, D. Pine, J. Ross, H. Howell, K. Brogan, N. Rieckmann, and L. Clemow. 2004. 'Women and Anxiety Disorders: Implications for Diagnosis and Treatment.' *CNS Spectrums* 9(9 Suppl. 8):1–16.

Cobb, J. 1983. 'Behaviour Therapy in Phobic and Obsessional Disorders.' *Psychiatric Developments* 1(4):351–65.

Coleman, M.D. 1982–3. 'Prestructural Determinants in a Case of Phobia.' *International Journal of Psychoanalytic Psychotherapy* 9:537–51.

Colp, R. 1997. 'The Dueling Diagnoses of Darwin (Discussion).' *Journal of the American Medical Association* 277:1275–6.

Compton, A. 1992a. 'The Psychoanalytic View of Phobias. Part I: Freud's Theories of Phobias and Anxiety.' *Psychoanalytic Quarterly* 61(2):206–29.

– 1992b. 'The Psychoanalytic View of Phobias. Part II: Infantile Phobias.' *Psychoanalytic Quarterly* 61(3):230–53.

– 1992c. 'The Psychoanalytic View of Phobias. Part III: Agoraphobia and Other Phobias of Adults.' *Psychoanalytic Quarterly* 61(3):400–25.

– 1992d. 'The Psychoanalytic View of Phobias. Part IV: General Theory of Phobias and Anxiety.' *Psychoanalytic Quarterly* 61(3):426–46.
– 1998. 'An Investigation of Anxious Thought in Patients with DSM-IV Agoraphobia/Panic Disorder: Rationale and Design.' *Journal of the American Psychoanalytic Association* 46(3):691–721.
Compton, W.C., M.G. Craske, D.F. Klein, J.F. Rosenbaum, M.A. Silverman, F. Busch, J.M. Meyer, and T. Shapiro. 1995. 'Agoraphobia and Panic States: Panel Report.' *Journal of the American Psychoanalytic Association* 43(1):207–21.
Cooksey, E.C., and P. Brown. 1998. 'Spinning on Its Axes: DSM and the Social Construction of Psychiatric Diagnosis.' *International Journal of Health Services* 28(3):525–54.
Cooper, R. 1984. 'A Note on the Biologic Concept of Race and Its Application in Epidemiologic Research.' *American Heart Journal* 108(3):715–22.
Cordes, E. 1872. 'Die Platzangst (Agoraphobie): Symptom einer Erschöpfungsparese.' *Archiv für Psychiatrie und Nervenkrankheiten* 3:521–74.
Cox, B.J., N.S. Endler, and R.P. Swinson. 1995. 'An Examination of Levels of Agoraphobic Severity in Panic Disorder.' *Behavior Research and Therapy* 33(1):57–62.
Cox, B.J., R.P. Swinson, G.R. Norton, and K. Kuch. 1991. 'Anticipatory Anxiety and Avoidance in Panic Disorder with Agoraphobia.' *Behavior Research and Therapy* 29(4):363–5.
Daigle, F. 1999. *Just Fine.* Trans. R. Majzels. Toronto: Anansi.
Davidoff, L., and C. Hall. 1987. *Family Fortunes: Men and Women of the English Middle Class, 1780–1850.* London: Hutchinson.
Deutsch, H. 1929. 'The Genesis of Agoraphobia.' *International Journal of Psycho-Analysis* 10:51–69.
Dillingham, W.P. 1911. *Reports of the Immigration Commission: Dictionary of Races or Peoples.* Washington, DC: United States Immigration Commission.
Dreyfus, H. 1987. 'Foucault's Critique of Psychiatric Medicine.' *Journal of Medicine and Philosophy* 12:311–33.
Drug Topics. 2002. 'US Top 200 Generic Drug Brands Ranked by Sales in Dollars for 2001.' *Drug Topics* 146(4):32. Available online at TableBase. Accessed 15 June 2004.
Drug Topics. 2003. 'US Top 200 Generic Prescription Drugs Ranked by Retail Sales in Dollars for 2002.' *Drug Topics* 147(7):57. Available online at TableBase. Accessed 15 June 2004.
Duffin, J.M. 1999. *History of Medicine: A Scandalously Short Introduction.* Toronto: University of Toronto Press.
Durkheim, E. 1933 [1893]. *The Division of Labor in Society.* New York: Free Press.

– 1951 [1897]. *Suicide: A Study in Sociology.* Glencoe, IL: Free Press.

Dyer, R. 2002. 'The Matter of Whiteness.' Pp. 9–14 in *White Privilege: Essential Readings on the Other Side of Racism*, ed. P.S. Rothenberg. New York: Worth.

Edlund, M.J. 1990. 'The Economics of Anxiety.' *Psychiatric Medicine* 8(2):15–26.

Ehrenreich, B., and D. English. 1979 [1978]. *For Her Own Good: 150 Years of the Experts' Advice to Women*. Garden City, NY: Anchor/Doubleday.

Ellenberger, H.F. 1970. *The Discovery of the Unconscious: The History and Evolution of Dynamic Psychiatry.* New York: Basic.

Emmelkamp, P.M., and A. Emmelkamp-Benner. 1975. 'Effects of Historically Portrayed Modeling and Group Treatment on Self-Observation: A Comparison with Agoraphobics.' *Behavior Research and Therapy* 13(2–3):135–9.

Emmelkamp, P.M., A.C. Kuipers, and J.B. Eggeraat. 1978. 'Cognitive Modification versus Prolonged Exposure In Vivo: A Comparison with Agoraphobics as Subjects.' *Behavior Research and Therapy* 16(1):33–41.

Engel, G.L. 1960. 'A Unified Concept of Health and Disease.' *Perspectives in Biology and Medicine* 3:459–85.

Engelhardt, H.T., Jr. 1976. 'Ideology and Etiology.' *Journal of Medicine and Philosophy* 1:256–68.

– 1978. 'Health and Disease: Philosophical Perspectives.' Pp. 599–606 in *Encyclopedia of Bioethics*, vol. 2, ed. W.T. Reich. New York: Free Press.

Errera, P. 1962. 'Some Historical Aspects of the Concept, Phobia.' *Psychiatric Quarterly* 36:325–36.

Evans, L.E., T.P. Oei, and H. Hoey. 1988. 'Prescribing Patterns in Agoraphobia with Panic Attacks.' *Medical Journal of Australia* 148(2):74–7.

Faravelli, C., C. Panichi, S. Pallanti, S. Paterniti, L.M. Grecu, and S. Rivelli. 1991. 'Perception of Early Parenting in Panic and Agoraphobia.' *Acta Psychiatrica Scandinavica* 84(1):6–8.

Fee, E. 1994. 'Man-Made Medicine and Women's Health: The Biopolitics of Sex/Gender and Race/Ethnicity.' Pp. 11–29 in *Women's Health, Politics, and Power: Essays on Sex/Gender, Medicine, and Public Health*, ed. E. Fee and N. Krieger. Amityville, NY: Baywood.

Fenichel, O. 1944. 'Remarks on the Common Phobias.' *Psychoanalytic Quarterly* 13:313–26.

Ferentz, K.S. 1990. 'Panic Disorder and Agoraphobia: Nondrug Treatment Options for Primary Care Physicians.' *Postgraduate Medicine* 88(2):185–92.

Fink, K. 1989. 'From Symmetry to Asymmetry.' *International Journal of Psycho-Analysis* 70(pt 3):481–9.

FitzGibbon, G.M. 1997. 'The Dueling Diagnoses of Darwin (Discussion).' *Journal of the American Medical Association* 277:1276.

Fodor, I. 1992. 'The Agoraphobic Syndrome: From Anxiety Neurosis to Panic

Disorder.' Pp. 177–205 in *Personality and Psychopathology: Feminist Reapprais-als*, ed. L.S. Brown and M. Ballou. New York and London: Guilford.

Foote, S.M., and L. Etheredge. 2000. 'Increasing Use of New Prescription Drugs: A Case Study.' *Health Affairs* 19(4):165–70. Available online at Pro-Quest. Accessed 21 September 2006.

Foucault, M. 1970. *The Order of Things: An Archaeology of the Human Sciences*. New York: Vintage.

– 1975 [1963]. *The Birth of the Clinic: An Archaeology of Medical Perception*. New York: Pantheon.

– 1978. *The History of Sexuality.* Vol. 1. New York: Vintage.

– 1979. *Discipline and Punish: The Birth of the Prison*. New York: Vintage.

– 1980. *Power/Knowledge: Selected Interviews and Other Writings by Michel Fou-cault, 1972–1977*. Ed. D. Gordon. New York: Pantheon.

– 1982. 'The Subject and Power.' Pp. 208–26 in *Michel Foucault: Beyond Structur-alism and Hermeneutics*, ed. H.L. Dreyfus and P. Rabinow. Chicago: Univer-sity of Chicago Press.

– 1984. 'Space, Knowledge, and Power.' Pp. 239–56 in *The Foucault Reader*, ed. P. Rabinow. New York: Pantheon.

– 1987. *Mental Illness and Psychology.* Berkeley: University of California Press.

– 1988. 'Technologies of the Self.' Pp. 16–49 in *Technologies of the Self: A Seminar with Michel Foucault*, ed. L.H. Martin, H. Gutman, and P.H. Hutton. Amherst, MA: University of Massachusetts Press.

– 1991. 'Questions of Method.' Pp. 73–86 in *Foucault Effect: Studies in Govern-mentality, with Two Lectures by and an Interview with Michel Foucault*, ed. C. Gordon, P. Miller, and G. Burchell. Chicago: University of Chicago Press.

– 1994a. 'The Birth of Biopolitics.' Pp. 73–9 in *Michel Foucault: Ethics: Subjectiv-ity and Truth*, vol. 1 of *Essential Works of Foucault, 1954–84*, ed. P. Rabinow. New York: New Press.

– 1994b. 'Genealogy and Social Criticism.' Pp. 39–45 in *The Postmodern Turn: New Perspectives on Social Theory*, ed. S. Seidman. Cambridge and New York: Cambridge University Press.

– 1994c. 'On the Government of the Living.' Pp. 81–5 in *Michel Foucault: Ethics: Subjectivity and Truth*, vol. 1 of *Essential Works of Foucault, 1954–84*, ed. P. Rabinow. New York: New Press.

– 1994d. 'The Politics of Health in the Eighteenth Century.' Pp. 90–105 in *Michel Foucault: Power*, vol. 3 of *Essential Works of Foucault, 1954–84*, ed. J. Faubion. New York: New Press.

– 1994e. 'Psychiatric Power.' Pp. 39–50 in *Michel Foucault: Ethics: Subjectivity and Truth*, vol. 1 of *Essential Works of Foucault, 1954–84*, ed. P. Rabinow. New York: New Press.

– 1994f. 'Truth and Power.' Pp. 111–33 in *Michel Foucault: Power*, vol. 3 of *Essential Works of Foucault, 1954–84*, ed. J. Faubion. New York: New Press.

– 2002. *Archaeology of Knowledge*. New York: Routledge.

Frances, A., and P. Dunn. 1975. 'The Attachment-Autonomy Conflict in Agoraphobia.' *International Journal of Psycho-Analysis* 56(4):435–9.

Franklin, D. 1987. 'The Politics of Masochism.' *Psychology Today* 21:52–7.

Franklin, S. 2001a. 'Biologization Revisited: Kinship Theory in the Context of the New Biologies.' Available online from the Department of Sociology, Lancaster University, at http://www.comp.lancs.ac.uk/sociology/papers/Franklin-Biologization.pdf. Version 28 November 2003. Accessed 13 August 2004. [This online paper may be cited in line with the usual academic conventions. You may also download it for your own personal use. This paper must not be published elsewhere (e.g., mailing lists, bulletin boards, etc.) without the author's explicit permission. But please note that it is a draft for discussion only. Many of the sources derive from presentations at recent seminars for which I have not cleared authors' permissions to make formal attributions. Please, therefore, do not quote from this paper. If you cite, copy, or quote this paper you must include this copyright note, this paper must not be used for commercial purposes or gain in any way, note you should observe the conventions of academic citation in a version of the following form: Sarah Franklin, 'Biologization Revisited: Kinship Theory in the Context of the New Biologies,' published by the Department of Sociology, Lancaster University, Lancaster LA1 4YL, UK at http:www.comp.lancs.ac.uk/sociology/papers/Franklin-Biologization.pdf]

– 2001b. 'Culturing Biology: Cell Lines for the Second Millennium.' Available online from the Department of Sociology, Lancaster University, at http://www.comp.lancs.ac.uk/sociology/papers/Franklin-Culturing-Biology.pdf. Version 28 November 2003. Accessed 13 August 2004. [This online paper may be cited in line with the usual academic conventions. You may also download it for your own personal use. This paper must not be published elsewhere (e.g., mailing lists, bulletin boards, etc.) without the author's explicit permission. But please note that it is a draft for discussion only. Many of the sources derive from presentations at recent seminars for which I have not cleared authors' permissions to make formal attributions. Please, therefore, do not quote from this paper. If you cite, copy, or quote this paper you must include this copyright note, this paper must not be used for commercial purposes or gain in any way, note you should observe the conventions of academic citation in a version of the following form: Sarah Franklin, 'Culturing Biology: Cell Lines for the Second Millennium,' published by the Department of Sociology, Lancaster University, Lancaster LA1 4YL, UK at http:www.comp.lancs.ac.uk/sociology/papers/Franklin-Culturing-Biology.pdf]

Freeman, H.P. 1998. 'The Meaning of Race in Science – Considerations for Cancer Research: Concerns of Special Populations in the National Cancer Program.' *Cancer* 82(1):219–25.

Freeman, J.K., J.H. Barnes, K.H. Summers, and S.L. Szeinbach. 1993. 'Modeling Physicians' Prescribing Decisions for Patients with Panic Disorder.' *Journal of Health Care Marketing* 13(1):34–9.

Freud, S. 1924 [1894]. 'The Defence Neuro-Psychoses.' Trans. J. Riviere. Pp. 59–75 in *Collected Papers*, vol. 1, ed. E. Jones. New York, London, Vienna: International Psycho-Analytic Press.

– 1950a [1909]. 'Analysis of a Phobia in a Five-Year-Old Boy.' Trans. A. and J. Strachey. Pp. 147–289 in *Collected Papers*, vol. 3, ed. E. Jones. London: Hogarth Press and the Institute of Psycho-Analysis.

– 1950b [1908]. '"Civilized" Sexual Morality and Modern Nervousness.' Trans. J. Riviere. Pp. 76–99 in *Collected Papers*, vol. 2, ed. E. Jones. London: Hogarth Press and the Institute of Psycho-Analysis.

– 1953 [1905, 1910]. 'Infantile Sexuality.' Trans. J. Strachey. Pp. 88–126 in *On Sexuality: Three Essays on the Theory of Sexuality and Other Works*, ed. A. Richards. London: Penguin.

– 1954a [1911]. 'A Hat as a Symbol of a Man (of Male Genitals).' Pp. 360–2 in *The Interpretation of Dreams*, trans. and ed. J. Strachey. London: George Allen & Unwin.

– 1954b [1911]. 'A "Little One" as the Genital Organ – "Being Run Over" as a Symbol of Sexual Intercourse.' Pp. 362–4 in *The Interpretation of Dreams*, trans. and ed. J. Strachey. London: George Allen & Unwin.

– 1954c. 'Arousal by Dreams – The Function of Dreams – Anxiety Dreams.' Pp. 573–87 in *The Interpretation of Dreams*, trans. and ed. J. Strachey. London: George Allen & Unwin.

– 1955a [1893]. 'Case Histories: Frau Emmy von N.' Pp. 48–105 in *The Standard Edition of the Complete Psychological Works of Sigmund Freud*, vol. 2, trans. and ed. J. Strachey et al. London: Hogarth Press and the Institute of Psycho-Analysis.

– 1955b [1893]. 'Case Histories: Miss Lucy R.' Pp. 106–24 in *The Standard Edition of the Complete Psychological Works of Sigmund Freud*, vol. 2, trans. and ed. J. Strachey et al. London: Hogarth Press and the Institute of Psycho-Analysis.

– 1955c [1918]. 'From the History of an Infantile Neurosis.' Pp. 7–124 in *The Standard Edition of the Complete Psychological Works of Sigmund Freud*, vol. 17,

trans. and ed. J. Strachey et al. London: Hogarth Press and the Institute of Psycho-Analysis.

– 1955d [1919]. 'Lines of Advance in Psycho-Analytic Therapy.' Pp. 157–68 in *The Standard Edition of the Complete Psychological Works of Sigmund Freud*, vol. 17, trans. and ed. J. Strachey et al. London: Hogarth Press and the Institute of Psycho-Analysis.

– 1955e [1919]. 'The Uncanny.' Pp. 217–56 in *The Standard Edition of the Complete Psychological Works of Sigmund Freud*, vol. 17, trans. and ed. J. Strachey et al. London: Hogarth Press and the Institute of Psycho-Analysis.

– 1955f [1919]. 'Introduction to *Psycho-Analysis and the War Neuroses*.' Pp. 205–16 in *The Standard Edition of the Complete Psychological Works of Sigmund Freud*, vol. 17, trans. and ed. J. Strachey et al. London: Hogarth Press and the Institute of Psycho-Analysis.

– 1959 [1925]. 'Inhibitions, Symptoms and Anxiety.' Pp. 87–156 in *The Standard Edition of the Complete Psychological Works of Sigmund Freud*, vol. 20, trans. and ed. J. Strachey et al. London: Hogarth Press and the Institute of Psycho-Analysis.

– 1962a [1894]. 'Obsessions and Phobias: Their Psychical Mechanism and Their Aetiology.' Pp. 74–82 in *The Standard Edition of the Complete Psychological Works of Sigmund Freud*, vol. 3, trans. and ed. J. Strachey et al. London: Hogarth Press and the Institute of Psycho-Analysis.

– 1962b [1894]. 'On the Grounds for Detaching a Particular Syndrome from Neurasthenia under the Description "Anxiety Neurosis."' Pp. 90–117 in *The Standard Edition of the Complete Psychological Works of Sigmund Freud*, vol. 3, trans. and ed. J. Strachey et al. London: Hogarth Press and the Institute of Psycho-Analysis.

– 1962c [1895]. 'A Reply to Criticisms of My Paper on Anxiety Neurosis.' Pp. 119–39 in *The Standard Edition of the Complete Psychological Works of Sigmund Freud*, vol. 3, trans. and ed. J. Strachey et al. London: Hogarth Press and the Institute of Psycho-Analysis.

– 1963 [1916–17]. 'Anxiety.' Pp. 392–411 in *The Standard Edition of the Complete Psychological Works of Sigmund Freud*, vol. 16, trans. and ed. J. Strachey et al. London: Hogarth Press and the Institute of Psycho-Analysis.

– 1964 [1932–6]. 'Anxiety and Instinctual Life.' Pp. 81–111 in *The Standard Edition of the Complete Psychological Works of Sigmund Freud*, vol. 22, trans. and ed. J. Strachey et al. London: Hogarth Press and the Institute of Psycho-Analysis.

– 1966a [1892–4]. 'Preface and Footnotes to the Translation of Charcot's Tuesday Lectures (1892–4).' Pp. 129–43 in *The Standard Edition of the Complete Psy-*

chological Works of Sigmund Freud, vol. 1, trans. and ed. J. Strachey et al. London: Hogarth Press and the Institute of Psycho-Analysis.

– 1966b [1893]. 'Extracts from the Fliess Papers (1950 [1892–1899]: Letter 14. (October 6, 1893).' Pp. 184–6 in *The Standard Edition of the Complete Psychological Works of Sigmund Freud*, vol. 1, trans. and ed. J. Strachey et al. London: Hogarth Press and the Institute of Psycho-Analysis.

– 1966c [1895]. 'Psychopathology.' Pp. 347–59 in *The Standard Edition of the Complete Psychological Works of Sigmund Freud*, vol. 1, trans. and ed. J. Strachey et al. London: Hogarth Press and the Institute of Psycho-Analysis.

– 1972 [1929]. *Civilization and Its Discontents*. Trans. J. Riviere. Ed. J. Strachey. London: Hogarth Press and the Institute of Psycho-Analysis.

– 1985 [1887–1904]. *The Complete Letters of Sigmund Freud to Wilhelm Fliess, 1887–1904*. Trans. and ed. J.M. Masson. Cambridge and London: Belknap Press of Harvard University Press.

Friedan, B. 1963. *The Feminine Mystique*. New York: Norton.

Friedman, D. 1974. 'Letter.' *British Medical Journal* 4:467–8.

Friedman, S. 1985. 'Implications of Object-Relations Theory for the Behavioral Treatment of Agoraphobia.' *American Journal of Psychotherapy* 39(4):525–40.

Frisby, D. 1986. *Fragments of Modernity: Theories of Modernity in the Work of Simmel, Kracauer, and Benjamin*. Cambridge, MA: MIT Press.

Fry, G. 1975. *Night Riders in Black Folk History*. Knoxville: University of Tennessee Press.

Fujimura, J. 1992. 'Crafting Science: Standardized Packages, Boundary Objects, and "Translation."' Pp. 168–211 in *Science as Practice and Culture*, ed. A. Pickering. Chicago: University of Chicago Press.

Fuss, D. 1998. 'Interior Chambers: The Emily Dickinson Homestead.' *Differences* 10(3):1–46.

Gamble, V.N. 1993. 'A Legacy of Distrust: African Americans and Medical Research.' *American Journal of Preventive Medicine* 9:35–8.

– 1997a. 'The Tuskegee Syphilis Study and Women's Health.' *Journal of the American Medical Women's Association* 52:195–6.

– 1997b. 'Under the Shadow of Tuskegee: African Americans and Health Care.' *American Journal of Public Health* 87:1773–8.

Garbowsky, M.M. 1989. *The House without the Door: A Study of Emily Dickinson and the Illness of Agoraphobia*. Rutherford, NJ, and London: Fairleigh Dickinson University Press and Associated University Presses.

Gardner, C.B. 1994. 'Out of Place: Gender, Public Places, and Situational Disadvantage.' Pp. 335–55 in *NowHere: Space, Time, and Modernity*, ed. R. Friedland and D. Boden. Berkeley: University of California Press.

Garfinkel, H. 1967. *Studies in Ethnomethodology.* Englewood Cliffs, NJ: Prentice-Hall.

Garland, A. 1992. 'In a Panic.' *Nursing Times* 88(52):25–7.

Gay, P. 1998. *Freud: A Life for Our Time.* New York and London: Norton.

Geertz, C. 1973. *The Interpretation of Cultures: Selected Essays.* New York: Basic.

Geiger, H.J. 1997. 'Annotation: Racism Resurgent – Building a Bridge to the 19th Century.' *American Journal of Public Health* 87(11):1765–6.

Gelder, M.G., and I.M. Marks. 1966. 'Severe Agoraphobia: A Controlled Prospective Trial of Behaviour Therapy.' *British Journal of Psychiatry* 112(484):309–19.

George, L.K., D.C. Hughes, and D.G. Blazer. 1986. 'Urban/Rural Differences in the Prevalence of Anxiety Disorders.' *American Journal of Social Psychiatry* 1:249–58.

Gibbs, P. 1929. '"Nerves" and City Civilization.' *Journal of Mental Science* 75(310):467–70.

Gilloch, G. 1996. *Myth and Metropolis: Walter Benjamin and the City.* Cambridge, UK: Polity Press in association with Blackwell.

Gilman, S.L. 1991. *The Jew's Body.* New York: Routledge.

– 1993. *Freud, Race, and Gender.* Princeton: Princeton University Press.

Gleason, M. 1999. *Normalizing the Ideal: Psychology, Schooling, and the Family in Postwar Canada.* Toronto: University of Toronto Press.

Goffman, E. 1961. *Asylums: Essays on the Social Situation of Mental Patients and Other Inmates.* Garden City, NY: Doubleday.

– 1963. *Stigma: Notes on the Management of Spoiled Identity.* Englewood Cliffs, NJ: Prentice-Hall and London: NLB.

Goisman, R.M., M.G. Warshaw, et al. 1994. 'Panic, Agoraphobia, and Panic Disorder with Agoraphobia. Data from a Multicenter Anxiety Disorders Study.' *Journal of Nervous and Mental Disease* 182(2):72–9.

Goisman, R.M., M.G. Warshaw, G.S. Steketee, E.J. Fierman, M.P. Rogers, I. Goldenberg, N.J. Weinshenker, R.G. Vasile, and M.B. Keller. 1995. 'DSM-IV and the Disappearance of Agoraphobia without a History of Panic Disorder: New Data on a Controversial Diagnosis.' *American Journal of Psychiatry* 152(10):1438–43.

Gordon, A.G. 1997. 'The Dueling Diagnoses of Darwin (Discussion).' *Journal of the American Medical Association* 277:1276.

Greenschpoon, R.R. 1936. 'A Case of Agoraphobia.' *Psychoanalytic Review* 23:383–94.

Greer, G. 1972 [1970]. *The Female Eunuch.* New York: Bantam.

Gregg, J. 2001. 'Are You a Phobia Expert?' Available online at http://

www.time.com/time/health/article/0,8599,103759,00.html. Accessed 26 April 2001.

Grob, G.N. 1985. *The Inner World of American Psychiatry, 1890–1940: Selected Correspondence*. New Brunswick, NJ: Rutgers University Press.

Guze, S.B. 1989. 'Biological Psychiatry: Is There Any Other Kind?' *Psychological Medicine* 19(2):315–23.

Hacking, I. 1995. *Rewriting the Soul: Multiple Personality and the Sciences of Memory*. Princeton: Princeton University Press.

Hadfield, J.A. 1929. 'Anxiety States.' *British Journal of Medical Psychology* 9:33–7.

Hallam, R.S. 1978. 'Agoraphobia: A Critical Review of the Concept.' *British Journal of Psychiatry* 133:314–9.

Hallfors, D.D., and L. Saxe. 1993. 'The Dependence Potential of Short Half-Life Benzodiazepines: A Meta-Analysis.' *American Journal of Public Health* 83(9):1300–4. Available online at ProQuest. Accessed 22 September 2006.

Hansen, B. 1992. 'American Physicians' "Discovery" of Homosexuals, 1880–1900: A New Diagnosis in a Changing Society.' Pp. 104–33 in *Framing Disease: Studies in Cultural History*, ed. J. Golden and C.E. Rosenberg. New Brunswick, NJ: Rutgers University Press.

Harding, J. 1986. 'Mood-Modifiers and Elderly Women in Canada: The Medicalization of Poverty.' Pp. 51–86 in *Adverse Effects: Women and the Pharmaceutical Industry*, ed. K. McDonnell and International Organization of Consumers' Unions. Toronto: Women's Educational Press.

Harnett, D.S. 1990. 'Panic Disorder: Integrating Psychotherapy and Psychopharmacology.' *Psychiatric Medicine* 8(3):211–22.

Hartman, M.S. 1974. 'Preface.' Pp. vii–xii in *Clio's Consciousness Raised: New Perspectives on the History of Women*, ed. M.S. Hartman and L. Banner. New York: Harper Torchbooks.

Hawkrigg, J.J. 1975a. 'Agoraphobia–1.' *Nursing Times* 71(33):1280–2.

– 1975b. 'Agoraphobia–2.' *Nursing Times* 71(34):1337–8.

Hayward, P., T. Ahmad, and J. Wardle. 1994. 'Into the Dangerous World: An In Vivo Study of Information Processing in Agoraphobics.' *British Journal of Clinical Psychology* 33(pt 3):307–15.

Headley Neale, J. 1898. 'Agoraphobia.' *Lancet* 2:1322–3.

Healy, D. 1990. 'The Psychopharmacological Era: Notes toward a History.' *Journal of Psychopharmacology* 4(3):152–67.

– 1997. *The Antidepressant Era*. Cambridge, MA: Harvard University Press.

– 2000. 'Good Science or Bad Business?' *Hastings Center Report* 30(2):19–22.

– 2001. 'The Dilemmas Posed by New and Fashionable Treatments.' *Advances in Psychiatric Treatment* 7:322–7.

– 2002. *The Creation of Psychopharmacology.* Cambridge, MA, and London: Harvard University Press.
– 2004a. *Let Them Eat Prozac: The Unhealthy Relationship between the Pharmaceutical Industry and Depression.* New York and London: New York University Press.
– 2004b. 'Shaping the Intimate: Influences on the Experience of Everyday Nerves.' *Social Studies of Science* 34(2):219–45.
Hermann, H.W. 1889. 'Clinical Memoranda: Cases of Agoraphobia.' *St. Louis Polyclinic* 1:232–4.
Herzig, R. 2000. '"Running True to the Female Type": Diagnosing Hypertrichosis before 1930.' Unpublished paper presented at the conference 'Writing the Past, Claiming the Future: Women and Gender in Science, Medicine and Technology,' St Louis, MO, 12–15 October.
Hodgkinson, P.E. 1981a. 'Agoraphobia. 2. Learning to Enjoy the Great Outdoors.' *Nursing Mirror* 153(2):40–1.
– 1981b. 'Agoraphobia: Far from the Madding Crowd.' *Nursing Mirror* 153(1):37–8.
Hoffart, A., and E.W. Martinsen. 1992. 'Personality Disorders in Panic with Agoraphobia and Major Depression.' *British Journal of Clinical Psychology* 31(pt 2):213–14.
– 1993. 'Coping Strategies in Major Depressed, Agoraphobic, and Co-morbid In-patients: A Longitudinal Study.' *British Journal of Medical Psychology* 66(pt 2, June):143–55.
Hollingshead, G. 1992. *Spin Dry: A Novel.* Oakville, ON: Mosaic.
Hout, M., A. van den Arntz, and R. Hoekstra. 1994. 'Exposure Reduced Agoraphobia but Not Panic, and Cognitive Therapy Reduced Panic but Not Agoraphobia.' *Behavior Research and Therapy* 32(4):447–51.
Huang, R. 2000. 'Phobias: Tough Love for Panicked People.' *Globe and Mail*, 19 December, p. R5.
Hudson, C.J. 1981. 'Agoraphobia and Its Implications for the Military: Case Reports.' *Military Medicine* 146(7):511–12.
Hudson, R.P. 1987. *Disease and Its Control: The Shaping of Modern Thought.* Westport, CT: Praeger.
Hughes, I., R. Budd, and S. Greenaway. 1999. 'Coping with Anxiety and Panic: A Factor Analytic Study.' *British Journal of Clinical Psychology* 38(3):295–304.
Hunter, D. 1983. 'Hysteria, Psychoanalysis, and Feminism: The Case of Anna O.' *Feminist Studies* 9(3):465–88.
Hunter, K.M. 1991. *Doctors' Stories: The Narrative Structure of Medical Knowledge.* Princeton: Princeton University Press.
Industry Canada. Health Industries Branch. 1997. *Pharmaceutical Industry, Part 1: Overview and Prospects.* Ottawa: The Branch.

Insane Asylum, The. 1998. 'Page of Lists.' Available online at http://
    www.cybercomm.net/~soulless/page-of-lists.html. Accessed 5 April 2001.
Jackson, H.J., and V. Elton. 1985. 'A Multimodal Approach to the Treatment of
    Agoraphobia: Four Case Studies.' *Canadian Journal of Psychiatry* 30(7):539–43.
Jackson, J.D. 1872. 'Agoraphobia: Eisophobia, Autophobia.' *The Clinic* 2(6):61–
    2.
Jarvis, L. 2000. 'Antidepressant Market Braces for Change: SSRIs Face
    Increased Competition.' *Chemical Market Reporter*, vol. 26 (7 August), p. 26.
    Available online at Business & Industry. Accessed 21 September 2006.
Jenike, M.A., H.L. Vitagliano, J. Rabinowitz, D.C. Goff, and L. Baer. 1987.
    'Bowel Obsessions Responsive to Tricyclic Antidepressants in Four Patients.'
    American Journal of Psychiatry 144(10):1347–8.
Johnson, E. 2000. 'Promoting Drugs through Patient Advocacy Groups.' CBC
    Marketplace. Broadcast 14 November. Available online at http://
    www.cbc.ca/consumers/market/files/health/drugmarketing/index.html.
    Accessed 30 November 2004.
– 2003. 'Inside the Business of Medical Ghostwriting.' CBC Marketplace.
    Broadcast 25 March. Available online at http://www.cbc.ca/consumers/
    market/files/health/ghostwriting/index.html. Accessed 30 November
    2004.
Jones, C.P., T.A. LaVeist, and M. Lillie-Blanton. 1991. '"Race" in the Epidemio-
    logic Literature: An Examination of the American Journal of Epidemiology,
    1921–1990.' *American Journal of Epidemiology* 134(10):1079–84.
Jones, R. 1898. 'A Case of Agoraphobia, with Remarks upon Obsessions.' *Lan-
    cet* 1:568–70.
Jones, R.B., G. Humphris, and T. Lewis. 1996. 'Do Agoraphobics Interpret the
    Environment in Large Shops and Supermarkets Differently?' *British Journal
    of Clinical Psychology* 35(4):635–7.
Joyce, P.R., J.A. Bushnell, M.A. Oakley-Browne, J.E. Wells, and A.R. Hornblow.
    1989. 'The Epidemiology of Panic Symptomatology and Agoraphobic
    Avoidance.' *Comprehensive Psychiatry* 30(4):303–12.
Kamieniecki, G.W., T. Wade, and G. Tsourtos. 1997. 'Interpretive Bias for
    Benign Sensations in Panic Disorder with Agoraphobia.' *Journal of Anxiety
    Disorders* 11(2):141–56.
Katan, A. 1951 [1937]. 'The Role of "Displacement" in Agoraphobia.' *Interna-
    tional Journal of Psycho-Analysis* 32:41–50.
Keller, E.F. 1992. *Secrets of Life, Secrets of Death: Essays on Language, Gender, and
    Science*. New York: Routledge.
Kennedy, F. 1916. 'Discussion re: Patrick, 1916.' *Journal of the American Medical
    Association* 67:185.

Kerber, L. 1988. 'Separate Spheres, Female Worlds, Woman's Lace: The Rhetoric of Women's History.' *Journal of American History* 75(1):9–39.

Khawaja, N.G., and T.P. Oei. 1998. 'Catastrophic Cognitions in Panic Disorder with and without Agoraphobia.' *Clinical Psychology Review* 18(3):341–65.

King, L. 1982. *Medical Thinking: An Historical Preface*. Princeton: Princeton University Press.

King, M. 1981. 'Dependency in Agoraphobia: A Woman in Need.' *Nursing Mirror* 152(4):34–6.

Kleinman, A. 1988. *Rethinking Psychiatry: From Cultural Category to Personal Experience*. New York: Free Press.

Kluger, J. 2001. 'Fear Not!' *Time Magazine*, vol. 157(13) (2 April), pp. 52–7, 59, 60–1.

Knapp, T.J., and M.T. Schumacher. 1988. *Westphal's 'Die Agoraphobie.'* Lanham, MD: University Press of America.

Knorr-Cetina, K. 1981. *The Manufacture of Knowledge: An Essay on the Constructivist and Contextual Nature of Science*. Oxford: Pergamon.

Knowles, C. 1996. 'Racism, Biography, and Psychiatry.' Pp. 47–67 in *Re-Situating Identities: The Politics of Race, Ethnicity, and Culture*, ed. V. Amit-Talai and C. Knowles. Peterborough, ON: Broadview.

Kohler Riessman, C. 1998. 'Women and Medicalization: A New Perspective.' Pp. 46–63 in *The Politics of Women's Bodies: Sexuality, Appearance, and Behavior*, ed. R. Weitz. New York and Oxford: Oxford University Press.

Kolko, D.J. 1984. 'Paradoxical Instruction in the Elimination of Avoidance Behavior in an Agoraphobic Girl.' *Journal of Behavior Therapy and Experimental Psychiatry* 15(1):51–7.

Kraepelin, E. 1962 [1918]. *One Hundred Years of Psychiatry*. Trans. W. Baskin. New York: Citadel.

– 1992 [1919]. 'Psychiatric Observations on Contemporary Issues.' Trans. E.J. Engstrom. *History of Psychiatry* 3:253–69.

Krieger, N. 1990. 'Racial and Gender Discrimination: Risk Factors for High Blood Pressure?' *Social Science and Medicine* 30(12):1273–81.

Krieger, N., and S. Sidney. 1996. 'Racial Discrimination and Blood Pressure: The CARDIA Study of Young Black and White Adults.' *American Journal of Public Health* 86(10):1370–8.

Kupers, T.A. 1995. 'The Politics of Psychiatry: Gender and Sexual Preference in DSM-IV.' *Masculinities* 3:67–78.

Kutchins, H., and S.A. Kirk. 1997. *Making Us Crazy: DSM: The Psychiatric Bible and the Creation of Mental Disorders*. New York and Toronto: Free Press.

Lancet, The. 1990. 'What Precipitates Agoraphobia?' *Lancet* 335(8701):1314–15.

Laing, R.D. 1969. *The Divided Self*. New York: Pantheon.

Langs, G., F. Quehenberger, K. Fabisch, G. Klug, H. Fabisch, and H.G. Zapo-toczky. 2000. 'The Development of Agoraphobia in Panic Disorder: A Pre-dictable Process?' *Journal of Affective Disorders* 58(1):43–50.

Last, C.G., D.H. Barlow, and G.T. O'Brien. 1984. 'Cognitive Change during Treatment of Agoraphobia: Behavioral and Cognitive-Behavioral Approaches.' *Behavior Modification* 8(2):181–210.

Latour, B. 1987. *Science in Action: How to Follow Scientists and Engineers through Society*. Cambridge, MA: Harvard University Press.

Latour, B., and S. Woolgar. 1979. *Laboratory Life: The Social Construction of Scientific Facts*. Beverly Hills, CA: Sage.

Laybourne, P.C., and J.G. Redding. 1985. 'Agoraphobia. Is Fear the Basis of Symptoms?' *Postgraduate Medicine* 78(5):109–12, 114, 117–18.

Lederer, S.E. 1995. *Subjected to Science: Human Experimentation in America before the Second World War*. Baltimore: Johns Hopkins University Press.

Lefebvre, H. 1991. *The Production of Space*. Oxford and Cambridge, MA: Blackwell.

Legrand du Saulle, M. 1876. 'De la peur des espaces (agoraphobie des Alle-mands).' *Annales Médico-Psychologiques* 34:405–33.

Lexchin, J. 1984. *The Real Pushers: A Critical Analysis of the Canadian Drug Indus-try*. Vancouver: New Star.

Liddell, A., and B. Acton. 1988. 'Agoraphobics' Understanding of the Develop-ment and Maintenance of Their Symptoms.' *Journal of Behavior Therapy and Experimental Psychiatry* 19(4):261–6.

Liebenau, J. 1987. *Medical Science and Medical Industry: The Formation of the American Pharmaceutical Industry*. Houndmills, Basingstoke: Macmillan in association with Business History Unit, University of London.

Liffiton, B. 1992. '"Brenda Goes to Town": A Case Study of a Woman with Ago-raphobia.' *Nursing Praxis in New Zealand* 7(3):33–5.

Lim, D. 1982. 'Nursing Care Study – Agoraphobia: Behind Closed Doors.' *Nursing Mirror* 154(16):50–1.

– 1985. 'Nursing Care Study. Imprisoned by Fear.' *Nursing Mirror* 161(4):18–19.

Logie, H.B., ed. 1933. *A Standard Classified Nomenclature of Disease*. New York: Commonwealth Fund.

– 1935. *Standard Classified Nomenclature of Disease*. New York: Commonwealth Fund.

London, L.S. 1963. 'Agoraphobia: A Case Report.' *Medical Times* 91(6):607–11.

Lopez, L.V. 1926. 'Fear.' *New Orleans Medical and Surgical Journal* 78:423–8.

Lopez-Munoz, F., C. Alamo, G. Rubio, P. Garcia-Garcia, B. Martin-Agueda, and E. Cuenca. 2003. 'Bibliometric Analysis of Biomedical Publications on SSRI during 1980–2000.' *Depression and Anxiety* 18(2):95–103.

Lunbeck, E. 1994. *The Psychiatric Persuasion: Knowledge, Gender, and Power in Modern America*. Princeton: Princeton University Press.

Lundh, L.G., S. Czyzykow, and L.G. Ost. 1997. 'Explicit and Implicit Memory Bias in Panic Disorder with Agoraphobia.' *Behavior Research and Therapy* 35:1003–14.

Lundh, L.G., U. Thulin, S. Czyzykow, and L.G. Ost. 1998. 'Recognition Bias for Safe Faces in Panic Disorder with Agoraphobia.' *Behavior Research and Therapy* 36(3):323–37.

Lutz, E.G., M.B. Lutz, and G.E. Lutz. 1987. 'Agoraphobia and Paroxysmal Cerebral Dysrhythmia.' *Journal of Clinical Psychiatry* 48(9):388–9.

Lydiard, R.B., and J.C. Ballenger. 1987. 'Antidepressants in Panic Disorder and Agoraphobia.' *Journal of Affective Disorders* 13(2):153–68.

Malleson, N. 1959. 'Panic and Phobia: A Possible Method of Treatment.' *Lancet* 1:225–7.

Margolis, J. 1976. 'The Concept of Disease.' *Journal of Medicine and Philosophy* 1:238–53.

– 1986. 'Thoughts on Definitions of Disease.' *Journal of Medicine and Philosophy* 11:233–6.

Marks, I. 1969. *Fears and Phobias*. New York: Academic Press.

Martin, E. 2000. 'The Rationality of Mania.' Pp. 177–96 in *Doing Science + Culture*, ed. R. Reid and S. Traweek. New York: Routledge.

Martin, I.C. 1979. 'Clinical Parable: Walking on Air.' *Nursing Times* 75(50):2170–1.

Marx, K. 1964 [1884]. *The Economic and Philosophic Manuscripts of 1844*. New York: International.

Mavissakalian, M. 1990. 'The Relationship between Panic Disorder/Agoraphobia and Personality Disorders.' *Psychiatric Clinics of North America* 13(4):661–84.

– 1993. 'Combined Behavioral Therapy and Pharmacotherapy of Agoraphobia.' *Journal of Psychiatric Research* 27(suppl. 1):179–91.

Mavissakalian, M., and M.S. Hamann. 1988. 'Correlates of DSM-III Personality Disorder in Panic Disorder and Agoraphobia.' *Comprehensive Psychiatry* 29(6):535–44.

– 1992. 'DSM-II Personality Characteristics of Panic Disorder with Agoraphobia Patients in Stable Remission.' *Comprehensive Psychiatry* 33(5):305–9.

Mavissakalian, M.R., and M.T. Ryan. 1998. 'Rational Treatment of Panic Disorder with Antidepressants.' *Annals of Clinical Psychiatry* 10(4):185–95.

May, E.M. 2004. 'Growing Little by Little.' *Medical Marketing and Media* 39(4):45–50. Available online at ProQuest. Accessed 18 June 2004.

McConnelly, E. 1926. 'Fear.' *New Orleans Medical and Surgical Journal* 78:427.

McIlroy, A. 2001. 'Drug Research Walks Thin Line.' *Globe and Mail*, 1 January, A1, A5.

McIntosh, P. 2003. 'White Privilege and Male Privilege: A Personal Account of Coming to See Correspondences through Work in Women's Studies.' Pp. 147–60 in *Privilege: A Reader*, ed. M.S. Kimmel and A.L. Ferber. Boulder, CO: Westview.

Med Ad News. 2002. 'Top 200 Prescription Drugs by Patent Expiration (Med Ad News 200).' *Med Ad News* 21(5):58(2). Available online at Business & Industry. Accessed 15 June 2004.

Medical Letter, The. 1981. 'Choice of Benzodiazepines.' *Medical Letter*, 1 May, 41–3.

– 1982. 'Alprazolam (Xanax).' *Medical Letter*, 16 April, 41–2.

– 1988. 'Choice of Benzodiazepines.' *Medical Letter*, 26 February, 26–8.

Mendlowicz, M.V., and M.B. Stein. 2000. 'Quality of Life in Individuals with Anxiety Disorders.' *American Journal of Psychiatry* 157(5):669–82.

Mercier, C. 1906. 'Agoraphobia – A Remedy.' *Lancet* 2:990–1.

Metzl, J.M. 2003. *Prozac on the Couch: Prescribing Gender in the Era of Wonder Drugs*. Durham, NC, and London: Duke University Press.

Metzl, J.M., and J. Angel. 2004. 'Assessing the Impact of SSRI Antidepressants on Popular Notions of Women's Depressive Illness.' *Social Science and Medicine* 58(3): 577–84.

Meyer, V., and M. Gelder. 1963. 'Behaviour Therapy and Phobic Disorders.' *British Journal of Psychiatry* 109:19–28.

Micale, Mark S. 1995. *Approaching Hysteria: Disease and Its Interpretations*. Princeton: Princeton University Press.

Miller, E. 1930. 'The Analysis of Agora-Claustrophobia: A Passive Anamnesis.' *British Journal of Medical Psychology* 10:253–67.

Millett, K. 1970. *Sexual Politics*. Garden City, NY: Doubleday.

Mills, C.W. 1959. *The Sociological Imagination*. New York: Oxford University Press.

Mitchell, S.A., and M.J. Black. 1995. *Freud and Beyond: A History of Modern Psychoanalytic Thought*. New York: Basic.

Mol, A. 1998. 'Missing Links, Making Links: The Performance of Some Atheroscleroses.' Pp. 145–65 in *Differences in Medicine: Unraveling Practices, Techniques, and Bodies*, ed. M. Berg and A. Mol. Durham, NC, and London: Duke University Press.

Mol, A., and J. Law. 1999. *Situated Bodies and Distributed Selves: Enacting Hypoglycaemia*. Available online from the Department of Sociology, Lancaster University, at http://www.comp.lancs.ac.uk/sociology/stslaw5.html. Version 17 February 1999. Accessed 3 March 2001. [This online paper may be cited in line with the usual academic conventions. You may also download it for your own personal use. This paper must not be published elsewhere (e.g., mailing lists, bulletin boards, etc.) without the author's explicit permission. But please note that it is a draft for discussion only. Many of the sources derive from presentations at recent seminars for which I have not cleared authors' permissions to make formal attributions. Please, therefore, do not quote from this paper. If you cite, copy, or quote this paper you must include this copyright note, this paper must not be used for commercial purposes or gain in any way, note you should observe the conventions of academic citation in a version of the following form: Annemarie Mol and John Law, 'Situated Bodies and Distributed Selves: Enacting Hypoglycaemia' (draft), published by the Department of Sociology, Lancaster University at http://www.lancaster.ac.uk/sociology/stslaw5.html]

Moncrieff, J., and M.J. Crawford. 2001. 'British Psychiatry in the 20th Century – Observations from a Psychiatric Journal.' *Social Science & Medicine* 53(3):349–56.

Mountjoy, C.Q., M. Roth, R.F. Garside, and I.M. Leitch. 1977. 'A Clinical Trial of Phenelzine in Anxiety Depressive and Phobic Neuroses.' *British Journal of Psychiatry* 131:486–92.

Myers, M.J. 1992. 'Marketing and Pharmaceutical Development.' *Journal of Drug Issues* 22(2):221–34.

Myerson, A. 1929 [1920]. *The Nervous Housewife*. Boston: Little, Brown.

National Institute of Health. 1993. 'Treatment of Panic Disorder: Summary of the NIH Consensus Statement.' *Maryland Medical Journal* 42:306–7.

Neidhardt, E., and I. Florin. 1999. 'Memory Bias for Panic-Related Material in Patients with Panic Disorder.' *Psychopathology* 32(5):260–6.

Norbury, F.P. 1916. 'Discussion re: Patrick, 1916.' *Journal of the American Medical Association* 67:183–4.

Norton, G.R., G.E. Allen, and J. Hilton. 1983. 'The Social Validity of Treatments for Agoraphobia.' *Behavior Research and Therapy* 21(4):393–9.

Nunn, J.D., R.J. Stevenson, and G. Whalan. 1984. 'Selective Memory Effects in Agoraphobic Patients.' *British Journal of Clinical Psychology* 23(pt 3):195–201.

Orr, J. 1990. 'Theory on the Market: Panic, Incorporating.' *Social Problems* 37:460–84.

Osborne, T., and N. Rose. 1999. 'Governing Cities: Notes on the Spatialisation of Virtue.' *Environment and Planning D: Society and Space* 17:737–60.

Parker, G. 1979. 'Reported Parental Characteristics of Agoraphobics and Social Phobics.' *British Journal of Psychiatry* 135:555–60.

Parpis, E. 2001. 'Fear Factor: How Should We Feel about Mental-Health Drug Ads?' *Adweek*, vol. 42(46) (12 November), p. 11. Available online at ProQuest. Accessed 18 June 2004.

Parry, V. 2003. 'The Art of Branding a Condition.' *Medical Marketing and Media* 38(5):43. Available online at ProQuest. Accessed 18 June 2004.

Parsons, T. 1951. *The Social System*. Glencoe, IL: Free Press.

– 1954. *Essays in Sociological Theory.* Glencoe, IL: Free Press.

– 1978. 'Health and Disease: A Sociological and Action Perspective.' Pp. 590–9 in *Encyclopedia of Bioethics*, vol. 2, ed. W.T. Reich. New York: Free Press.

Patrick, H.T. 1916. 'The Factor of Fear in Nervous Cases.' *Journal of the American Medical Association* 67:180–3, 185–6.

Pecknold, J.C. 1987. 'Behavioural and Combined Therapy in Panic States.' *Progress in Neuropsychopharmacology and Biological Psychiatry* 11(2–3):97–104.

Pecknold, J.C., and R.P. Swinson. 1986. 'Taper Withdrawal Studies with Alprazolam in Patients with Panic Disorder and Agoraphobia.' *Psychopharmacology Bulletin* 22(1):173–6.

Pfizer. 2003. 'Financial Report 2003.' Available online at http://www.pfizer.com/are/mn_investors.cfm. Accessed 15 June 2004.

Pharmacia & Upjohn. 1998. 'Powering the Turnaround: Annual Report.' Bridgewater, NJ: Pharmacia & Upjohn.

Pickles, A.J., and M.D. van den Broek. 1988. 'Failure to Replicate Evidence for Phobic Schemata in Agoraphobic Patients.' *British Journal of Clinical Psychology* 27:271–2.

Pinto, R. 1972. 'A Case of Movement Epilepsy with Agoraphobia Treated Successfully by Flooding.' *British Journal of Psychiatry* 121(562):287–8.

Pohl, R., R. Berchou, and J.M. Rainey. 1982. 'Tricyclic Antidepressants and Monoamine Oxidase Inhibitors in the Treatment of Agoraphobia.' *Journal of Clinical Psychopharmacology* 2(6):399–407.

Pollard, C.A. 1986. 'Respiratory Distress during Panic Attacks Associated with Agoraphobia.' *Psychological Reports* 58:61–2.

Pollard, C.A., and J.G. Henderson. 1987. 'Prevalence of Agoraphobia: Some Confirmatory Data.' *Psychological Reports* 60(3 pt 2):1305.

Pollard, C.A., R.C. Tait, D. Meldrum, I.H. Dubinsky, and J.S. Gall. 1996. 'Agoraphobia without Panic: Case Illustrations of an Overlooked Syndrome.' *Journal of Nervous and Mental Disease* 184:161–2.

Pollock, L.J. 1928. 'Phobias and Neurology of the Viscera.' *Medical Clinics of North America* 12(1):31–47.

Poovey, M. 1987. '"Scenes of an Indelicate Character": The Medical "Treatment" of Victorian Women.' Pp. 137–68 in *The Making of the Modern Body: Sexuality and Society in the Nineteenth Century*, ed. C. Gallagher and T.W. Laqueur. Berkeley: University of California Press.

– 1988. *Uneven Developments: The Ideological Work of Gender in Mid-Victorian England*. Chicago: University of Chicago Press.

Porter, R. 1997. *The Greatest Benefit to Mankind: A Medical History of Humanity from Antiquity to the Present*. New York and London: Norton.

Potter, L.T. 1882. 'Agoraphobia: A Contribution to Clinical Medicine.' *Chicago Medical Journal and Examiner* 45:472–5.

PR Newswire. 2003. 'Pharmacia Corporation Reports 11% Increase in Earnings per Share for Fourth Quarter.' *PR Newswire*. 19 February. Available online at http://www.lexisnexis.com. Accessed 15 June 2004.

Prosser White, R. 1884. 'Agoraphobia.' *Lancet* 2:1140–1.

Pyke, J.M., and M. Longdon. 1985. 'Agoraphobia.' *L'infirmière canadienne* 27(6):24–7.

Rabinow, P. 1983. 'Ordonnance, Discipline, Regulation: Some Reflections on Urbanism.' *Humanities in Society* 5(3–4):267–78.

– 1989. *French Modern: Norms and Forms of the Social Environment*. Cambridge, MA: MIT Press.

– 1996 [1992]. 'Artificiality and Enlightenment: From Sociobiology to Biosociality.' Pp. 91–111 in *Essays on the Anthropology of Reason*, ed. P. Rabinow. Princeton: Princeton University Press.

Rajchman, J. 1991. 'Foucault's Art of Seeing.' Pp. 68–102 in *Philosophical Events: Essays of the '80s*, ed. J. Rajchman. New York: Columbia University Press.

Ravaris, C.L. 1981. 'Current Drug Therapy for Agoraphobia.' *American Family Physician* 23(1):129–31.

Records, B.F. 1896. 'Agoraphobia.' *Kansas City Medical Index* 17:306–8.

Reeves, J.B., and S.F. Austin. 1986. 'Toward a Sociology of Agoraphobia.' *Free Inquiry in Creative Sociology* 14:153–8.

Reik, T. 1948. *Listening with the Third Ear: The Inner Experience of a Psychoanalyst*. New York: Farrar Straus.

Reuter, S.Z. 2001. '"The Very Opposite of Calm": A Socio-Cultural History of Agoraphobia.' Unpublished Ph.D. dissertation, Department of Sociology, Queen's University.

– 2002. 'Doing Agoraphobia(s): A Material-Discursive Understanding of Diseased Bodies.' *Sociology of Health and Illness* 24(6):750–70.

Reuters UK. 2004. 'Doctors Peer into Brains to Gauge Antidepressants.' Available online at http://www.reuters.co.uk/newsPackageArticle.jhtml?type= scienceNews&storyID=5295196&section=news. Accessed 15 June 2004.

Rhodes, F. 1916. 'Discussion re: Patrick, 1916.' *Journal of the American Medical Association* 67:185.

Risse, G. 1978. 'History of the Concepts [of Health and Disease].' Pp. 579–85 in *Encyclopedia of Bioethics*, vol. 2, ed. W.T. Reich. New York: Free Press.

212   References

Roberts, A.H. 1964. 'Housebound Housewives – A Follow-up Study of a Phobic Anxiety State.' *British Journal of Psychiatry* 110:191–7.

Roberts, F.T. 1882. 'Agoraphobia.' Pp. 17–18 in *Dictionary of Medicine Including General Pathology, General Therapeutics, Hygiene, and the Diseases Peculiar to Women and Children*, ed. R. Quain. New York: Appleton.

Rogler, L.H. 1997. 'Making Sense of Historical Changes in the Diagnostic and Statistical Manual of Mental Disorders: Five Propositions.' *Journal of Health and Social Behavior* 38(1):9–20.

Rohs, R.G., and R. Noyes. 1978. 'Agoraphobia: Newer Treatment Approaches.' *Journal of Nervous and Mental Disease* 166(10):701–8.

Rose, G. 1985. 'Sick Individuals and Sick Populations.' *International Journal of Epidemiology* 14:32–8.

Rose, N. 1989. *Governing the Soul: The Shaping of the Private Self.* London and New York: Routledge.

– 1994. 'Medicine, History, and the Present.' Pp. 48–72 in *Reassessing Foucault: Power, Medicine, and the Body: Studies in the Social History of Medicine*, ed. C. Jones and R. Porter. London and New York: Routledge.

– 1998. *Inventing Our Selves: Psychology, Power, and Personhood.* Cambridge: Cambridge University Press.

– 1999. *Powers of Freedom: Reframing Political Thought.* Cambridge: Cambridge University Press.

– 2000. 'Identity, Genealogy, History.' Pp. 313–26 in *Identity: A Reader*, ed. P. du Gay, J. Evans, and P. Redman. London, Thousand Oaks, CA, New Delhi: Sage.

– 2001a. 'Biopolitics in the Twenty First Century – Notes for a Research Agenda.' *Distinktion* 3:25–44.

– 2001b. 'The Politics of Life Itself.' *Theory, Culture & Society* 18(6):1–30.

Rosenbaum, J.F., R.A. Pollock, M.W. Otto, and M.H. Pollack. 1995. 'Integrated Treatment of Panic Disorder.' *Bulletin of the Menninger Clinic* 59(2 suppl. A):A4–26.

Rosenberg, C.E. 1974. 'Social Class and Medical Care in Nineteenth-Century America: The Rise and Fall of the Dispensary.' *Journal of the History of Medicine and the Allied Sciences* 29(1):32–54.

– 1992. *Explaining Epidemics and Other Studies in the History of Medicine.* Cambridge: Cambridge University Press.

Rosenberg, C.E., and J. Golden. 1992. *Framing Disease: Studies in Cultural History.* New Brunswick, NJ: Rutgers University Press.

Roth, M., and N. Argyle. 1988. 'Anxiety, Panic and Phobic Disorders: An Overview.' *Journal of Psychiatric Research* 22(suppl. 1):33–54.

Roth, W.T., M.J. Telch, C.B. Taylor, J.A. Sachitano, C.C. Gallen, M.L. Kopell, K.L. McClenahan, W.S. Agras, and A. Pfefferbaum. 1986. 'Autonomic

Characteristics of Agoraphobia with Panic Attacks.' *Biological Psychiatry* 21(12):1133–54.

Ruddick, B. 1961. 'Agoraphobia.' *International Journal of Psycho-Analysis* 42:537–43.

Ruttle, R. 1889. 'Agoraphobia.' *British Medical Journal* 2:818.

Sakai, M., and M. Takeichi. 1996. 'Two Cases of Panic Disorder Treated with Autogenic Training and In Vivo Exposure without Medication.' *Psychiatry and Clinical Neurosciences* 50(6):335–6.

Salkovskis, P.M., D.M. Clark, A. Hackmann, A. Wells, and M.G. Gelder. 1999. 'An Experimental Investigation of the Role of Safety-Seeking Behaviours in the Maintenance of Panic Disorder with Agoraphobia.' *Behavior Research and Therapy* 37(6):559–74.

Salomon Smith Barney. 2002. 'Pharmacia Corp.'s Top 10 Brand Name Pharmaceutical Products Ranked by Global Sales in Dollars for 2000, with Each Drug's US Launch Date, Generic Name, Class/Category and Percent Share of Pharmacia's Total Sales.' *Salomon Smith Barney* [brokerage report]. 4 February. Available online at TableBase. Accessed 15 June 2004.

Salzman, C. 1993. 'Benzodiazepine Treatment of Panic and Agoraphobic Symptoms: Use, Dependence, Toxicity, Abuse.' *Journal of Psychiatric Research* 27(suppl.) 1:97–110.

Schmideberg, W. 1951. 'Agoraphobia as a Manifestation of Schizophrenia: The Analysis of a Case.' *Psychoanalytic Review* 38:343–52.

Schwartz, L.S., and E.R. Val. 1984. 'Agoraphobia: A Multimodal Treatment Approach.' *American Journal of Psychotherapy* 38(1):35–46.

Sciuto, G., G. Diaferia, M. Battaglia, G. Perna, A. Gabriele, and L. Bellodi. 1991. 'DSM-III-R Personality Disorders in Panic and Obsessive-Compulsive Disorder: A Comparison Study.' *Comprehensive Psychiatry* 32(5):450–7.

Seidenberg, R., and K. DeCrow. 1983. *Women Who Marry Houses: Panic and Protest in Agoraphobia*. New York: McGraw-Hill.

Shean, G., and U. Uchenwa. 1990. 'Interpersonal Style and Anxiety.' *Journal of Psychology* 124(4):403–8.

Shear, M.K. 1996. 'Factors in the Etiology and Pathogenesis of Panic Disorder: Revisiting the Attachment-Separation Paradigm.' *American Journal of Psychiatry* 153(7 suppl.):125–36.

Sheehan, D.V., J. Ballenger, and G. Jacobsen. 1980. 'Treatment of Endogenous Anxiety with Phobic, Hysterical, and Hypochondriacal Symptoms.' *Archives of General Psychiatry* 37(1):51–9.

Sheehan, D.V., K.E. Sheehan, and W.E. Minichiello. 1981. 'Age of Onset of Phobic Disorders: A Reevaluation.' *Comprehensive Psychiatry* 22(6):544–53.

Sheikh, J.I., G.A. Leskin, and D.F. Klein. 2002. 'Gender Differences in Panic Disorder: Findings from the National Comorbidity Survey.' *American Journal of Psychiatry* 159(1):55–8.

Shephard, Ben. 2001. *A War of Nerves: Soldiers and Psychiatrists in the Twentieth Century.* Cambridge, MA: Harvard University Press.

Shilling, C. 1993. *The Body and Social Theory.* London and Newberry Park, CA: Sage.

Showalter, E. 1985. *The Female Malady: Women, Madness, and English Culture, 1830–1980.* New York: Pantheon.

Silove, D. 1986. 'Perceived Parental Characteristics and Reports of Early Parental Deprivation in Agoraphobic Patients.' *Australian and New Zealand Journal of Psychiatry* 20(3):365–9.

Silverman, M., and P.R. Lee. 1974. *Pills, Profits & Politics.* Berkeley and Los Angeles: University of California Press.

Simmel, G. 1950. *The Sociology of Georg Simmel.* Trans., ed., and with an introduction by Kurt H. Wolff. Glencoe, IL: Free Press.

– 1978. *The Philosophy of Money.* London and Boston: Routledge & Kegan Paul.

Sitte, C. 1965. *City Planning According to Artistic Principles.* New York: Random House.

Smith-Rosenberg, C. 1972. 'The Hysterical Woman: Sex Roles and Role Conflict in 19th-Century America.' *Social Research* 39:652–78.

Snowden, M.B. 1934. 'Phobia.' *Practitioner* 133:315–20.

Soja, E.W. 1989. *Postmodern Geographies: The Reassertion of Space in Critical Social Theory.* London and New York: Verso.

– 2000. *Postmetropolis: Critical Studies of Cities and Regions.* Malden, MA: Blackwell.

Solyom, L., M. Silberfeld, and C. Solyom. 1976. 'Maternal Overprotection in the Etiology of Agoraphobia.' *Canadian Psychiatric Association Journal* 21(2):109–13.

Solyom, L., C. Solyom, and B. Ledwidge. 1991. 'Fluoxetine in Panic Disorder.' *Canadian Journal of Psychiatry* 36(5):378–80.

Spillers, H.J. 1987. 'Mama's Baby, Papa's Maybe: An American Grammar Book.' *Diacritics* 17(2):64–81.

Spitzer, R.L., and J.B. Williams. 1988. 'Revised Diagnostic Criteria and a New Structured Interview for Diagnosing Anxiety Disorders.' *Journal of Psychiatric Research* 22(suppl. 1):55–85.

Stamm, J.L. 1972. 'Infantile Trauma, Narcissistic Injury, and Agoraphobia.' *Psychiatric Quarterly* 46(2):254–72.

Stantworth, H.M. 1982. 'Nursing Care Study: Agoraphobia – An Illness or a Symptom?' *Nursing Times* 78(10):399–403.

Stone, M. 1988. 'Shellshock and the Psychologists.' Pp. 242–71 in *The Anatomy of Madness: Essays in the History of Psychiatry,* vol. 2, ed. W.F. Bynum, R. Porter, and M. Shepherd. London and New York: Tavistock.

Strange, C. 1995. *Toronto's Girl Problem: The Perils and Pleasures of the City, 1880–1930.* Toronto: University of Toronto Press.

Street, L.L., M.G. Craske, and D.H. Barlow. 1989. 'Sensations, Cognitions, and the Perception of Cues Associated with Expected and Unexpected Panic Attacks.' *Behavior Research and Therapy* 27(2):189–98.

Suckling, C.W. 1890. 'Agoraphobia and Allied Morbid Fears.' *American Journal of the Medical Sciences* 99(new series):476–83.

'Surgeon.' 1885. 'Letter.' *Lancet* 1:93.

Sutherland, H. 1877. 'On "Agoraphobia" (So Called).' *Journal of Psychological Medicine and Mental Pathology* 3 (new series):265–9.

Swaan, A. de. 1990. *The Management of Normality: Critical Essays in Health and Welfare.* London and New York: Routledge.

Swinson, R.P., B.J. Cox, and C.B. Woszczyna. 1992. 'Use of Medical Services and Treatment for Panic Disorder with Agoraphobia and for Social Phobia.' *Canadian Medical Association Journal* 147(6):878–83.

Szasz, T.S. 1974. *The Myth of Mental Illness: Foundations of a Theory of Personal Conduct.* New York: Harper & Row.

Taylor, N. 1895. 'A Case of Agoraphobia.' *New York Medical Journal* 61:397–8.

Telch, M.J., B.H. Tearnan, and C.B. Taylor. 1983. 'Antidepressant Medication in the Treatment of Agoraphobia: A Critical Review.' *Behavior Research and Therapy* 21(5):505–17.

Terhune, W.B. 1949. 'The Phobic Syndrome.' *Archives of Neurology and Psychiatry* 62:162–72.

– 1959. 'Fear and Phobias.' *Connecticut Medicine* 23:765–71.

Theriot, N. 1997. 'Women's Voices in Nineteenth-Century Medical Discourse: A Step toward Deconstructing Science.' Pp. 156–86 in *History and Theory: Feminist Research, Debates, Contestations,* ed. B. Laslett, R.B. Joeres, M. Mayres, E.B. Higginbotham, and J. Barker-Nunn. Chicago: University of Chicago Press.

Thomas, T.H. 1922. 'The Phobia as the Fundamental Factor in the Psychoneurosis.' *Journal of Neurology and Psychopathology* 3:128–33.

Thomas, W.I., and D.S. Thomas. 1928. *The Child in America: Behavior Problems and Programs.* New York: Knopf.

Thomaselli, R. 2003. 'DTC Ads Influence Majority of Consumers, Say Doctors.' *Advertising Age,* vol. 74(3) (20 January), p. 6. Available online at ProQuest. Accessed 18 June 2004.

Tomes, N. 1994. 'Feminist Histories of Psychiatry.' Pp. 348–83 in *Discovering the History of Psychiatry,* ed. M.S. Micale and R. Porter. New York and Oxford: Oxford University Press.

Toni, C., G.B. Cassano, G. Perugi, L. Murri, M. Mancino, A. Petracca, H. Akiskal, and S.M. Roth. 1996. 'Psychosensorial and Related Phenomena in Panic Disorder and in Temporal Lobe Epilepsy.' *Comprehensive Psychiatry* 37(2):125–33.

Tönnies, F. 1957 [1887]. *Community and Society (Gemeinschaft und Gesellschaft)*. New York: Harper & Row.

Tucker, W.I. 1956. 'Diagnosis and Treatment of the Phobic Reaction.' *American Journal of Psychiatry* 112:825–30.

Underwood, N. 1999. 'Don't Panic!' *President's Choice Magazine*, November, pp. 25–6.

United States Census Bureau. 1999. *Statistical Abstract of the United States*. Vol. 119. Washington, DC: United States Census Bureau.

– 2000. 'Statistical Abstract of the United States: 2000 (Table No. 191).' 120th ed. Washington, DC.

United States Department of Health and Human Services. 1986. 'Health Status of the Disadvantaged Chartbook 1986, DHHS Publication No. (HRSA) HRS-P-DV86-2.' Washing, DC: Bureau of Health Professions Division of Disadvantaged Assistance.

– 1987. 'Health Care Coverage by Sociodemographic and Health Characteristics, United States, 1984, Data from the National Health Survey Series 10, No. 162.' Hyattsville, MD: National Center for Health Statistics.

UselessKnowledge.com. n.d. 'Phobias of the Rich and Famous.' http://www.uselessknowledge.com/vmd/phobias.shtml. Accessed 5 April 2001.

Van Dyke, F.W. 1908. 'Three Reasons Why Men Break Down.' *Transactions of the Oregon State Medical Society* 34:178–84.

Van Horn, A.K. 1886. 'A Case of Agoraphobia.' *Chicago Medical Journal and Examiner* 52:600–4.

Veith, I. 1965. *Hysteria: The History of a Disease*. Chicago and London: University of Chicago Press.

Verster, J.C., and E.R. Volkerts. 2004. 'Clinical Pharmacology, Clinical Efficacy, and Behavioral Toxicity of Alprazolam: A Review of the Literature.' *CNS Drug Review* 10(1):45–76.

Vickery, A. 1993. 'Golden Age to Separate Spheres? A Review of the Categories and Chronology of English Women's History.' *Historical Journal* 36(2):383–414.

Vidler, A. 1991. 'Agoraphobia: Spatial Estrangement in Georg Simmel and Siegfried Kracauer.' *New German Critique* 54:31–45.

– 1993. 'Bodies in Space/Subjects in the City: Psychopathologies of Modern Urbanism.' *Differences* 5:31–51.

– 1994. 'Psychopathologies of Modern Space: Metropolitan Fear from Agoraphobia to Estrangement.' Pp. 11–29 in *Rediscovering History: Culture Politics and the Psyche*, ed. M.S. Roth. Stanford: Stanford University Press.

– 2000. *Warped Space: Art, Architecture, and Anxiety in Modern Culture*. Cambridge, MA: MIT Press.

– 2002. 'A City Transformed: Designing "Defensible Space."' *Grey Room* 7:82–5.

'Vincent.' 1919. 'Confessions of an Agoraphobic Victim.' *American Journal of Psychology* 30:295–99.

Waldby, C. 1996. *AIDS and the Body Politic: Biomedicine and Sexual Difference*. London and New York: Routledge.

– 2000. *The Visible Human Project: Informatic Bodies and Posthuman Medicine*. London and New York: Routledge.

Waldron, I. 1977. 'Increased Prescribing of Valium, Librium, and Other Drugs – an Example of the Influence of Economic and Social Factors on the Practice of Medicine.' *International Journal of Health Services* 7(1):37–62.

Wangh, M. 1959. 'Structural Determinants of Phobia: A Clinical Study.' *Journal of the American Psychoanalytic Association* 7:675–95.

Warner, J.H. 1986. *The Therapeutic Perspective: Medical Practice, Knowledge, and Identity in America, 1820–1885*. Cambridge, MA: Harvard University Press.

Warren, R., G. Zgourides, and A. Jones. 1989. 'Cognitive Bias and Irrational Belief as Predictors of Avoidance.' *Behavior Research and Therapy* 27(2):181–8.

Webber, S.G. 1872a. 'Agoraphobia.' *Boston Medical and Surgical Journal* 10(18) (new series):297–8.

– 1872b. 'Agoraphobia Again.' *Boston Medical and Surgical Journal* 10(18) (new series):445–7.

Weber, M. 1958 [1904–5]. *The Protestant Ethic and the Spirit of Capitalism*. New York: Scribner.

Weekes, C. 1973. 'A Practical Treatment of Agoraphobia.' *British Medical Journal* 2(5864):469–71.

Weiss, E. 1935. 'Agoraphobia and Its Relation to Hysterical Attacks and to Traumas.' *International Journal of Psycho-Analysis* 16:59–83.

Weissman, M.M. 1990a. 'Epidemiology of Panic Disorder and Agoraphobia.' *Psychiatric Medicine* 8(2):3–13.

– 1990b. 'Panic and Generalized Anxiety: Are They Separate Disorders?' *Journal of Psychiatric Research* 24(suppl. 2):157–62.

Weissman, M.M., P.J. Leaf, D.G. Blazer, J.H. Boyd, and L. Florio. 1986. 'The Relationship between Panic Disorder and Agoraphobia: An Epidemiologic Perspective.' *Psychopharmacology Bulletin* 22(3):787–91.

Welter, B. 1966. 'The Cult of True Womanhood: 1820–1860.' *American Quarterly* 18(2):151–74.

Westphal, C.F.O. 1871. 'Die Agoraphobie: Eine neuropathische Erscheinung.' *Archiv für Psychiatrie und Nervenkrankheiten* 3:138–61.

– 1988 [1871]. 'Die Agoraphobie.' Trans. T.J. Knapp and M.T. Schumacher. Pp. 59–92 in Knapp and Schumacher, *Westphal's 'Die Agoraphobie.'* Lanham, MD: University Press of America.

Wiborg, I.M., and A.A. Dahl. 1997. 'The Recollection of Parental Rearing Styles in Patients with Panic Disorder.' *Acta Psychiatrica Scandinavica* 96(1):58–63.

Williams, E.T. 1872. 'Agoraphobia.' *Boston Medical and Surgical Journal* 87:351–3.

Williams, S.L., P.J. Kinney, S.T. Harap, and M. Liebmann. 1997. 'Thoughts of Agoraphobic People during Scary Tasks.' *Journal of Abnormal Psychology* 106(4):511–20.

Williams, T.A. 1916. 'Discussion re: Patrick, 1916.' *Journal of the American Medical Association* 67:184–5.

– 1919. 'Differentia Regarding Obsessions and Phobias with Reference to Their Pathogenesis and Treatment, Showing the Relatively Greater Importance of the Mechanism Than of the Form of Phobia.' *International Clinics* 4:180–201.

– 1930. 'The Management of Hyperemotionalism and States of Anxiety.' *Medical Journal and Record* 132:435–9.

Williamson, F. 1974. 'The Fourth Is Freedom from Fear.' *Nursing Times* 70:1840–5.

Wilson, E. 1992. *The Sphinx in the City: Urban Life, the Control of Disorder, and Women.* Los Angeles: University of California Press.

– 1995. 'The Rhetoric of Urban Space.' *New Left Review* 209:146–60.

Wilson, M. 1993. 'DSM-III and the Transformation of American Psychiatry: A History.' *American Journal of Psychiatry* 150(3):399–410.

Wittchen, H.U., V. Reed, and R.C. Kessler. 1998. 'The Relationship of Agoraphobia and Panic in a Community Sample of Adolescents and Young Adults.' *Archives of General Psychiatry* 55(11):1017–24.

Wolff, J. 1989. 'The Invisible *Flâneuse*: Women and the Literature of Modernity.' Pp. 141–56 in *The Problems of Modernity: Adorno and Benjamin*, ed. A. Benjamin. London and New York: Routledge.

Wondrak, R. 1980. 'Nursing Care Study. Agoraphobia: Another Brick in the Wall.' *Nursing Mirror* 150(16):42–4.

Wood, A. Douglas. 1974. '"The Fashionable Diseases": Women's Complaints and Their Treatment in Nineteenth-Century America.' Pp. 1–22 in *Clio's Consciousness Raised: New Perspectives on the History of Women*, ed. M.S. Hartman and L. Banner. New York: Harper Torchbooks.

Wyke, A. 1987. 'Pharmaceuticals: Harder Going.' *Economist*, 7 February, pp. 4–14.

Yaniv, G. 1998. 'Phobic Disorder, Psychotherapy, and Risk-Taking: An Economic Perspective.' *Journal of Health Economics* 17(2):229–43.

Young, A. 1995. *The Harmony of Illusions: Inventing Post-Traumatic Stress Disorder.* Princeton: Princeton University Press.

Young, P.L. 2004. 'The Crushing Cost of Fear.' *Globe and Mail,* 14 April, C1, C4.

Ziporyn, T.D. 1992. *Nameless Diseases.* New Brunswick, NJ: Rutgers University Press.

Zucker, D., C.B. Taylor, M. Brouillard, A. Ehlers, J. Margraf, M. Telch, W.T. Roth, and W.S. Agras. 1989. 'Cognitive Aspects of Panic Attacks: Content, Course, and Relationship to Laboratory Stressors.' *British Journal of Psychiatry* 155:86–91.

Index

24; and planners, 24, 26; public
space in, 91; shocks and stimuli of,
30
urbanism: as context for Atwood's
'rapid methods of living,' 23–4; as
detrimental to well-being, 24–5

Vanderbilt Clinic, New York, 85
Van Dyke, F.W., 73
Van Horn, A.K., 36
vertigo, 33, 36, 44, 45–6
Vidler, Anthony, 24, 26
visual representations and agoraphobia, 46
vitalism, 42
von Brücke, Ernst Wilhelm, 6–7

Waldby, C., 153–4
Waldron, I., 83
walking, pleasure of, 49
Wangh, Martin J., 58
war neurosis, 52, 77–8; and agora-
phobia, 182n3
Washington, D.C., 58
Watson, J.B., 65
Weaver, Signourney, 177n1
Webber, S.G., 36, 38–40
Weber, Max, 26–7
Weiss, Edoardo, 54, 57
Weissman, M.M., 140
Welter, Barbara, 74–5
Western Europe, agoraphobia in,
178n7
West London Hospital Post-Gradu-
ate College, 67
Westphal, Carl Friedrich Otto, 7, 15,
33–4, 36, 163
White, R. Prosser. See Prosser White,
R.

white men as a homogeneous population, 92
white middle class, 8; and neuroses,
172; private sphere of, 30; as privileged subject of medicine, 89; as
qualifying for 'normality,' 88
whites: annual family income of in
the United States, 90–1; lack of
colour of, 88; normalization of, 86;
as the privileged, 86
white upper class: as privileged subject of medicine, 89; as qualifying
for 'normality,' 88
white women, 'passing' of as True
Women, 90, 92. See also women
Wigan, England, 35
Williams, Edward T., 36
Williams, Janet, 155
Williams, Tom A., 51, 67–8
Wilson, E., 74
Wilson, Mitchell, 109
withdrawal: from amphetamines,
121; from caffeine, 121; from substances, 121
Wolpe, J., 68
Woman As She Was, Is, and Should Be
(deportment manual), 74
women: African American, 89, 92–3;
and agoraphobia, 37, 71, 80, 182n2;
and anxiety disorders, 4; and
childbearing, 39; and control, 74;
and emancipation, 76–7; employment of in London, 76; exclusion
of from clinical studies, 92; and
experiences of public space, 76;
and fear of crime and violence, 93;
history of hysteria in, 10–12; and
'housekeeping,' 149; inequality of,
85; lives of, 75–6; nervous systems

of, 39; normality for bourgeois, 75; panic disorder without agoraphobia in, 130; reproductive systems of, and agoraphobia, 38–9; and the sociality of agoraphobia, 9–12; and the stresses of modern urban life, 74; treatment programs for, 80. *See also* Jewish women; white women
Women and Madness (Chesler), 10
Wood, Ann Douglas, 10–11; 'The "Fashionable Diseases": Women's Complaints and Their Treatment in Nineteenth-Century America,' 10
working classes, 75

World Health Organization, *International Classification of Diseases (ICD-10)*, 103, 127–8

Xanax. *See* alprazolam (Xanax)

Yale University, 66
Yaniv, G., 181n16
Yellow Creek, Illinois, 35–6
Young, Allan, 77
Young Lady's Book: A Manual of Elegant Recreations, Exercises, and Pursuits, The (deportment manual), 74